S0-ABQ-160

Jean McNiff &
Jack Whitehead

ALL YOU NEED TO KNOW ABOUT
Action Research

Los Angeles • London • New Delhi • Singapore • Washington DC

© Jean McNiff and Jack Whitehead 2006

First published 2006

Reprinted 2009

Apart from any fair dealing for the purposes of
research or private study, or criticism or review, as
permitted under the Copyright, Designs and Patents
Act, 1988, this publication may be reproduced, stored
or transmitted in any form, or by any means, only with
the prior permission in writing of the publishers, or in
the case of reprographic reproduction, in accordance
with the terms of licences issued by the Copyright
Licensing Agency. Inquiries concerning reproduction
outside those terms should be sent to the publishers.

SAGE Publications Ltd
1 Oliver's Yard
55 City Road
London EC1Y 1SP

SAGE Publications Inc.
2455 Teller Road
Thousand Oaks, California 91320

SAGE Publications India Pvt Ltd
B 1/I 1 Mohan Cooperative Industrial Area
Mathura Road
New Delhi 110 044

SAGE Publications Asia-Pacific Pte Ltd
33 Pekin Street #02-01
Far East Square
Singapore 048763

British Library Cataloguing in Publication data

A catalogue record for this book is available from the
British Library

ISBN 978 1 4129 0805 4
ISBN 978 1 4129 0806 1 (pbk)

Library of Congress Control Number 2005931969

Typeset by C&M Digitals (P) Ltd, Chennai, India
Printed on paper from sustainable resources
Printed in Great Britain by
CPI Antony Rowe, Chippenham, Wiltshire

FSC
Mixed Sources
Product group from well-managed
forests and other controlled sources
Cert no. SGS-COC-2953
www.fsc.org
© 1996 Forest Stewardship Council

Contents

Acknowledgements

We wish to thank all those who have contributed to this book, and we acknowledge that your work is your intellectual copyright.

We also wish to thank our editor, Patrick Brindle, at Sage, for his enthusiasm for this project throughout, and Vanessa Harwood for her expert advice about production.

We commend this book to all educators who are committed to realizing their educational values that contribute to enhancing the life experience of all.

Introduction

This book is a complete guide to action research. It is written to help you to undertake an action enquiry, and produce a quality report for publication and further dissemination. It explains how to identify a research question, map out an action plan, use appropriate methodologies, and generate evidence from the data to test your findings against the most stringent critique. It also explains why you should do action research and the potential benefits for your own learning and the learning of others.

There are two main reasons for doing action research. First, you can improve learning in order to improve educational practices. Second, you can advance knowledge and theory, that is, new ideas about how things can be done and why. All research aims to generate knowledge and theory. As a practitioner-researcher, you are aiming to generate theories about learning and practice, your own and other people's.

This is a key point. Most of the action research literature talks about improving practice, but talks less about improving learning as the basis of improved practice, and even less about how this should be seen as new theory and an important contribution to the world of ideas. The literature tends to reinforce the portrayal of practitioners as doers who are competent to be involved in improving practice, but not as thinkers who are competent to be involved in debates about knowledge, or who have good ideas about what is important in life and how we should live. Consequently, in wider debates, including policy debates, practitioners tend to be excluded, on the assumption that they are good at practice, but perhaps they should leave it to official theorists to explain what, how and why people should learn, and how they should use their knowledge. So strong is this discourse that many practitioners have come to believe it themselves, and collude in their own subjugation by refusing to believe that they are competent theorists, or by dismissing 'theory' as above their heads or irrelevant.

We do not go along with this. We believe that practitioners can, and should, get involved. We also believe that theory itself needs to be reconceptualized, not as an abstract, seemingly esoteric field of study, but as a practical way of thinking about social affairs and how they can be improved. This is why doing action research is so important. You can show how you have learned to improve practice, in terms, say, of achieving better working conditions or increased opportunities for learning, and you can also show how this has enabled you to produce your own personal theory about why it worked (or didn't, if that is the case), and what you need to do differently next time. Theorizing your practice like this shows that you are producing ideas which can influence the learning of others. Your practice is the grounds for your own theory.

This view of theory is barely evident in the mainstream literatures, which largely maintain that theory should be expressed as sets of propositions, or statements, produced by official knowledge creators in universities and think tanks. Such propositional theories do exist, of course, and are important, for example, for predicting social trends and keeping track of national economies. However, this is not the only kind of theory. People's living theories are just as important as propositional theories, but they tend not to be seen as such. There should be room enough for both kinds, and discussions about how one can contribute to the development of the other.

We authors subscribe firmly to Foucault's idea that knowledge is power. We urge you to regard yourself as a researcher, well capable of creating your own theories by studying your living practice. You have important things to say, both in relation to workplace practices, and also in relation to the world of ideas and theory. We have written this book to help you to say those things in such a way that others will listen and want to hear more. The book aims to help you take your rightful place as a publicly acknowledged competent professional and as a brilliant knower.

Reading this book

The book is organized as seven parts, which deal with what and why you need to know, how you learn and test your learning, and how you disseminate your knowledge for public use. The chapters follow a coherent sequence, and each deals with a separate issue. The material is organized like this so that you can see action research as a whole, and also focus on particular issues as needed. The chapters are reasonably short and snappy, with case stories throughout. We do emphasize that whenever we present ideas as free standing, this is for analysis only. Action research is an integrated practice, comprising multiple practices, all of which contribute to everything else, so it is important to see the holistic connections and their potentials for generating further connections.

You should note the form of the book as you work with it. We have presented it as an example of the generative transformational nature of living systems, which is one of the key themes that underpin our work. This idea, which is a recurrent theme throughout the history of ideas, is that each living organism has its own internal generative capacity to transform itself into an infinitude of new forms. Each new form is a more fully realized version than the previous one. Caterpillars metamorphose into butterflies, and acorns into oak trees. Here we explain how values can turn into practices, and beginning action researchers into doctoral candidates. The organization of the ideas in the text also reflects this idea of relentless and unstoppable growth. 'How to do action research' turns into 'Why do action research?' and 'What can you achieve for social good?' We do not stop at how to do the action, but develop into how your action can transform into the grounds for your own and other people's new learning, and what the implications of your work may be.

This transformational process mirrors our own commitments as professional educators. We believe, like Habermas (1975), that people cannot not learn. We all learn, potentially every moment of every waking day. What we learn is at issue, and what we do with that learning. Do we transform our learning into new learning and new practices that will benefit ourselves and others? In other words, what educational influence do we have in our own learning, in the learning of others, and in the learning of social formations? Do we celebrate our living, in the certainty that one day we will be gone? What kind of legacy will we leave? What do we do, to try to ensure a better world today for tomorrow?

Working with the text itself can be seen as you engaging in your action enquiry about how you can learn about action research and generate your own ideas about how to do it and what some of the implications may be for your own practice. On page 79 we explain that doing action research involves asking a range of questions, such as the following:

- What is my concern?
- Why am I concerned?
- How do I gather evidence to show reasons for my concern?
- What do I do about the situation?
- How can I check whether any conclusions I come to are reasonably fair and accurate?
- How do I evaluate the validity of my account of learning?
- How do I modify my practice in the light of my evaluation?
- How do I explain the significance of my work?

In the introduction to each part we draw your attention to where you are in this action–reflection cycle. As you read and work with the ideas, you may become aware of your own process of becoming increasingly critical, and more aware of the values base of what you are doing in your real-life contexts.

We invite you to engage with these ideas, and to transform your own understanding about how you can make your contribution. While you may be concerned initially with how to do action research, we urge you to think about what you can achieve through your own enquiry, and how this can benefit yourself and others.

Writing the book

The book is part of our own writing and dissemination programme, as we pursue our research into how we can encourage practitioners to believe in themselves as they produce their descriptions and explanations (their theories) of practice and produce accounts that will contribute to new learning. We believe passionately in the right of all to speak and be listened to, and we believe in the need for individual practitioners, working collectively, to show how they hold themselves accountable for what they do. We aim to do the same. Although we do not appear much in this book as real persons, you can easily contact us and access our work via our websites, which show how we also test our ideas against public critique. If you contact us, we will respond.

We hope that this book speaks to your experience.

Jean McNiff and Jack Whitehead

You can contact Jack at A.J.Whitehead@bath.ac.uk. His website is http://www.actionresearch.net.

You can contact Jean at jeanmcniff@mac.com. Her website is http://www.jeanmcniff.com.

Part I

What Do I Need To Know?

Action research is about practitioners creating new ideas about how to improve practice, and putting those ideas forward as their personal theories of practice. This is different from traditional social science, which is about official researchers producing theory, which practitioners apply to their practice, so immediately we are into a context of power and politics around the struggle for knowledge and recognition as a knower.

Part I provides the setting for a discussion of these ideas. It contains the following chapters.

Chapter 1   What is action research?
Chapter 2   Who does action research?
Chapter 3   The underpinning assumptions of action research
Chapter 4   Where did action research come from?

We said in the Introduction that you could regard working with the ideas in this book as your own action enquiry into how you can learn about action research and how to do it. At this point in your action–reflection cycle you are asking, 'What is my concern?' You are articulating the idea that you need to find out what the core ideas of action research are, so that you have a firm grasp of the basics in order to begin an action enquiry from an informed position.

1

What Is Action Research?

The action research family is wide and diverse, so inevitably different people say different things about what action research is, what it is for, and who can do it and how. You need to know about these issues, so that you can take an active part in the debates. Taking part also helps you to get to grips with why you should do action research and what you can hope to achieve.

This chapter is organized into four sections that deal with these issues.

1   What action research is and is not
2   Different approaches to action research
3   Purposes of action research
4   When to use action research and when not

1   WHAT ACTION RESEARCH IS AND IS NOT

Action research is a form of enquiry that enables practitioners everywhere to investigate and evaluate their work. They ask, 'What am I doing? What do I need to improve? How do I improve it?' Their accounts of practice show how they are trying to improve their own learning, and influence the learning of others. These accounts come to stand as their own practical theories of practice, from which others can learn if they wish (see McNiff and Whitehead 2002).

Action research has become increasingly popular around the world as a form of professional learning. It has been particularly well developed in education, specifically in teaching, and is now used widely across the professions. One of the attractions about action research is that everyone can do it, so it is for 'ordinary' practitioners as well as principals, managers and administrators. Students can also do, and should do, action research (Steinberg and Kincheloe 1998). You can gain university accreditation for your action enquiries. Case studies appear in this book from action researchers who never thought when they began their enquiries that they would get their masters and doctoral degrees.

Action research can be a powerful and liberating form of professional enquiry because it means that practitioners themselves investigate their own practice as they find ways of living more fully in the direction of their educational values. They are not told what to do. They decide for themselves what to do, in negotiation with others. This can work in relation to individual and also collective enquiries. More and more groups of practitioners are getting together to investigate their collective work and put their stories of learning into the public domain. Your story can add to that collection and strengthen it.

This is what makes action research distinctive. It is done by practitioners themselves rather than a professional researcher, who does research on practitioners, as is often the case in traditional forms of social science research. Social scientists tend to stand outside a situation and ask, 'What are those people over there doing? How do we understand and explain what they are doing?' This kind of research is often called spectator research, and is usually outsider research. Action researchers, however, are insider researchers. They see themselves as part of the situation they are investigating, and ask, individually and collectively, 'Is my/our work going as we wish? How do we improve it where necessary?' If they feel their work is already reasonably satisfactory, they evaluate it to show why they believe this to be the case. If they feel something needs improving, they work on that aspect, keeping records and producing regular oral and written progress reports about what they are doing.

Here are some examples of social science questions and action research questions to show the difference between them.

Social science questions	Action research questions
What is the relationship between teacher motivation and teacher retention?	How do I influence the quality of teachers' experience in school, so that they decide to stay?
Does management style influence worker productivity?	How do I improve my management style to encourage productivity?
Will a different seating arrangement increase audience participation?	How do I encourage greater audience participation through trying out different seating arrangements?

Action research aims to be a disciplined, systematic process. A notional action plan is:

- take stock of what is going on
- identify a concern
- think of a possible way forward
- try it out
- monitor the action by gathering data to show what is happening
- evaluate progress by establishing procedures for making judgements about what is happening

- test the validity of accounts of learning
- modify practice in the light of the evaluation.

(This is a modified version of the plan in McNiff et al. 2003.)

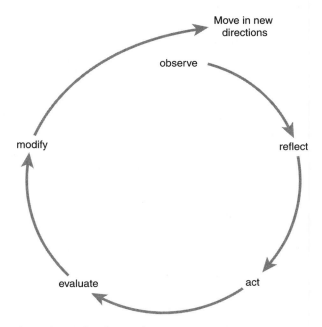

FIGURE 1.1   An action–reflection cycle

In your action enquiry you would identify something of concern, try a different way of doing things, reflect on what was happening, and in the light of your reflections try a new way that may or may not be more successful. For example, Caitríona McDonagh (2000) tried out different reading programmes for her children with reading difficulties, none of which seemed to help. She realized that she had to change her pedagogies and teach in a way that helped the children to learn. Geoff Mead (2001) tells of his professional learning in the police service, where he transformed personal and institutional constraints into a context in which he could theorize police leadership as an inclusive, holistic practice.

The process of 'observe – reflect – act – evaluate – modify – move in new directions' is generally known as action–reflection, although no single term is used in the literature. Because the process tends to be cyclical, it is often referred to as an action–reflection cycle (Figure 1.1). The process is ongoing because as soon as we reach a provisional point where we feel things are satisfactory, that point itself raises new questions and it is time to begin again. Good visual models exist in the literature to communicate this process (for example Elliott 1991).

2   DIFFERENT APPROACHES TO ACTION RESEARCH

Different approaches have emerged within the action research family. While all action researchers ask questions about influencing processes of change, different perspectives ask different kinds of questions. To appreciate the differences, we need to go back to the idea mentioned above of outsider and insider research.

Throughout the twentieth century, new forms of enquiry became established. A shift took place in some quarters, away from a positivist view towards an interpretive view. Positivism held that the world was a 'thing', separate from an observer. It was possible to observe and comment on the world in an objective, value-free way. In the same way, knowledge was a 'thing', separate from a knower, so it was possible also to comment on knowledge in an objective, value-free way. This view led to a tradition in which the world and its phenomena could be studied, experimented with and analysed, and outcomes could be predicted and controlled by manipulating variables in the form of objects, people and practices.

The emergent interpretive tradition, however, held that people were part of and created their own reality, so it did not make sense to see the world as separate from the people who inhabited it, or practices as separate from the people who were doing them. Rather than study the world and practices as separate phenomena, the focus shifted to understanding how people interacted with one another and their environment. In many instances, the focus in the physical sciences has shifted over time to understanding how the world can be sustained, and in the social sciences to how personal and social practices interact with one another so that people can sustain their own life practices, and, in some cases, come to understand how these can contribute to sustaining the planet itself. The purpose of much research therefore has shifted from a wish to control the environment and human practices by imposing change from without to a commitment to understanding and improving the environment and human practices by changing them from within.

These different perspectives can be seen as influenced by the different values commitments of researchers themselves. People's values are part of their ontological perspectives. 'Ontology' means 'a theory of being', so how we perceive ourselves (our theory of being) can influence how we perceive others and our environment. If we perceive ourselves as discrete, self-contained identities, we will tend to see others as separate from us, whereas if we see ourselves as constantly creating our identities, we may come to see others as sharing our lives within a shared environment. This does not mean that we relinquish our uniqueness as individuals. Rather, we see ourselves as unique human beings who are inevitably in company with other unique human beings. Further, some people have come to see themselves as so deeply involved in the co-creation of new identities, and trying to understand how this process of transformative self-creation can come to influence how they can work collectively for sustainable personal and collective wellbeing, that a distinct focus has emerged to do with how persons understand and accept their own responsibility for accounting for why they live as they do.

It has to be noted that some researchers still maintain a strictly positivist stance, while many others prefer to adopt a more reflective attitude. Lively debates take place in the literature to argue these different perspectives.

Ontological perspectives and boundaries

An understanding of how ontological perspectives influence personal and social practices is essential to understanding different perspectives in action research.

Some action researchers maintain an almost exclusive self-perception as external researchers who are watching what other people are doing. They set up rigid boundaries that come to act as demarcations between themselves and others. Standing outside the situation, they observe other people doing action research and ask, 'What are those people doing? How can their practice be described? How can it be explained?'

Often, however, the researcher becomes involved in the situation, and can become an insider researcher. Sometimes the researcher gets so involved that they become a participant. Then they ask, 'What are we doing? How can our action be described and explained?' A good deal of participatory and collaborative action research adopts this perspective. The boundaries between people begin to dissolve, as people see themselves as united in a common endeavour to improve their own circumstances. However, this stance can be problematic in the reporting stage, because questions can arise about who tells the research story, whose voice is heard, and who speaks on behalf of whom. In much interpretive research, the researcher's voice is usually heard rather than the participants'. Participants are sometimes viewed as sources of data rather than as actors, so further questions arise about how power relationships are used, and why.

A new focus on self-study, which is the basis of this book, has emerged in recent times. Self-study places individual researchers at the centre of their own enquiries. Researchers ask, 'What am I doing? How do I describe and explain my actions to you?' The individual 'I' is always seen to exist in company with other individual 'I's', and each asks, 'How do I hold myself accountable to myself and to you?' The boundaries begin to dissolve, as researchers come to see themselves as sharing meanings, that is, developing a common understanding about what they are doing and why. Boundaries become permeable membranes (Capra 2003), where meanings and commitments flow between lives, and people perceive themselves not as separate entities, though still unique individuals, but as sharing the same life space as others (Rayner 2002; 2003; Whitehead 2005).

The idea of self-study has become popular worldwide, and many accounts show its potential for generating personal, organizational and social change.

For example, Jackie Delong, working as a superintendent in the Grand Erie District Board in Ontario, has done much to embed action research organizationally, so that all teachers have the opportunity of evaluating their work as the basis for their career-long learning pathways (Delong 2002); and Je Kan Adler-Collins, a nursing supervisor in the Faculty of Nursing in Fukuoka University, Japan, is developing a curriculum that encourages nursing practitioners to understand and improve their work (Adler-Collins 2004).

Ironically, some of the new self-study literature adopts a spectator approach. Some authors analyse self-study in an abstract way, rather than talk from the experience of their own self-studies. Other practitioners, however, show the reality of their self-studies by explaining what their values are and showing whether or not they are realizing them. Madeline Church (2004; Church et al. 2003), for example, a consultant in the development of evaluations in international networks, undertook her self-study to explore ways of developing the work of international networks as emancipatory processes that liberate individuals to work together for common educational processes; and Máirín Glenn (2003; 2004), a primary school teacher, investigated her learning as she helped children and colleagues to come to appreciate their capacity for original thinking and creativity.

Personal theories are especially powerful for sustainable educational change. Sustainable change happens when people create and implement their own ideas rather than only accept and implement the ideas of others. Existing power relationships between 'experts' and 'trainees' are demolished and more democratic forms of working developed. While an external researcher may make suggestions about what a practitioner may do, it is for the practitioner to make decisions and stand over them.

3   PURPOSES OF ACTION RESEARCH

The purpose of all research is to generate new knowledge. Action research generates a special kind of knowledge.

Action research has always been understood as people taking action to improve their personal and social situations. Some see its potential for promoting a more productive and peaceful world order (Heron 1998; Heron and Reason 2001). A strong new theme is emerging about how action researchers can find more democratic ways of working for sustainable organizational development (McNiff and Whitehead 2000). Educational action research is coming to be seen as a methodology for real-world social change.

As noted, much educational research (and action research) is written about from a spectator perspective. Researchers offer conceptual analyses and explanations of action research and its possible uses, which tend to stay at the level of words. Mill (1985) said that such analyses often produce 'dead dogma'.

According to Mill, ideas that stay on a page remain lifeless, because they do not make the real-world link with action.

The potential of action research becomes real when ideas are linked with action. People can give meaning to their lives, because they stop talking about action research and start talking about themselves as action researchers. They communicate their ideas as theories of real-world practice, by explaining what they are doing, why they are doing it, and what they hope to achieve. These personal theories are also living theories, because they change and develop as people change and develop themselves. The purpose of action research is to generate living theories about how learning has improved practice and is informing new practices.

The best accounts show the transformation of practice into living theories. The individual practitioner asks, 'What am I doing? How do I understand it in order to improve it? How can I draw on ideas in the literature, and incorporate them into my own understanding? How do I transform these ideas into action?' Asking these questions can help practitioners to find practical ways of living in the direction of their educational and social values. Breda Long (2003) explains how she influenced people's understandings of processes of organizational change; and Alon Serper (2004) explains how he has come to understand his own ontological being in the world.

4   WHEN TO USE ACTION RESEARCH AND WHEN NOT

You can use action research for many purposes, but not for all.

When to use action research

Use action research when you want to evaluate whether what you are doing is influencing your own or other people's learning, or whether you need to do something different to ensure that it is. You may want to:

Improve your understanding

- Relations are strained in your workplace. How are you going to find out why, so that you can do something about it?
- Your students are achieving remarkably high scores. Why? Is it your teaching, their extra study, or a new classroom environment?

Develop your learning

- How do you learn to encourage people to be more positive?
- How do you learn to improve your own timekeeping?

Influence others' learning

- How do you help colleagues to develop more inclusive pedagogies?
- How do you encourage your senior management team partners to listen more carefully to employees?

When not to use action research

Do not use action research if you want to draw comparisons, show statistical correlations, or demonstrate a cause and effect relationship. For example:

- If you want to see whether adults who are accompanied by children are more likely to wait at pedestrian crossings than those who are not accompanied by children, you would do an observational study and include statistical analyses of a head count.
- If you want to see why some male teachers seem reluctant to teach relationships and sexuality education, you would probably do a survey and analyse the results. You may also possibly do a comparative analysis of results from your survey and one you have read about, which aims to find out which subjects teachers find most attractive.
- If you want to show the effects of good leadership on teaching motivation you could interview a sample of teachers and analyse their responses in terms of identified categories. You would probably also interview a sample of educational leaders and get their opinions on the relationship between their leadership and the quality of teachers' motivation.

These are social science topics where researchers ask questions such as, 'What are those people doing? What do they say? How many of them do it?' Action research questions, however, take the form, 'How do I understand what I am doing? How do I improve it?', and place the emphasis on the researcher's intent to take action for personal and social improvement.

We said in the Introduction that educational research should make room for all kinds of research and encourage interchange of ideas by researchers working in different traditions. One way is to show how living theories can draw on the findings of abstract spectator theories. 'How do I ...?' questions often incorporate questions of the form 'What is happening here?' (see page 15, for example).

This kind of fact-finding can often be the beginning of an action enquiry. John Elliott (1991) rightly calls it a reconnaissance phase. However, it is necessary to go beyond fact-finding and into action if real-world bullying is to stop or engaged reading begin.

'How do I ...?' questions	'What is happening here?' questions
How do I stop the bullying in my class?	How many children are being bullied? Who is bullying whom? Why are they bullying them?
How do I encourage my students to read?	What kind of books do my students read at present? How many categories of books are in the college library? How much time is given to independent reading in the curriculum?

SUMMARY

This chapter has set out some core issues in action research. It has explained that, unlike social science, action research places the individual 'I' at the centre of an enquiry. Different forms of action research have emerged over the years, which prioritize different aspects. Action research can be useful when investigating how to improve learning and take social action. It is inappropriate for investigations that aim to draw comparisons or establish cause and effect relationships.

The next chapter deals with the interesting and contested question of who does action research, and who says.

2

Who Does Action Research?

Anyone and everyone can do action research. You do not need any specialized equipment or knowledge. All you need is curiosity, creativity, and a willingness to engage. You can do action research virtually anywhere, in institutional settings, in homes, and on safaris.

Investigating your work and finding ways to improve it means that you now become a knowledge creator. This idea has implications for the politics of knowledge, because not all people would agree that practitioners should be knowledge creators. Some people think that practitioners should concern themselves only with workplace practice, and not get involved in research or generating knowledge. Others think that practitioners should credit themselves as working with their intellects and contributing to policy debates. These differences of opinion can be traced back to differences of interests (see page 249). The question arises: whose interests are served by perpetuating the mythology that practitioners cannot do research or think for themselves, or that those currently positioned as knowledge workers should not see themselves also as practitioners?

This chapter is organized into four sections, which address the following issues.

1   Who is a practitioner?
2   Why is practitioner knowledge important?
3   What is special about practitioners' theories?
4   How can practitioners contribute to new practices and new theories?

1   WHO IS A PRACTITIONER?

The contested nature of the territory is well illustrated by a famous metaphor by Donald Schön about the topology of professional landscapes.

The topology of professional landscapes

In 1983, and later in 1995 (see page 239), Schön developed a metaphor that was to become an enduring theme in the social sciences and education. He wrote

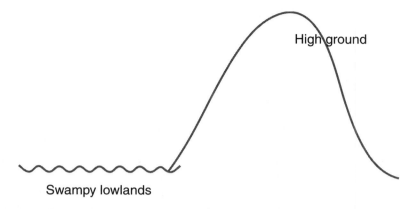

High ground

Swampy lowlands

FIGURE 2.1   The topology of professional landscapes

about the topology (the contours and different heights) of professional landscapes, where there is a high ground and a swampy lowlands. The high ground is occupied mainly by academics, perceived as official researchers, who produce 'pure' conceptual theory about education and other matters. This theory is regarded as legitimate both by themselves and by practitioners. Practitioners occupy the swampy lowlands. They are involved in everyday practices and so create the kind of knowledge that is valuable for conducting everyday lives. However, it is held both by academics and by practitioners that practitioner knowledge should not be regarded as theory, nor should practitioners regard themselves as legitimate knowledge creators. In this metaphor, Schön returns us to the issue addressed in the Introduction. The entire research community, including educational researchers, have been persuaded to believe that there are 'real' theorists, whom Schön (1983) calls 'professional elites', who produce abstract conceptual theory, and there are practitioners, those in workplaces, who create practical knowledge, which is useful knowledge but not 'real' theory. The irony for Schön in all this is that the knowledge produced in the swampy lowlands is the kind of knowledge that is of most benefit to ordinary people, while the knowledge produced on the high ground is often far removed from the practicalities of everyday life, and so often does not touch ordinary people in a meaningful and relevant way. Its remoteness is accentuated by the kind of language used. Professional elites tend to use their own language to talk to one another. This language can often be obscure and in code, and, in Schön's opinion (which is shared by other researchers such as Jenkins 1992 and Thomas 1998), the elites deliberately keep it that way.

Schön maintained that practitioners in the swampy lowlands should create their own knowledge through investigating their practice, and submit their emergent personal theories to the same rigorous processes of testing and critique as happens in the creation of high-ground theory. This was important if practitioners wanted to demonstrate the validity of their arguments, and have their ideas accepted as bone fide theory by the high-ground research community and the wider public.

Schön's ideas were definitely appropriate for former times, and still hold true for some quarters today, but things have changed considerably with the advent of action research. The topology is beginning to level out. Many people working in higher education and managerial positions now perceive themselves as practitioners in a workplace with the responsibility of supporting people in other workplaces, while also generating their theories of practice about how they do this. Self-study as a recognized discipline has legitimized their positioning as practitioners who are supporting other practitioners, and who are creating democratic communities of practice committed to a scholarship of educational enquiry (Whitehead 1999). Patricia Mannix McNamara (2003), for example, tells how she regards herself as an academic in a higher education setting, whose work is to support the enquiries of others, while herself a part-time PhD candidate. What she learns from her doctoral studies informs her practice with masters students, and what she learns from them informs her doctoral studies. She sees her professional identity not in terms of a formal role but in terms of how she understands her relationships with others. The changing topology has highlighted the need for all to regard themselves as practitioners and to study their practice collaboratively, in a disciplined and scholarly way, and to make their accounts of practice public, so that others in their communities and elsewhere can learn and benefit.

The implications for recognition and accreditation are considerable. Those who are not seeking accreditation for workplace learning come to be regarded as competent professionals. Those who are seeking accreditation come to be seen as practitioner academics whose studies are supported by academic practitioners. Any previously existing hierarchies of power between academics and practitioners are demolished, and power is shared among equals for the benefit of others.

2   WHY IS PRACTITIONER KNOWLEDGE IMPORTANT?

Practitioner knowledge is central to practical and theoretical sustainability.

Practical sustainability

Sustainability refers to the idea that living systems have the capacity for interdependent self-renewal, which is indispensable for continuing development. Reliance on an external agency means that a system may collapse if the agency is withdrawn, whereas internal capacity means the interdependent creation of renewable resources for growth.

Practitioners' personal theories constitute these renewable resources. All are free to stake their claim about what needs to be done to enable themselves and others to grow in ways that are right for them. This was the idea that first inspired action research. Lewin (1946), one of the originators of action research (page 36), believed that if all members of a workforce were involved collaboratively in implementing and testing strategy, the organization itself would grow. This view is developed in important new literatures. Amartya Sen (1999), winner of the 1998 Nobel Prize in Economic Science, distinguishes between an economic theory of human capability and theories of human capital. He talks about the need to move from seeing capital accumulation in primarily physical terms to seeing it as a process in which human beings are integrally involved in the production of their own futures. Through education, learning, and skill formation, people can become more productive over time, which contributes greatly to the process of economic expansion.

Theoretical sustainability

Practitioners' theories of practice are also core to sustainable theoretical development, in the sense that educational research needs to show its own capacity for self-renewal. It can do this by developing new forms that increasingly demonstrate their capacity for internal transformation. Grand theory, that is, the idea of a body of knowledge that deals with eternal truths, is now complemented by local forms of theory that celebrate individual narratives. New 'movements' such as postmodernism explain how researchers need to regard themselves as influenced by, and influencing, the situation they are investigating. Some researchers such as John Law (2004) explain that the stories people tell about research actually come to inform how they do research in the future.

Action research has this self-transforming capacity. Practitioners can show how they have contributed to new practices, and how these new practices can transform into new theory. When researchers claim that they have generated new theory, they are saying that they have created knowledge that never existed before. Perhaps pieces of knowledge existed, but what practitioners do with that knowledge and how they have reconfigured it in relation to their own contexts can be seen as their original theorizing. This capacity for ongoing creativity contributes greatly to sustainability.

3   WHAT IS SPECIAL ABOUT PRACTITIONERS' THEORIES?

The basis for many practitioners' research is that they are trying to live in the direction of their educational values (see page 46). If they hold values of justice and compassion, they try to live in a way that is just and compassionate. They make practical judgements about the extent to which they can show that they are living in the direction of these values.

For example, Bernie Sullivan, who is a traveller resource teacher in Ireland, has deep commitments to the rights of traveller children to celebrate their own culture, dialect, and ways of knowing. Traveller children in mainstream schools, however, are often required to fit in with the conventions and cultures of the settled community, a situation which can lead to conflict and distress when, for example, traveller children are required to speak in a standard dialect, or their intellectual capacity is judged by means of standardized tests. This situation denies Bernie's values of justice and compassion, and she works hard to raise awareness among her colleagues of the importance of valuing the traditions of minority cultures such as the traveller community. She also works hard to influence discourses at a wider level by offering her theories of justice, which are rooted in her classroom practice, as legitimate ways of thinking about justice and compassion (Sullivan 2004).

Like Bernie, many practitioners work in contexts where their values of justice and compassion are denied in practice. Nor are external forces the only sources of this denial. Most of us often deny our own values by acting in a way that is contrary to what we believe in. Then we put our best efforts into trying to practise in a way that is consistent with our values, and we assess the quality of our work in those terms. We gather data and generate evidence that we believe show instances of ourselves at work with others in ways that can be understood as in keeping with our values, such as justice and compassion, and we invite critical feedback on our perceptions. If other people agree that we are acting in accordance with our values, we can claim that we now know better, and put forward our claims for public consideration.

This is a rigorous and stringent research process that can be seen as systematic enquiry and an uncompromising testing of claims to knowledge. The account that a practitioner produces contains descriptions of the research (what was done) and explanations (why it was done and what was aimed for). This account then constitutes the practitioner's own theory.

4   HOW CAN PRACTITIONERS CONTRIBUTE TO NEW PRACTICES AND NEW THEORIES?

Many people believe that 'theory' is something mysterious, which it is not. We often say things like, 'I have a theory about cats', or 'This is my theory about the way things work.' A theory is a set of ideas about what we claim to know and how we have come to know. If we can show that what we know (our theory) stands up to public scrutiny, we can claim that our theory has valildity (has truth value and is trustworthy).

By doing your research, you can claim to have generated your theory of practice, that is, you can say with confidence that you know what you are doing and why you are doing it. You are showing that you are acting in a systematic way, not *ad hoc*, and that you are developing a praxis, which is morally committed practice.

Your theory of practice may contain other theories, such as a theory of learning or a theory of management. Mary Hartog (2004), a tutor in higher education in the UK, created her own theory of learning – her own theory of education – by showing how she supported teachers who were studying for their masters degrees in a way that enabled them to learn effectively. Pip Bruce Ferguson (1999), also a tutor in higher education in New Zealand, created her theory of educational management by showing how she ensured equal opportunities for Maori and white practitioners. Moira Laidlaw (2002), a volunteer worker supporting teachers and administrators in China, has shown how she is creating a theory of sustainable development by enabling teachers to engage in new practices that encourage people to take control of their individual and collective lives for social benefit. All these theories are valid theories, because they have been demonstrated as having truth value through a rigorous process of stringent public critique. They are not just a matter of their authors' opinions. The accounts of practice recount what are now social facts. Social situations have changed for the better because of these practitioners' committed interventions.

SUMMARY

This chapter has set out a debate about the politics of knowledge, in relation to who should be regarded as a practitioner or a member of an elite, and who decides. It has addressed the questions:

- Who is a practitioner?
- Why is practitioner knowledge important?
- What is special about practitioners' theories?
- How can practitioners contribute to new practices and new theories?

The point has been made that all should regard themselves as practitioners, regardless of role or setting, who are involved in learning and influencing the learning of others.

The next chapter develops some of these ideas as we consider the main features of action research and its underpinning assumptions.

3

The Underpinning Assumptions of Action Research

In order to see how action research is different from other kinds of research, it is useful to look at the underpinning assumptions, and see how these can transform into different kinds of practices. Doing this also reveals the main features of action research.

Action research is one form of research among many. You use different forms of research to achieve different goals, in the same way as you use different vehicles for different purposes. You use a tractor to plough a field and a fast car to get somewhere quickly. You use action research when you want to find ways of taking action to improve learning with social intent.

We also need to remember that all kinds of research, including action research, share common features, which distinguish them as research and not just activity. Those features include the following:

- They identify a research issue.
- They identify research aims.
- They set out a research design (plan).
- They gather data.
- They establish criteria and standards of judgement.
- They generate evidence from the data.
- They make a claim to knowledge.
- They submit the claim to critique.
- They explain the significance of the work.
- They disseminate the findings.
- They link new knowledge with existing knowledge.

(See McNiff et al. 2003: 10–12 for further discussion of these points.)

Where research traditions differ is how they perceive the positioning of the researcher (ontological commitments), the relationship between the knower and what is known (epistemological commitments), the processes of generating knowledge (methodological commitments), and the goals of research in terms of how the knowledge will be used (social commitments). It is not only action research that is different from other kinds of research. All research methodologies are different from one another according to these underpinning assumptions. However, self-study action research has made a gigantic leap from other research methodologies, in that the researcher is placed at the centre of the enquiry, and accepts the responsibility of showing how they account for themselves.

This chapter sets out these underpinning assumptions. It is in four sections.

1   Ontological assumptions
2   Epistemological assumptions
3   Methodological assumptions
4   Social purposes of action research

1   ONTOLOGICAL ASSUMPTIONS

Ontology is the study of being. Our ontologies influence how we view ourselves in our relationships with others. The ontological commitments that underpin action research include the following.

- Action research is value laden.
- Action research is morally committed.
- Action researchers perceive themselves as in relation with one another in their social contexts.

Action research is value laden

Positivist forms of research are notionally value free. The researcher stays out of the research, so as not to 'contaminate' it, and reports are written in the third person ('the researcher did'), which is supposed to reduce bias in the claim to objectivity. Some social science adopts this perspective, but not all.

Action research is done by people who are trying to live in the direction of the values and commitments that inspire their lives. You may be passionate about justice, or about people being free to run their own lives. You may see your patients as real people who can make decisions about their treatments. Your values come to act as your guiding principles. Action research often begins by articulating your values and asking whether you are being true to them. Cruelty is a value as much as kindness. It is up to you to decide which values you want to live by and be accountable for.

Action researchers often experience themselves as 'living contradictions' (Whitehead 1989) (see page 46), in that they hold a set of values, yet do not live according to them. You may believe in justice but act in an unjust way. You set out to find ways of living in the direction of your values. This can be difficult, because investigating one's practice involves other people who have values of their own, and these may not be commensurate with your own. It is then a case of negotiating meanings and practices, which is easy to say but difficult to do (see Chapter 18 for some implications).

Action research is morally committed

Action researchers choose which values they subscribe to, and they show how they hold themselves accountable for their choices. Doing your action enquiry involves explaining what inspires you to do things as you do, and what you hope to achieve. If you are aiming to improve some aspect of your practice, you are doing it for a reason, consistent with what you believe to be better practice, which involves explaining what you understand as 'good' and 'better', to avoid being seen as imposing your values on others. This can be tricky, because people hold different views of 'good'. We live and learn in different cultures, which have their own values system. You have to decide which values system to live by, within your own culture. You may sometimes choose to seek a cultural transformation because your values conflict with cultural norms. Whatever you decide, you will aim to make yours a purposeful, morally committed practice, that is, praxis.

Remember that you cannot hold yourself responsible for other people's decisions. They decide for themselves, just like you. It is your responsibility to hold yourself accountable for yourself, and how you try to influence other people's learning. This has big implications. Do you do it in a coercive way, insisting that people listen to you, or in a more educational way, respecting others' points of view but inviting them to consider other options?

Holding these views can get you into trouble within established contexts. For example, Mary Roche (2003), a primary teacher, encourages her four- and five-year-old children to think critically and to ask questions about the status quo. When the children were instructed to form straight lines in the playground during a fire drill, one of them asked, 'What's so good about straight lines anyway?' Critical pedagogies that encourage such questions can often get researchers into trouble if they work in institutions that are run according to bureaucratic values. The richness of Mary's critical pedagogy is demonstrated by the capacity of her young children to question their own and other people's assumptions, which is the basis of quality citizenship (see also Roche 2000).

Action researchers perceive themselves as in relation with one another in their social contexts

An increasingly important perspective in action research is the development of relational and inclusional values (see also Chapter 25). The idea of establishing inclusive relationships refers not only to the social world, where we see ourselves in relation with others, but also to the mental world, where we see how ideas are in relation with other ideas. The core idea of transformative capacity enables us to incorporate the insights of others and transform them as we create our theories of practice.

Action researchers always see themselves in relation with others, in terms of their practices and also their ideas, and the rest of their environment. They do not adopt a spectator approach, or conduct experiments on others. They undertake enquiries with others, recognizing that people are always in company. Even when we are alone, we are still in the company of others, who are perhaps absent in time and space, but their influence is evident. The pen or computer you use was created by someone else. The ideas you express began as other people's ideas. What is special is that you have made the equipment and the ideas your own. You have mediated them through your own unique capacity for creativity, perhaps using your computer in special ways or reconfiguring other people's ideas in your own original way. Your beginnings, however, were in other people. You have transformed those beginnings into new opportunities and practices.

The idea of never being alone is key. Although the focus of the enquiry is you, as you ask, 'How do I improve what I am doing?', your question automatically assumes that any answer will involve other people's perceptions of your influence in their learning. You are also in company with others who are asking the same question, and who also assume that their answers will involve other people's perceptions of their influence in learning. It is not a case of you as a free-standing 'I', in the company of other free-standing 'I's', because each one of you recognizes that you are in company, and that you form a community of 'I's', all of whom understand that their claims to educational influence will be evaluated by others within their range of influence.

Action researchers therefore aim to develop inclusional methodologies that nurture respectful relationships. This does not mean that everyone has to agree on how we should live in terms of social practices. Differences of opinion are understood as the basis for creative engagement. It does, however, mean that everyone recognizes the uniqueness of the other, even though the other acts and thinks in ways that are sometimes radically different from oneself, and they let this attitude inform their practices. The underpinning ethic of inclusion of the other (Habermas 1998) contains a hope, not a requirement, that the other will hold the same view. If all sign up to an inclusional ethic, difficulties can be reduced. The task for action researchers is especially demanding when the other does not sign up to an inclusional ethic, which means that they have to find ways of living in the direction of their values within a context of being with others who do not share the same underpinning ethic of inclusion.

Ontological assumptions at a glance

Given the emphasis on inclusional and relational values:

- Action research is value laden and morally committed, which is a transformation of the assumption that research can be value free.
- It aims to understand what I/we are doing, and not only what 'they' are doing. This demonstrates a shared commitment towards 'we–I' forms of enquiry.
- It assumes that the researcher is in relation with everything else in the research field, and influences, and is influenced by, others. The research field cannot be studied in a value-free way, because the researcher brings their own values with them.

2   EPISTEMOLOGICAL ASSUMPTIONS

Epistemology is to do with how we understand knowledge, and how we come to acquire knowledge. The epistemological assumptions underpinning action research include the following.

- The object of the enquiry is the 'I'.
- Knowledge is uncertain.
- Knowledge creation is a collaborative process.

The object of the enquiry is the 'I'

'The object of enquiry' refers to the focus of the research. In self-study action research, the focus of the research is you. You study yourself, not other people. The questions you ask are of the kind, 'What am I doing? How do I improve it?', not of the kind, 'What are they doing? How do they improve it?' You aim to show how you hold yourself accountable for what you do.

This idea of personal accountability has big implications. One is that you cannot accept responsibility for what others do and think, but you must accept full responsibility for what you do and think. This can be difficult, because it sometimes means being prepared to let go of favourite positions, which may even have become entrenched prejudices. Why do conversations stop when you say something? Are people so impressed with what you say that they are awe-struck, or could it be that they resist the imposition of your ideas?

Another implication is that you always need to recognize that you may be mistaken. Testing your ideas rigorously against the feedback of others is not a sufficient safeguard. Public approval does not necessarily mean that practices and their underpinning assumptions are socially beneficial, or that claims to, for example, national security and a safer world are believable. The case of Galileo is a classic example. Galileo was shown instruments of torture as if they were to be used on him to make him recant the belief he knew to be true. The most stringent safeguard against the hubris of believing that one is right beyond a reasonable doubt is to take into account the opinions of all whose lives are involved. In your case, this refers to your research participants. In the case of governments, it refers to all citizens of the world.

Knowledge is uncertain

Traditional researchers tend to believe that knowledge is certain, and assume the following (see Berlin 1998).

- There is an answer to everything. Knowledge is certain and true, and is 'out there', waiting to be discovered.
- Knowledge can be discovered using specific methodologies such as the 'scientific method', which aims to predict and control outcomes.
- Answers to questions are fixed for all time. All possible answers are compatible and commensurable.

This perspective may be valuable when it is a case of genetic engineering or weather forecasting, but it does not necessarily work in relation to real human practices, because humans are unique, unpredictable, and make their own choices.

Action researchers tend to assume the following (see Berlin 1998).

- There is no one answer. Knowledge is uncertain and ambiguous. A question may generate multiple answers.
- Knowledge is created, not discovered. This is usually a process of trial and error. Provisional answers, and the process itself, are always open to critique.
- Any answer is tentative, and open to modification. Answers are often incommensurable and cannot be resolved. People just have to live with the dissonance and do the best they can.

This means that action researchers do not look for a fixed outcome that can be applied everywhere. Instead they produce their personal theories to show what they are learning and to invite others to learn with them. They judge their work not in terms of its generalizability or replicability, which are social science criteria, but in terms of whether they can show how they are living in the direction of their educational and social values, using those values as their living standards of judgement (see page 149). It also means that it is legitimate for action researchers to have different aims. In some participatory action research, for example, the motivation to act is to resolve a common problem, whereas other researchers may wish to find ways of living in situations where people disagree, often fundamentally, about how they should live.

Knowledge creation is a collaborative process

Although the 'I' is central, the 'I' should never be understood as in isolation. We all live and work in social situations. Whatever we do in our professional practices potentially influences someone somewhere. Action research means working with others at all stages of the process. At the data gathering stage you (singular or plural) are investigating your practice in relation with others; at the validation stage you negotiate your findings with others. It is definitely not a solitary activity. As well as this, the people you are working with are also possibly doing their action research into their practice, so the situation becomes one of collectives of individuals investigating their practices, a question of the 'I/we' investigating the 'I/we' in company with others who are also investigating their individual or collective practices.

Innovative practices have developed recently, where groups of action researchers have undertaken their joint enquiries. In this case the focus shifts from 'I' to 'we'. This is particularly helpful when the aim of the research is to improve whole organizational practices (see Marshall 1999; 2004). Underpinning such initiatives is the understanding that groups share certain collective values that they wish to realize.

For example, a group of faculty at St Mary's University College in London decided to form themselves into a research group. At an institutional level they wished to show how they were research active. At a personal level, they wished to improve their personal and collective learning about their practice, and about the processes of collaborative learning. Here is the abstract they submitted for a symposium at an international conference (Penny et al. 2004).

Accounting for ourselves as we develop a new scholarship of educational enquiry in our college

In this paper we explain how we are holding ourselves accountable for our educational practices as a group of ten faculty members in a London teacher training college who are working to raise our research capacity for the benefit of ourselves and the teachers we support, and to meet the legislative criteria involved for our College to achieve taught degree-awarding powers. Because we locate our work within the new scholarship of teaching, we regard the study of our practice as our research. By undertaking our self-study action enquiries we show how we are both influencing professional learning for improving practices, and also developing a research culture in our College. We aim to test the validity of our claims to knowledge by submitting them to public critique in this conference forum.

We explain that these innovations involve developing new perspectives about the nature of our work and an acceptance of responsibility for our influence. We hold ourselves accountable for the production of authenticated evidence in support of our claims to knowledge as we ask, 'How do I/we improve my/our work?' We also explain how we are reconceptualizing ourselves as a community of enquiry, and the considerable implications this may have for redefining what counts as institutional forms of teaching and learning practice.

We believe that the educational significance of our work lies in our capacity to clarify the processes we engage in as we explicate the meanings of our lives in educational relation with others. We believe that we are building new professional relationships through our emergent community of enquiry, which have considerable implications for reconceptualizing educational enquiry both as a living educational form of theory and also as a process by which a community of enquiry is formed and sustained.

Epistemological assumptions at a glance

Given the emphasis on inclusional and relational values:

- In action research the object of enquiry is not other people, but the 'I' in relation with other 'I's'.
- Knowledge is uncertain. Answers are created through negotiation. Often answers cannot be negotiated, so people have to learn to live with the situation. Answers can be in how we live as much as in what we say.
- Knowledge is a property of individuals, so it is often subjective and biased. Individuals have to negotiate their meanings with other knowing individuals.

3   METHODOLOGICAL ASSUMPTIONS

Methodologies refer to the way research is conducted. The main methodological assumptions of action research include the following.

- Action research is done by practitioners who regard themselves as agents.
- The methodology is open-ended and developmental.
- The aim of the research is to improve learning with social intent.

Action research is done by practitioners who regard themselves as agents

The idea of agency is that people are able to, and should, take an active part in decisions about how they and others should live. An agent, says Sen (1999: 19), is 'someone who acts and brings about change, and whose achievements can be judged in terms of her own values and objectives, whether or not we assess these in terms of some external criteria as well'.

The main responsibility of agents is to ask questions, and not accept complacency or self-righteous justification, their own or anyone else's. In this sense, they act as public intellectuals (Said 1994) whose job is to interrupt and question the status quo. Why are things as they are? Are they satisfactory? If not, how can they be changed? For action researchers this means that they need always to ask questions and not accept final answers.

Traditional forms of research assume that the researcher is a neutral, value-free operative who observes, collects data and generates evidence to support their findings, but should not influence or be influenced by the research itself. Action researchers accept full responsibility for exercising influence. This involves taking action and considering what influence they may be having in their own and other people's learning. Therefore, when you ask, 'How do I improve what I am doing?' you raise questions about two related processes. The first process refers to what is going on 'out there', in the social situation you are investigating. The second process is about what is going on 'in here', in relation to your own learning. You ask critical questions about why things are as they are. Why do you think as you do? Do you think for yourself, or what someone else tells you? Who writes your script? Further, how can you show that your own capacity for critique influences other people's capacity also to critique?

The methodology is open-ended and developmental

Unlike traditional social science, action enquiries do not aim for closure, nor do practitioners expect to find certain answers. The process itself is the methodology (Mellor 1998), and is frequently untidy, haphazard and experimental. Richard Winter (1998) talks about 'improvisatory self-realisation in action research', where a certain degree of entrepreneurialism is involved; and Marian Dadds and Susan Hart (2001) talk about 'methodological inventiveness', where we try multiple innovative ways until we find the one that is right for us. We look out for what might be a useful way forward, and try it out. One step leads to another, and one cycle of action–reflection leads to another. Answers are held as provisional because any answer already has new questions within itself. This emphasizes the value of being open to new possibilities, and understanding learning as never complete. Traditional ways of doing research offer a completed story. Action researchers let their own story evolve. It is as much about the storyteller as about the story. In a story of the growth of his educational knowledge Whitehead explains how his educational enquiry moved through four social science methodologies of the analytic scientist, the conceptual theorist, the conceptual humanist and the particular humanist (Mitroff and Kilman 1978) before he evolved an educational research methodology for his educational enquiry, 'How do I improve what I am doing?' (Whitehead 1985).

As well as being exciting, this way of working is also risky. Action researchers constantly stand on the edge. The next moment is unknown. They commit to the risk of creating a new future. This is a different mental set from traditional assumptions that knowledge is given. Action researchers anticipate new problematics. Concrete answers do not pre-exist but are created by real people, in negotiation with others. This can be destabilizing for people who are used to being told what to do. Instead of beginning with a hypothesis, which they aim to accept or reject, action researchers start with an idea and follow it where it leads them.

The aim of the research is to improve learning with social intent

Traditional research tends to try to show a cause and effect relationship. It works on the assumption that if people do this, that will happen. The logic abides by the law of contradiction that eliminates statements that are contradictory to 'correct' thought, even though we can experience ourselves in our practice as living contradictions. Many workplace and education programmes work on the principle of cause and effect. Sometimes managers or principals are expected to ensure that specific inputs are arranged to produce certain outputs, which often appear as targets. Many curricula are organized to generate learning outcomes consistent with official policy. Learners are expected to internalize messages. They are expected not to think for themselves but to do as they are told.

If all people have agency, they can, and should, think for themselves and make decisions. Managers and educators need to provide appropriate conditions for this. They should not be overly concerned with behavioural outcomes, unless of course the behaviours in question are hindering the educative process. Their task is to enable people to work with their new knowledge in ways that are right for them, and help them to create their own new futures.

This idea, however, carries conditions. If people wish to create their own futures, they have to accept responsibility for the present. This means generating their theories of practice to show whether the practice is consistent with their values. They generate theories to explain how they are improving their own and other people's learning with social intent, and they subject these theories to stringent critique, before putting them into the public domain for further testing and wider consideration about how new practices can be developed.

Methodological assumptions at a glance

Given the emphasis on inclusional and relational values:

- Action researchers do not do research on others, but do it on themselves, in company with others. Action research is participatory and collaborative in the sense that it takes place in social contexts and involves other people.
- Action research begins with the experience of a concern and follows through a developmental process which shows cycles of action and reflection. It aims to demonstrate relationships of influence.
- Action researchers aim to investigate their practice with a view to improving it. They aim for new beginnings. The idea of closure is transformed into the idea of one state metamorphosing into another. Change is understood as people improving learning to improve practices.

4   SOCIAL PURPOSES OF ACTION RESEARCH

Social purpose refers to why we do research in relation to informing and improving its social contexts. The main social purposes of action research include the following.

- It aims to improve workplace practices through improving learning.
- It aims to promote the ongoing democratic evaluation of learning and practices.
- It aims to create good social orders by influencing the education of social formations.

It aims to improve workplace practices through improving learning

Action research can be workplace based (see Williams and Dick 2004), not exclusively higher education based as traditional research tends to be, and is undertaken by practitioners who regard themselves as researchers, who may or may not be supported by higher education personnel. The aim is to improve practice through improving learning. Improved practices do not just happen. They can improve when people think carefully about what they need to do differently in relation to others. It is then the responsibility of practitioners to produce public accounts that show how their improved learning has led to improved practices. These accounts would contain practitioners' theories of practice, which have arisen from within the practice, and now connect with the accounts and theories of others. As they study what they do and offer these public accounts of practice, practitioners produce accounts that themselves come to constitute a body of theory. These are the personal practical theories of practitioners, which describe and explain processes of working as a living practice. These living theories are different from the conceptual theories of spectator researchers. This is why it is important for you to put your story of practice into the public domain, because you can show how you are contributing to new discourses about how practice should be seen as a living form of theory (see Chapter 7).

It aims to promote the ongoing democratic evaluation of learning and practices

Action research is such a common-sense approach to personal and professional development that, when people first meet the idea, they often say, 'That's what I do in any case. What's different?'

What is different is that action research insists on justifying claims to knowledge by the production of authenticated and validated evidence, and then making the claims public in order to subject them to critical evaluation.

However, evaluation itself is a problematic concept, because different people have different views about what it entails. While most would agree that evaluation aims to establish the value of something, what is valuable for one person is not necessarily valuable for another. Consequently different views exist about who should do evaluation and why, and what they are supposed to be evaluating.

Traditional perspectives regard evaluation as evaluating a thing or a product. Action research, however, is an ongoing process of developing learning and action, and reflection on the learning and action. The process is generative and transformational, because the end of one thing becomes the beginning of something else. All organic systems have their own internal generative capacity to transform themselves into ever more fully developed versions of themselves (McNiff et al. 1992; McNiff and Whitehead 2000). It is not a case of working towards a notional perfect end state, because a living system always has the potential to transform into even more fully realized states. Action research is this kind of generative transformational process, where claims to improved learning and practice generate further learning to improve practice.

The question therefore arises, who evaluates what? In traditional interpretive approaches, which work from a spectator's point of view, an external researcher makes judgements on what other people are doing. From a self-study perspective, the researcher evaluates their own work. If action research is a process in which the 'I' studies the 'I' in company with other 'I's', then evaluation can be seen as the 'I' making judgements about what the 'I' is doing in relation to others. This calls for considerable honesty, and the capacity to listen to and act on critical feedback. It also calls for the articulation of standards of judgement that, consistent with the idea of Sen (see page 19), draw on the practitioner's own values and objectives, as explained throughout the work of Jack Whitehead (see page 46). This discussion continues in Chapter 15.

It aims to create good social orders by influencing the education of social formations

In action research, the situation changes from an external person studying 'them', to an individual studying 'me', or a collective of individuals studying 'us'. Each person asks, 'How do I improve what I am doing for my own and others' benefit?' Each person is seen as an agent with the capacity for influencing their own and others' practices. A collective has the potential to influence wider social change.

In Part VII we discuss fully the idea of the education of social formations and how this can be a contributing factor in the creation of good social orders. In summary, the idea is to do with how social groupings learn to work together. This tends to be much more difficult than it sounds, because working together means working in a way that regards all as legitimate participants whose different traditions and ways of thinking need to be valued. This may be straightforward in contexts where all share more or less the same values base and come from more or less the same tradition, but can be problematic in contexts where parties hold different values perspectives and come from radically different traditions. Further, in politically contested contexts, where one party is dominant, that party may mobilize their resources to continue subjugating the other. The subjugated party then comes to be seen, and sometimes to believe, that they are not worthy of being regarded as a legitimate participant, but remain as peripheral and subservient. In many cases, the oppression leads to such frustration that feelings spill over into violence. How, then, do social groupings learn to see the other as a valuable participant whose opinion and voice may be different, but who needs to be listened to if the dialogue is to go forward? How do the Democratic Unionist Party and Sinn Fein learn to understand the other's point of view? How do Palestinians and Israelis learn to listen, so that they can talk as equals?

In action research, people begin by holding themselves accountable. They do not make judgements on others without first making judgements on themselves, and they do not expect others to do anything they are not prepared first to do themselves. The education of social formations begins with each participant learning to recognize themselves as other to the other (McNiff 2005), and subject to the same conditions of entry to a community that they wish to enforce for others.

Social purposes of action research assumptions at a glance

Given the emphasis on inclusional and relational values:

* Action research can be workplace based, which raises questions about who is seen as a worker, and what is seen as a workplace. It can also take place within non-work based relationships in the family and community.

- Practitioners evaluate their own work in relation to their values. They do not need 'external' evaluation, but they understand the need for stringent testing and evaluation at all stages of the research, which involves the critical insights and judgements of others.
- Practitioners constitute their own social orders, and need to learn how to change their thinking in order to improve their practices. The capacity of individuals to think for themselves and to hold themselves accountable for their educational influence can act as the grounds for the creation of good societies.

SUMMARY

This chapter has set out some of the main features of action research and its underpinning assumptions. The assumptions are ontological, epistemological, method-ological, and to do with social purpose.

The main ontological assumptions are that action researchers see themselves as trying to live in a way that is consistent with their values. These values are to do with the need to see oneself as in relation with others, and how inclusional and relational practices can strengthen those relationships.

The main epistemological assumptions are that knowledge is always in process, so it is impossible to create final answers. Processes of knowledge creation involve social processes, so while knowing may be a property of the individual knower, all answers should be regarded as provisional and subject to social critique.

The main methodological assumptions are that action research is done by practi-tioners who perceive themselves as agents, regardless of their social and institu-tional contexts. Their methodologies are open-ended and developmental as they ask how they can learn to improve social practices.

The main assumptions underpinning the social purposes of action research are that learning can be improved in relation to all social practices, and that the way societies operate can be improved if their members reflect on what they are doing and hold themselves responsible for their own thinking and actions.

We now turn to an outline of the historical development of action research. To appreciate the significance of this, have a look at Part VII to see how the under-pinning assumptions of action research are being realized as social practices. If Chapter 4 sets out what action research is about, and where it has come from, Part VII sets out what its achievements are and where it may be going.

4

Where Did Action Research Come From?

This chapter traces the emergence of action research from its beginnings in the 1930s and 1940s to its current position of world importance. It discusses the historical journey of action research through social science and educational research, and places it within the emergence of different paradigms. The chapter is organized into two sections, which discuss these questions.

1 Where did action research come from?
2 Where is action research located in different research paradigms?

This chapter has implications for the question, 'Where is action research going?', which is dealt with fully in Part VII.

1 WHERE DID ACTION RESEARCH COME FROM?

Action research has been around for some 70 years. It has always been linked with social change for social justice. Noffke (1997) says that the term 'action research' appeared in a 1961 speech by Martin Luther King. An emphasis on learning by Whitehead (1976) shows how people can learn to act in ways that improve learning while connected to democratic processes of evaluation.

It is generally understood that action research began with the work of John Collier in the 1930s, acting as commissioner for Indian affairs, and Kurt Lewin in the 1940s. Lewin, a Jewish refugee from Nazi Germany who worked as a social psychologist in the US, believed that people would be more motivated about their work if they were involved in decision-making about how the workplace was run. He researched what happened when people did become involved (Lewin 1946). Lewin's original ideas have remained influential, and, following his ideas, many researchers organize their work and reports as a cycle of steps: observe – reflect – act – evaluate – modify. This cycle can turn into another cycle. Figure 4.1 shows this process.

In the 1950s action research was taken up in education, specifically by the teaching profession, and Stephen Corey's (1953) book *Action Research to Improve*

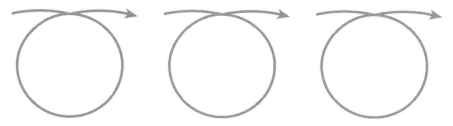

FIGURE 4.1   A cycle of action–reflection cycles

School Practices became influential in America. This could also be seen in the context of the free schools and progressive education movements of the 1960s (Miller 2002), in which the emphasis was on education for the promotion of democratic practices that would enable all people to take a full and active part in political life. Education came to be seen as about the production of thoughtful and responsible citizens.

Action research went into decline in America during the late 1950s because of the focus on the need for technical excellence after the launch of Sputnik and the emergence of new research and development models. It did, however, begin to take hold in Britain, mainly through the influence of Lawrence Stenhouse, who was working in contexts of teacher education. Departing from the previously dominant disciplines approach to education, in which teachers studied the psychology, sociology, history and philosophy of education, Stenhouse advocated a view of teachers as highly competent professionals who should be in charge of their own practice. He maintained that professional education involved:

> The commitment to systematic questioning of one's own teaching as a basis for development;
>
> The commitment and the skills to study one's own teaching;
>
> The concern to question and to test theory in practice by the use of those skills.
> (Stenhouse 1975: 144)

Stenhouse believed that teachers in classrooms should be supported by higher education personnel: 'fruitful development in the field of curriculum and teaching depends upon evolving styles of co-operative research by teachers and using full-time researchers to support the teachers' work' (1975: 162). Full-time researchers should therefore continue to have primary responsibility for reporting the research. This situation was ironic, because the same power relationships that action research sought to combat were evident within contexts of the professional education of teachers.

The work of Stenhouse was developed by a group of action researchers who were situated in and around the Centre for Applied Research in Education, some of whom later went their separate ways and developed ideas in other contexts. Stephen Kemmis, for example, became active in Australia, and has had worldwide influence by developing ideas with a participatory focus.

This theme of teachers being in charge of their own practice was developed specifically by two prominent researchers, but from different perspectives. John Elliott, a colleague of Stenhouse's at the University of East Anglia, developed an interpretive approach (page 11), and Jack Whitehead, at the University of Bath, developed a self-study perspective (page 11). These different perspectives had implications for how professional education should be understood and conducted, and also for how action research itself could be seen as fulfilling its own values of social justice. In general terms, action research became known as a form of practical research that legitimated teachers' attempts to understand their work from their own point of view. Instead of learning about the disciplines and applying theory to themselves, teachers were encouraged to explore what they were doing and propose ways of improving it. In this way, the practical wisdom of teachers was awarded greater status, as well as their professional standing. Action research is now widely accepted as a form of professional learning across the professions.

Creating your own living educational theories

The issue remains, however, about who is competent to research practice and make judgements about it. It would seem that, if action research is about social justice, action research itself should promote just practices, that is, do away with hierarchies of power in relation to who knows, and recognize that practitioners themselves should be acknowledged as the creators of their own knowledge. This view has been relentlessly developed by Whitehead. He has said consistently that teachers should both study their own practice and regard their practice as the grounds for the generation of their own personal theories of practice (Whitehead 2003). They then make their theories available for public critique and testing. Action research should be seen as not simply about problem solving, but about learning and creating knowledge. The kind of knowledge created can contribute to personal and social wellbeing.

This is a powerful stance. A living theory perspective places the individual practitioner at the heart of their own educational enquiry. Individuals undertake their research with a view to generating their own living educational theory, which would be an account containing the descriptions and explanations of practice that individuals offer as they address the question, 'How do I improve my practice?' (Whitehead 1989). It is the responsibility of the individual researcher to hold themselves accountable for their potential influence in the learning of others.

In the 1980s, Jack Whitehead's work was complemented by the work of Jean McNiff, who developed the idea of the generative transformational nature of evolutionary processes. In this view, all living systems are in constant transformation, and each new transformation holds within itself its next potential transformation. This idea, together with the idea of living theories, has implications for inclusive and relational practices, which are part of the foundation of social justice. Although the individual researcher is placed at the heart of their own enquiries, the researcher is seen as in company with others in the research and in the wider community. People are always in relation with other people and with the rest of their environment. The quality of the relationship is important for sustainable development, because sustainability depends on the freedom of the individual to make decisions about their own lives. Freedom, however, comes with responsibility. The individual action researcher has to accept that they have a responsibility to others, and, in their educational relationships as professional educators, to place the interests of the other above their own. Action research therefore may be undertaken by individuals, singly or collectively, but it is always a participative and collaborative exercise, not individualistic. The methodologies of living enquiry are both rigorous and scientific, and always grounded in care and consideration for the other, while still maintaining the integrity and unique capacity of the individual to know and make judgements about the validity of claims to knowledge.

2 WHERE IS ACTION RESEARCH LOCATED IN DIFFERENT RESEARCH PARADIGMS?

If you are studying for higher degree accreditation, you need to know where action research is located within different methodological and epistemological developments.

Most research methods texts draw on different theories of scientific and social progress to explain the emergence of new paradigms. A paradigm is a set of ideas or theories appropriate to a specific context. These different theories see progress in different ways. The work of Kuhn and Lakatos, for example, is often cited when discussing models of progress. Kuhn (1970) maintained that paradigm change was often a case of replacement, whereas Lakatos (1970) saw progress as the incorporation of old ideas into new ones (see Losee 2004 for an excellent overview). You should make up your own mind about how processes happen, but try to avoid assuming a cut and dried sequential process, because paradigm shifts often involve a good deal of overlap, repetition and back-tracking. Also one paradigm may borrow from another, and sometimes it is difficult to see where one paradigm begins and the other leaves off.

Many research methods texts (see, for example, Hitchcock and Hughes 1995; Usher 1996) explain that understanding educational research means understanding that it involves different paradigms. Some authors (for example Ernest 1994) specifically identify the following:

- technical rational (often called empirical) research
- interpretive research
- critical theoretic research.

Each of these paradigms, or approaches, has different views about the nature of knowledge, how it is acquired, and how it is used.

Technical rational (empirical) research

This form of research assumes that:

- The researcher stays outside the research field to maintain objectivity. Knowledge generated is uncontaminated by human contact.
- There is a cause and effect relationship throughout: 'If I do this, that will happen', more generally, 'if x, then y'.
- Results are generated usually through statistical analysis, and remain true for all time.
- The results can be applied and generalized to other people's practices, and will be replicable in similar situations.

Technical rational research is used throughout scientific enquiry, and has led to massive developments in technology, medical care and space travel. However, many rational researchers assume that the methodologies of the natural sciences can be applied to human practices, so they tend to view humans as machines, or as data. Stringent critiques say that rational research is a myth (Thomas 1998), and objectivity is unattainable. Some ask what is so special about objectivity anyway.

Interpretive research

This form of research assumes that:

- Researchers observe people in their natural settings, and offer descriptions and explanations for what the people are doing.
- Analysis of data tends to be qualitative, in terms of meanings of behaviours.
- The people in the situations offer and negotiate their own understandings of their practices with the interpretations of external researchers, but it is still the external researcher's story that goes into the public domain.

Interpretive research is used widely in social science and educational research, often taking the form of case study. The aim is to understand what is happening in social situations and negotiate meanings.

Critical theoretic research

This form of research assumes that:

- It is important to understand a situation in order to change it.
- Social situations are created by people, so can be deconstructed and reconstructed by people.
- Taken for granted situations need to be seen in terms of what has brought them into existence, especially in terms of relationships of power.

Critical theory emerged as a critique of existing forms of research, on the basis that research is never neutral, but is used by a researcher for a specific purpose, which is often linked with the desire to predict and control. It is important, in this tradition, to understand the human interests involved both in social situations (page 249) and in the means used to find out about them.

IMPORTANT NOTE! FORM OF THEORY

The chapter so far has set out what different approaches say. It is important also to note how they say it, that is, the form of logic used, and to consider the form of theory generated.

The stance of researchers working in these traditions remains external. They speak about research and ideas as things 'out there'. What is known is assumed to be separate from a knower. Reality, and ideas about reality, are turned into free-standing things, which can be studied, taken apart, and put back together in new ways. Many researchers working in these traditions do not seem to appreciate that they are part of the same reality they are studying.

This tendency has been exported into many forms of action research. People talk about action research, but do not always see themselves as living participants, doing action research.

Some implications are developed in the next section.

Action research

Action research developed out of critical theory, and went beyond. Critical theory asked, 'How can this situation be understood in order to change it?' but aimed only for understanding, not for action. Action research went into action and asked, 'How can it be changed?' Some researchers, however, still like to locate action research within a broad framework of critical theory, emphasizing its participatory nature to combat relations of power.

What distinguishes a living theory form of action research is that it is grounded in the ontological 'I' of the researcher, and uses a living logic, that is, researchers organize their thinking in terms of what they are experiencing at the moment. While many research approaches still tend to adopt an externalist stance, using a form of thinking that sees things as separate from one another, action researchers working with a living theory approach use a form of thinking that sees things as in relation with one another. The aim of the researcher is to hold themselves accountable for their learning and their influence in the learning of others.

This has important implications for how action research is conducted in the world, and also how it is theorized. Currently a lot of work goes on that is called action research, but is actually social science research, when an official researcher observes, describes and explains what other people do. Adopting this stance does not do much to move people to develop inclusional or relational practices. Instead, it reinforces a view of aristocrats and subservients, and asymmetrical relationships of power.

Power sharing happens when all parties perceive the other as powerful, potentially able to speak for themselves and exercise their own agency, and agree to talk with one another on those terms. It happens because people see themselves as in relation with one another, as participants who are creating their life world. They may even sometimes feel that they are in a combative relationship with the other, but at least the recognition of a relationship is a start, which can be developed. The worst point is when one party perceives the other party as a non-person, which is no basis at all for the development of life-affirming human practices.

SUMMARY

This chapter has given a brief summary of where action research has come from. We have traced its development from its beginnings in social science in the 1930s and 1940s, through its use in the work of Lawrence Stenhouse and his idea of 'teacher as researcher', and on to its most up-to-date position in the work of Jack Whitehead and his idea of living educational theories and, together with Jean McNiff, in our idea of 'practitioner as theorist'. We have set out its location within different research paradigms, while emphasizing that living theory approaches have made a leap into new forms of thinking about research and its underpinning logics and values.

As well as considering where it has come from, it is also important to ask, 'Where is it going?' Where it is going can be seen in the reality of multiple interconnected branching networks of communication, all of which recount stories of action researchers using their best efforts to ask, 'How do I improve my learning? How do I improve my work?', and holding themselves accountable to themselves and one another for what they are doing. These themes will be developed in Part VII.

Part II

Why Do I Need To Know?

Part II sets out why you should do action research. The emphasis shifts from what action research is to why it is important. It contains the following chapters.

At this stage in your own action enquiry, you are asking, 'Why am I concerned?' By asking the question, you show how you are engaging with the underpinning values and commitments of action research (Chapter 5). These are to do with the ideas of freedom, democracy and accountability. You exercise your creative capacity as you learn to improve your practice (Chapter 6); you show your capacity for collaborative and negotiated forms of working as you contribute to new forms of theory (Chapter 7); and you demonstrate your accountability as you evaluate your own research (Chapter 8).

5

Why Do Action Research?

We said on page 1 that action researchers undertake their enquiries for two main purposes:

- to contribute to new practices (this is the *action* focus of action research)
- to contribute to new theory (this is the *research* focus of action research).

Both aspects are intertwined and interdependent.

Many practitioners would probably feel at ease with the idea that they are contributing to new practices, but perhaps fewer would immediately see their work as contributing to theory or new ideas or new knowledge. In fact, practitioners are often suspicious of the idea of theory and research, some having had the experience of being researched on by officially appointed researchers. However, it is vital that practitioners do see themselves as both practitioners and researchers. The public acknowledgement of practitioners as practice innovators and theory creators is a key factor if practitioners are to be seen as legitimate participants in public debates about what is worth striving for in life, and which lives are important. However, public acknowledgement begins with the private acknowledgement of practitioners themselves. It is no good expecting someone else to value your work if you don't value it yourself. You need to appreciate the importance of your work in relation to your capacity to generate both new practice and new theory, and to see how this ties in with policy formation and implementation.

This chapter deals with these aspects. It is in two sections.

1 The importance of seeing yourself as a capable practitioner
2 The importance of seeing yourself as a capable theorist

1   THE IMPORTANCE OF SEEING YOURSELF AS A CAPABLE PRACTITIONER

In Chapter 2 we set out Donald Schön's ideas about the topologies of professional landscapes. Schön was, as we are here, making the point that practitioners should be regarded as competent professionals whose practical knowledge is key to developing human capabilities, their own and other people's.

This idea of developing human capability is core to action research. Sen (1999) describes capabilities as people's ability to think for themselves, and to make their own decisions about how they wish to live their lives. He also makes the point that realizing these capabilities requires people to be free, and, in turn, to exercise their freedom to ensure the continued development of their own capabilities and the capabilities of others. This is done, he says, by 'support in the provision of those facilities (such as basic health care or essential education) that are crucial for the formation and use of human capabilities' (1999: 42). The task for practitioners then becomes how they can exercise their own capability to think for themselves and make decisions about their own lives, and also to encourage others to do the same. Because practitioners are also professionals, they do not assume that this is just happening, but carry out stringent tests to see whether it is. The values that inspire their work are to do with their own and other people's capacity to think for themselves and make decisions about how they live their lives, so they check whether they really are living in the direction of those values.

These ideas can provide a useful background context for starting an action enquiry.

Starting an action enquiry

People have different reasons for starting an action enquiry. You may feel that your current practice is really good, and other people can learn from you. You evaluate your work to explain how you can claim that this is the case. Sometimes you have a hunch and you ask, 'I wonder what would happen if …?' Perhaps something could improve, and you may want to try out a new style or strategy. This means also evaluating what happens. Is it working? Should you change something? For example, as a chef you want to know how customers respond to a new menu. As a care service manager you want to evaluate the effectiveness of new work schedules. This involves asking, 'How do I understand what I am doing? How do I improve it?', and generating evidence to support any claim that you have improved practice by studying it systematically.

Experiencing oneself as a living contradiction

Many action researchers begin their enquiries on the grounds that they want to improve certain aspects of their work or work situation, in order to live more fully in the direction of their social and educational values. Sometimes, in Jack Whitehead's words, they experience themselves as 'living contradictions' when their values are denied in their practice. By this he means that we hold values about what is important in life, which act as our guiding principles, and we try to live accordingly. Sometimes we do, and sometimes we don't. Many people are guided by the principles of fairness and equity, and try to work in a way that is fair and equitable. Often they succeed. Caroline Muir (2004) showed how she involved people in credit unions in workplace decision-making, and how this participative working influenced people's economic and personal-social wellbeing. Thérèse Burke (1997) tells how she involved children with special needs in planning their own curriculum, and the beneficial influences in school and family life.

Sometimes, however, we do not live according to our values. Perhaps we have built up habits over the years. Perhaps, like Mary Geoghegan, a principal, you find that you tend to run business meetings yourself, even though you believe in participative working. Mary explains how she experienced herself as a living contradiction by denying her values in her practice during staff meetings. She introduced a rotating chair system, which meant everyone had the chance to lead. She explains (Geoghegan 2000) how some people developed confidence in their capacity for leadership, even to the extent of questioning Mary's decisions. Mary could claim that she was living in the direction of her values, and realizing them in some cases.

Often we do not live according to our values because external circumstances stop us. Margaret Cahill (2004), a special needs resource teacher, works in an education system that espouses the rhetoric of equity and entitlement, yet these values are consistently denied when some children are labelled by terms such as having 'special educational needs'. These children are bright and articulate, many with significant visual or kinaesthetic intelligence (Gardner 1983). Because numerical and verbal intelligence are valued in the education system, and verbal and kinaesthetic intelligences are less valued, the children are relegated to lower status. Margaret shows how she lives in the direction of her values in her own class context, yet is prevented from doing so in wider contexts. The conflict of values (Sowell 1987) that such situations create can lead to emotional dissonance for the people involved. Margaret's research question became, 'How do I create contexts of fairness and democracy for the children in my care?' (Cahill 2004). She shows how she transformed an existing situation, where marginalization was practised systematically, to one of fairness and democracy. Thousands of such stories are now available (you can access some on www.actionresearch.net and www.jeanmcniff.com).

What goals do action researchers wish to achieve?

Traditional social science tends to describe and explain the status quo, to maintain and reproduce it. Social science researchers ask, 'What is happening here? How can we predict and control future outcomes?' Their ideas make up a body of theory that practitioners can apply to their practices, if that is what they want to do. Action researchers also describe and explain the status quo, often drawing insights from the social sciences, and show how and why they are changing it. They ask, 'What is happening here? How do we ensure that it manifests our commitments to the capacity of all to think and act responsibly?' Action research is rooted in the ideas of social and intellectual freedom, that people can think for themselves, can make their own life decisions, and will come together on an equal footing to negotiate their life plans. The goals of action researchers include supporting public institutions that will safeguard people's social and intellectual freedom and the exercise of those freedoms. When people ask, 'How do I/we improve what we are doing …' they imply '… for our benefit?' In answering these questions, they generate their theories of human capability (Sen 1999) that encourage sustainable forms of personal and social development, rooted in freedom, and they use that freedom to support new freedoms. They make their theories public through their research accounts, which others can access and learn from, if that is what they wish to do.

For example, Winnie Hignell (2004) explains how she and others worked collaboratively to enable so-called 'disabled' people with physical and mental trauma to be part of the social economy in a special way. Winnie's job was to ensure that the 'disabled' were included in other people's activities, and also developed their own capacity for creative work. She tells how she and her colleagues supported groups to set up their own businesses to produce texts and videos designed to inform the public about disability, explaining that disability should be reconceptualized not as a property of people with trauma but as a social practice of people who construct disabling terms such as 'disability'. She and others developed sustainable work practices that were committed to enabling people to decide for themselves what to do and take responsibility for the consequences of their actions.

2   THE IMPORTANCE OF SEEING YOURSELF AS A CAPABLE THEORIST

When you tell other people about your work, whether orally or in a written report, you are showing two things. First, you are showing how you have developed innovative practices. Second, you are showing how these ideas about practice are brand new. You may have adopted, or incorporated, other people's ideas into your own work, but the work is yours, an original contribution. Other people can now learn from you, and adapt or incorporate your ideas if they wish. You explain that you are contributing to the practical life world by adding your story of practice, and you are contributing to the intellectual life world by offering your explanations for practice, your theory of practice. The idea of contributing to the intellectual life world is important. Edward Said (1994) talks about professionals as public intellectuals. Perhaps all practitioners should be seen as potentially public intellectuals. Many shopkeepers and pop singers have as worthwhile contributions to make as professional elites. The fact remains that as a professional you are in a privileged position where you can use your voice. Unless you use your voice and profess your status as a public intellectual, you will not be heard. If you are not heard you will continue to be marginalized and not be taken seriously.

Here is an example of this situation from the teaching profession. Although the issues are about teachers, they are relevant to all practitioners.

Getting recognized

In the United Kingdom, and following the reforms of recent years, teachers are now recognized as the best judges of their own practice, and best placed to take main responsibility for the initial education of those entering the profession, as well as the ongoing professional education of those already in service. This new explicit recognition of the professional expertise of teachers has done much to enhance their status as professionals, and is manifested in a variety of ways, for example, in terms of the changed relationship between themselves and higher education institutions (HEIs). Whereas previously the work of HEIs was to pass on received wisdom about practice to teachers, teachers themselves are now seen as in charge of their own practice.

However, these changes are happening largely at the level of practice, and not so much at the level of theory. Although the professional competence of teachers is recognized, they still tend to be seen as competent practitioners, whose professional knowledge is about work in schools and classrooms. They are not widely recognized as competent theory generators, whose theoretical knowledge can inform policy. While these issues are aspects of debates about what should be the work of teachers and the extent of their capacity for influence, the issues are actually rooted in debates about what kind of knowledge should be seen as theory, and who should be regarded as a knower. Should practice be seen as a form of applied theory, or should it be seen as the grounds for theory generation? Should teachers be seen as appliers of other people's theory, such as academics in HEIs and business, or should teachers themselves be seen as practitioner-theorists?

These are core issues for the teaching profession, because the directions the profession takes are decided mainly by policy. However, as noted earlier, policy formation and implementation tend to be informed not by research-based theory but by the values-based political commitments of politicians, who use research-based evidence selectively to support their politically motivated policies. Furthermore, the kind of research-based theory that politicians take seriously tends to be of the kind generated by professional elites, that is, academics in HEIs, business, and think tanks, and also in the civil service and quangos, many of whom subscribe to neo-liberal and neo-conservative agendas (Furlong et al. 2000), and some of whom articulate a determination to keep teachers out (for example Gorard 2002; McIntyre 1997). Teachers, so the story goes, may certainly be recognized as best placed to make professional judgements about practice, and to look after the internal affairs of the profession, but they should not aspire to be seen as theorists whose ideas will actually inform policy. Given the market orientation of many governments in the developed world to secure power and privilege for themselves, frequently driven by the values of self interest, and given the educational goals of many teachers to work for social regeneration, frequently driven by the values of democratic ways of working, it is not surprising that the clashes of the underpinning values manifest as clashes of policy and political will. Consequently, and given that governments are kept in power by the publics who elect them, it then becomes a question both of whose ideas are more powerful and acceptable in public perceptions, and also of whose voices are most persuasive in making a case for their own positions.

The issue is highlighted by John Furlong who, in his 2003 Presidential Address to the British Educational Research Association, made the point that teachers also still tend to regard their action research as a form of professional development that can lead to school improvement, and seldom make the link to the need to produce texts that will stand as quality theorizing (Furlong 2004). He has also made the point that teachers do not yet take themselves seriously as practical theorists, which involves 'learning how to assess evidence, and address the values implicit in different courses of action; learning how to utilise such knowledge to inform practical judgements; fostering the abilities and dispositions to undertake practical theorising in relation to one's work' (Furlong 2000: 13–14). These are core issues. Unless teachers are prepared to engage in these processes, their work will continue to be seen as a form of applied theory, and they will continue to be regarded as practitioners who are implementing other people's ideas rather than knowledge creators themselves.

So what does it take to turn your practice into a form of theorizing? It takes mainly two things:

- showing how you are learning to improve your practice
- showing how your learning can stand as a contribution to new theory.

These issues are discussed in the following two chapters.

SUMMARY

This chapter has addressed the question, 'Why do action research?', and has put forward two main reasons, to do with the importance of seeing yourself as both a competent practitioner and also a competent theorist. Currently, practitioners tend to see themselves as working in a practice context but not in a knowledge context, and action research tends to be seen as a form of professional development rather than a form of practical theorizing. In order to have your work taken seriously as a potential contribution to wider debates, including policy debates, you have to regard yourself as contributing to both practice and theory. These two issues are addressed in the following two chapters.

both
practice
and
theory

6

Learning To Improve Practice

As a practitioner-researcher, your real work is to improve learning, both your own and others', in order to improve practice. Improvement is not something done by one person to another, but is a matter of influence. You do not set out to impose change on people and their ways. Change imposed by an external agency does little for sustainable renewal. Change that comes from within, and in accordance with people's own felt wishes, does. Your work is to contribute to your own and other people's capacity to think independently and decide how you wish to live, recognizing that individuals are always in company with others. How do people learn to live responsibly? How do you influence their thinking about these things?

This chapter deals with these issues. It is in two sections.

1 Understanding influence
2 Exercising influence to improve practice

The chapter includes a case study by Liu Xia, who shows how she learned to exercise her educative influence to improve her own and others' practices.

1 UNDERSTANDING INFLUENCE

People sometimes think influence is sinister and negative. This is not so. We are all influenced all the time. We learn how to think and act and make choices. This doesn't just happen. We learn from our books, families, friends and colleagues, according to the specific traditions of our particular culture. Some people choose not to be influenced by social norms, and do their own thing, but this choice is itself influenced by other voices. Our relationships of influence are multidimensional. They are horizontal, in terms of who we are interacting with at the time, and vertical, existing through space and time. Most of us are influenced by what went before, and by visions of the future.

As well as being influenced by others, each person has the capacity for influence. What we say and do potentially influences others, whether we realize it or not. This has enormous implications for you. How do you ensure that your influence contributes in a life-affirming way? How do you help yourself and others to grow? In which direction do you want to grow – towards critical self-reflection or towards reinforcing prejudices?

Visiting other theorists

Some visits to the literature can help. Some theorists such as Rousseau and Hume believed that a child is born as a 'blank slate' or an 'empty vessel' into which learning, usually information, is poured. They seemed to believe that people have to learn to become human. On the other hand, Chomsky (1986) says that people have an infinite capacity for knowledge generation as part of their genetic make-up. On this view, we have unlimited potentials to learn an infinite amount of new knowledge. Polanyi (1958) says much the same, also maintaining that we know more than we can say. We know how things are, but cannot always explain why, and we know how to do some things without knowing how we do it – riding a bike, for example. Polanyi calls this personal, or tacit, knowledge.

Processes of coming to know (learning) are complex. One view is that we raise our deep tacit knowledge to an explicit level. This idea can be linked with Chomsky's (1965) and Goethe's (1988) ideas about generative transformational capacity, a developmental process that enables a present form to emerge as a new form.

Combining these ideas gives rise to a theory of learning that accepts the infinite capacity of humans to create an infinite number of new forms of knowledge, and to transform their existing knowledge into new improved forms. This means that each person should be recognized as having the capacity for creative choice and for making original contributions.

Now let's link this with an idea from Habermas (1975), that people are not capable of *not* learning, that is, we *must* learn as part of our genetic make-up. The question arises, how do people decide what to learn? This has implications for practitioners with agency. Do we exercise our influence in ways that respect each person's uniqueness of mind and unlimited capacity for unlimited acts of creation, or do we aim to influence so that we deny those opportunities? Do we give others the choice to exercise their capacity for choice?

Influence does not 'just happen', although it can appear to. A vegetarian friend said that she bought a can of chicken sauce from watching a TV advert. Accepting or rejecting influence is a matter of choice. We hear voices everywhere. Which ones we attend to is up to us. We are all able to exercise our critical judgement when deciding what to think and how to think. Having said this, it has to be recognized that some people choose not to think for themselves, and other people are persuaded to believe certain things. This is a case of insidious influence. More will be said in Chapter 18.

It is a matter not only of you influencing others, but also of how you are influenced. What you do and how you do it is your choice. Choosing is one of your freedoms. While imprisoned in a concentration camp, Victor Frankl (1963) chose to adopt life-affirming attitudes, and Etty Hillesum (1983, quoted in Todorov 1999) chose to forgive her persecutors. Most of us are able to choose, even though we may live in prisons of one kind or another. Retaining this capacity is sometimes impossible when a direct assault is made on controlling our minds.

Choices frequently involve tension, which can be both creative and obstructive. Try choosing between two equally attractive pairs of shoes. Choices are also not simply a matter of right and wrong, but often a question of choosing between competing rights. A trade union of postal workers has currently chosen not to deliver what they see as racially charged political leaflets. Their choice, as part of their contractual rights, not to deliver the post, denies their legal obligations and customers' rights to receive their post. Most moral debates are about choosing between rival claims to rights and knowledge. Often these cannot be settled, so unless we choose to resort to force, we have to learn how to negotiate a way through so that all can live as we wish in company with others who want to do the same.

2   EXERCISING INFLUENCE TO IMPROVE PRACTICE

You can show how you are improving practice by exercising your influence to improve learning, in other words, how you are exercising your educational influence. Does your account of practice show you thinking for yourself and encouraging others to think for themselves? Do you create the kinds of relationships that will encourage people to feel safe enough to critique? This means they can also critique you. How do you show that you are influencing in an educational way and not cleverly manipulating?

Sometimes these matters are too complex to resolve, and we have to go on trust. You can, however, do some things that will help people to trust you. If they have reason to trust you in some things, they will be more likely to trust you in the intangibles.

Trust can be established when you show that

- you are committed to your own knowledge, and
- you produce evidence to support what you are saying.

Making a commitment to your own knowledge

Polanyi (see above) says that any act of knowing involves commitment, a personal faith that the knowledge we create is potentially right. It can be difficult, he says, to make such a commitment while also accepting the possibility that one might be mistaken. Nevertheless, this should not prevent each one of us from making our claims to knowledge with universal intent (Polanyi 1958: 327), that is, saying that we have learned something, with the intent of helping others to learn from our learning. We must also be open to ongoing critique, so that we can refine our learning in light of the critique.

Here is an edited version of Thérèse Burke's (2001) proposal to study for a PhD through action research, which shows how she is prepared to do this.

DOCTORAL RESEARCH PROPOSAL

Thérèse Burke

I have taught in second level schools since the early seventies, amid change and flux. I am particularly interested in the purpose of schools. Has school become a function of our economic culture which deskills as it produces conformists? I am also interested in the role of the teacher as 'gatekeeper' of knowledge (Spender 1981). Equally I am attracted by 'the emancipatory possibilities of teaching and learning as part of a wider struggle for democratic life and critical citizenship' (Aronowitz and Gadotti 1991: 189).

It has been my experience as a teacher that the education system as I knew it was disadvantaging and debilitating for many young people. I want to be part of a system that values all learners equally, where each child is helped to find her or his special way to learn. My belief in the value of education as emancipatory and the uniqueness of the individual has been consistently denied. In order to address the changing needs of students, it is necessary to examine what I know about knowing, as well as ways of knowing myself and the world. I find Giroux's idea of teacher as transformative intellectual who empowers students to participate in their own self-formation particularly provocative. However the important question whether emancipatory education is possible or just a utopian vision remains to be explored.

I intend to examine and challenge my practice as an educator. Am I an emancipatory educator? How can I best promote an emancipatory style of education? How do I resolve the contradiction that currently exists between my educational values and the educational system within which I practise? Like Polanyi (1958), 'Having decided that I must understand the world from my own point of view, as a person claiming originality and exercising [her] personal judgement responsibly with universal intent' (p. 327), I intend to find ways to improve my practice and test my findings against public critique.

The evidence base of your claim to knowledge

The idea of evidence is crucial in all research, not only in action research. Research is a process of finding out in order to create new knowledge. If you say you now know something that you didn't know before, you can be reasonably sure someone will say, 'Prove it.' While you can't 'prove' it, nor should you even get into using such language, you can produce reasonable evidence to support your claim to knowledge (see Chapter 15). At this point we want to return to the question of how you can demonstrate how you are exercising your influence to improve learning for improving practice.

When you produce your research report you will make the claim that you have improved your practice by improving your learning, and you have encouraged others to do the same. The others in question would be people such as your students, colleagues, peers, and those in senior positions. Perhaps a significant triumph would be if you could say you had influenced policy makers to improve their learning about these things.

Your claim to improved learning would be supported by validated evidence (see Chapter 15 for generating evidence). This can be problematic. It is straightforward enough to produce illustrative material to show people in action, but it is a far more rigorous process to produce evidence, which is about extracting from your data instances which you believe are manifestations of your values in practice. For you, your commitment to learning is a value that inspires your work. How to produce evidence of learning?

Producing evidence of your own learning is not difficult. You can, for example, show your learning journal, and point to instances when you really did learn something new, and were able to articulate what you had learned, and the significance of that learning for you. You can produce memos and letters when you seemed to be saying new things, influenced by new learning. These also could stand as evidence of learning.

Producing evidence of other people's learning is more problematic, and means producing instances also of them saying and doing different things. You can surmise that they are doing this because of their learning, but your evidence would be much more robust if you could get their testimony that this actually was influenced by their learning. This means asking the people themselves to say what they have learned, and how their learning is significant for them. You would need to ask them, 'What were you thinking when you did this? What had you learned?' Their accounts of what they were learning would stand as evidence of their learning, and could also supplement images and descriptions of them in action. In this way, it is possible to show how learning enters into action, so action is shown to be purposeful and committed and not just spur of the moment reaction.

A further step is needed, however, if you want to produce evidence of your influence in other people's learning. Again, this means asking them, using your own form of words, 'Have I influenced you? How?' The fact that they may learn to copy what you say, or use your language, is no evidence that they have learned to think for themselves. You can produce, say, video clips of people debating and using their capacity for creativity, but to claim that they are doing that because of your influence means getting their testimony that this is the case.

Producing evidence of your educative influence can be difficult, but it can be done. Here is an example from the work of Liu Xia, a teacher in the Guyuan Teachers College in Ningxia Province, the People's Republic of China. This is an edited version of her report, which you can access at http://www.bath.ac.uk/~edsajw/moira/LiuXia.htm.

HOW DO I HELP STUDENTS TO DEVELOP SELF-CONFIDENCE THROUGH RESPECT AND ENCOURAGEMENT?

Liu Xia

Context

I work as a teacher in Guyuan Teachers College. I undertook my action enquiry to promote learning through respect and encouragement. I wanted to help students to develop confidence in learning in order to improve their English, and my report shows how I helped them to believe in themselves as learners. Further, it shows how I took this new pedagogical knowledge into my family to help my nephews and my own son in their learning of English. My new educational knowledge enables me to make recommendations about the conditions for teaching and learning a foreign language.

Why did I choose this topic?

My first reason for choosing this topic is to do with my educational values. I believe that love and respect are essential to human welfare. I was concerned that students in my classes said they lacked self-confidence, even though they acknowledged its importance to their sense of self-worth.

My second reason was that our Chinese traditions tend to suggest that teachers must be strict with their students. Beating is a kind of love, they say. Being strict with your students is necessary, they say.

Here is a conversation with an English teacher colleague in a middle school.

> 'Every time I go to my classroom, I take a long stick in my hand,' she said.
> 'What do you do with it?' I asked.
> 'To deal with the students who don't study hard,' she answered.

(Continued)

> 'Do you really beat your students when they haven't done well?'
>
> 'Not really. I just threaten them by knocking my stick on the desk.'
>
> 'Does this work?'
>
> 'Sometimes it really works, but not always. The students will repeat their mistakes after ten days. I don't think this is a good way to teach, but I have no better method.'

On the other hand, some theorists believe that teachers should be kind to their students. I agree. I wanted to help my students develop their confidence through respect and encouragement.

My third reason was my introduction to action research, through a meeting with Moira Laidlaw [read about the work of Moira Laidlaw on page 196]. I was especially moved and influenced by Moira's words in a public lecture (Laidlaw 2004):

> I have been consciously influenced in my life by humanitarianism and liberalism, and most recently, by Christianity. I don't believe life is simple and without problems. However, as far as I can see, striving to overcome adversity is a way to grow.

What did I do to use this idea in my practice?

I undertook an action enquiry into my own practice as an English teacher. My practice context was my class of Mixed Western and Chinese Medicine.

I tried various strategies to encourage self-confidence. My first was to say 'thank you' to students who answered my questions in class. When I was a college student a warm-hearted English woman, Susan, impressed me deeply by saying 'thank you' every time I answered her question. I felt my answer was important to her, so I struggled to answer her questions. I had never heard Chinese teachers saying 'thank you' to their students, so when I became a teacher I never forgot to thank my students. After my words, students invariably blushed a little, but next time willingly answered my questions. Saying 'thank you' is not difficult, but to have such a sense in oneself when this is not a cultural norm is not easy.

My second strategy was to praise students when they got an answer right. After receiving praise, one of the students, Wu Jiandong, said to me, 'I was greatly encouraged by your words. I know I made many mistakes, but you and my classmates didn't laugh at me, which is different from my experience in high school. I feel I earned your respect.'

My strategy seemed to work, because the quality of spoken English improved considerably. Furthermore, some of them attested to the importance of my influence. Here is a written comment from Yu Li Bin:

> 'When I was in high school I didn't like studying English because my teacher always insulted me and called me stupid. I was angry but I dared not say a word because he was the teacher. I didn't get a high mark in the Entrance Examination.

(Continued)

Hence I am in Guyuan Teachers College, where I have been fortunate to meet you. It was you who let me realise that I was not so stupid. I could do what others did. I could even do it better. Failure cannot defeat a person. The most important thing is to have confidence. I have become a real student through your encouragement.'

Four of my students have gone on to take the National Proficiency Examination in English, in the second term of their first grade. No matter what results they achieve, this is a really exciting development.

Giving written praise

I tried giving written praise. Zhang Ling was once the monitor in his class. However, he was consistently absent or late to arrive, so he was demoted, and after that his absences increased and he showed little interest in study.

In one class, I set an assignment, which Zhang Ling accomplished. On reading his work, I found that the quality of his English was in fact rather good. I wrote in his exercise book, 'You are clever. Don't waste your intelligence.'

Wonder of wonders, his attendance improved, and he began to hand in homework. In the second term of 2003–2004, he was second in class. I never praised him in public, because I knew that with a reputation of being a 'bad boy', he would feel embarrassed. I did continue encouraging him through my written comments: 'You have really made progress. Well done.'

Offer constructive criticism to some good students publicly and privately

This is a most important point. I was reminded by one of my students, Mu Feng Xia, that students did not always wish to be praised publicly, when she said: 'If I am always praised by the teacher I will ask myself, "Am I so excellent? Am I really worthy of such praise? Did the teacher make a mistake?"' I worried whether praise may encourage some good students to begin to feel arrogant, and whether constructive critical feedback may be a better route to encouragement. The nature of the feedback would be crucial. For example, when handing back examination papers to a class I said, 'It is a pity if someone falls behind just because of careless mistakes. Although perhaps a student is usually in the top grades, this should be a warning sign.' This was said specifically for Xu Baifang, who had always been in the top five but had made some careless errors in her examination. She made an opportunity to talk with me later and assure me that she would not take her excellence for granted but would continue to make every effort in her studies.

Widening the range of my educational influence

I decided to widen my range of potential educational influence. This shift was prompted by conversations with students. When I asked them, 'Do you think it is important to improve

(Continued)

your confidence as children?' they responded with a definite yes. I therefore decided to shift the emphasis to personal-life action research. Here is what I mean by this idea and how I put it into practice.

Education is everywhere. In my view, it is not only in classrooms, but extends to all life contexts. This realisation was brought home to me during the winter holiday of 2004, when my two sisters asked me to help their sons to study English. I willingly agreed to do so, thinking that this would also help me to understand how I could widen the scope of my action research.

The next morning I called my nephews and my son. 'Gentlemen, get up! We are going to play basketball in the school playground.'

They got ready in a surprisingly short time. Before we began playing I said, 'Anyone who can say "basketball" in English gets to choose his partner.' What a surprise. All answered correctly.

> 'Another word. Who knows what "Cao Chang" means in English?'
> 'Playground,' from Song Chenwei.
> 'Do you two want to learn this word?'
> 'Yes, of course,' they responded.
> 'Right. Listen and repeat …'

I taught them at least fifteen words and five simple sentences. 'Tomorrow we will play football. Those who know about football in English will get special treatment. Those who can remember today's words will get a present from me.' The next day the three boys got up early without being asked, did their English preparation, and waited patiently until I had distributed my gifts of rulers and pencils. Bai Chenguang said, 'Aunt, you must be the person who encourages me most. My teachers never play games with us. Some people force me to learn. They sometimes beat me when I don't obey. You never scold me. I think I am more interested in English now.'

This was the beginning of a long and intensive educational conversation between us.

Because of this experience, I became aware of the needs of my own son. I was often so busy with my work that I neglected his requests for us to speak more together. One day, looking very downhearted, he asked, 'Mother, can you please spare just a little time to have a talk?' Shocked into attention, I responded,

> 'Of course, dearest, you are my sunshine. Of course I will talk with you.'
> 'Thank you, Mother. Can you talk with me every day?'
> 'Yes. How about a regular conversation just before we go to sleep?'

Our conversations often took unexpected turns. I not only got to know his thoughts and feelings, but we also probed important aspects of life. Here is such a conversation.

(Continued)

My son: Mother, will everyone die one day?

I: Yes, it's natural. All beings will die some day.

My son: Will you also die?

I: Yes.

My son: What will I do if you die?

I: You will grow up and become a man. You will need less and less care from me.

My son: I will need your care for ever.

I: Maybe you can do something to postpone my death and the death of others.

My son: What can I do?

I: If you study hard you may develop a new medicine to prolong life. Some people devote their lives to this kind of work. Also, studying English will help you to achieve this.

My son: How?

I: Because many scientific studies are reported in English. You can access them by learning English.

My son: Mother, is English difficult?

I: Not at all. You are so clever, and such a lovable person, that I am sure you will succeed. We can learn it together at any time and anywhere, but you do need to have interest and confidence.

My son: I want to learn English. Can you help me?

I: With pleasure. Let's begin now by saying, 'Let's have a good sleep,' and do as we say.

Our conversations continued. One day I told him, 'Your Chinese teacher told me that she admired you because you answer questions in class. She was happy to see you making such good progress.'

He was proud, but asked, 'Why didn't our teacher tell me that herself?'

'They are not used to giving praise in front of students,' I responded.

Yes, in China, teachers tend not to express their real feelings in front of students, for fear of losing their dignity as a teacher. This attitude is because of our long tradition of feudal society. Yet humanitarianism and liberalism do seem to be entering the Chinese mind. More and more teachers are accepting these ideas and incorporating them into their own teaching pedagogies, as part of the New Curriculum and its emphasis on opening up opportunities for education in China. Local education authorities are organising training courses for teachers to help them learn from advanced person-centred education methods from America and England. More needs to be done, and action research can help.

Here are some of the ways in which I have evaluated my own action research, and come to some conclusions about whether I am exercising my influence in an educational way.

(Continued)

- I observed students in my class. Most students' behaviours changed for the better. They became more active in role play, in pair work and group work, and in answering questions.
- I asked students to assess themselves. Their self-assessments revealed that they tended to have a higher opinion of themselves than before.
- I set tests and assignments. I was able to gather information about their improved capacity for knowledge creation.

I was greatly assisted by Moira Laidlaw and other colleagues in Guyuan Teachers Centre. Moira developed her own strategies for offering support, one of which was to praise one of my papers in public, saying it was 'groundbreaking'. She further convened a meeting, including the Dean, Dean Tian Fengjun, and both senior and junior members of department. They offered helpful critical feedback. For example, Zhao Xiaohong said, 'As an action research report, it lacks sufficient evidence. It should be written in a systematic way.' Others commented on the lack of references and substantive evidence for the claims I made. This was most useful advice, which I accepted gratefully. I subsequently improved and expanded that paper into the one you are reading now.

What have I learned from the process?

I have learned many things from the experience, including the following.

Things don't always run smoothly. Encouragement and respect sometimes don't work in a systematic way. My experience of working with one particular student brought this home to me. The student in question is often absent. I knew that his parents had divorced recently, and, according to the law, he therefore has to live with his father. He doesn't get on well with his stepmother, and he is the butt of his classmates' scorn because of his loss of face. He prefers to stay away from school and spend his time in internet cafés. I did my best to per-suade him to study hard, but he just offered me a hopeless smile, without saying a word. I said to him, 'Everyone has the power to choose their own life. We should all live a free and happy life. You have the right to choose a hopeful future. I can help you at any time.' He gave me an indifferent smile. He continued to stay away. Conversations with other educational leaders revealed that they had also tried to encourage him, but to no avail.

This experience led to my conviction that I, like other action researchers, should involve myself in all aspects of society. Educational action research should not be confined to teachers and students, but has the potential to be concerned with different sections of society. Just as with that boy. I could spare only a little time for him during class, because of my responsibilities to other students. I had no other time to talk with him. But he was already feeling unworthy of others' concern. If everyone neglected him he would neglect himself. This would be a tragedy, and we have had so many tragedies. Shall we continue to see children going forward towards a hopeless future? I call for the concern of all those people around him. These children need very little – only respect and encouragement. We can do this, if only each one of us believes.

(Continued)

Conclusion

I believe there was a generally changed attitude in my class over the course of my action research project. Students became more active and successful, and many said that it was because of their enhanced self-esteem. Some took part in competitions, including the American and English Cultural Knowledge competition. No matter what results they achieved, their courage deserved praise.

My nephews and my son said they were also greatly encouraged. They were able to write and talk to me in English, and seemed to have confidence in me and in themselves.

I learned that to be successful, you have to adopt a professional attitude to your work, and, more importantly, you have to understand that everyone needs respect and encouragement. Once people feel respected and encouraged their potential will tend to emerge in some way. Respect and encouragement can work wonders. They can make a coward into a hero. Further, anyone who respects and encourages others, also earns respect and encouragement. My students now regard me as their friend. Some call me just to have a chat. This has also enabled me to develop confidence. I need encouragement too.

To appreciate the quality of Moira Laidlaw's educational responses to Lin Xia, see: http://www.bath.ac.uk/~edsajw/moira/mlliuxia80605.htm

SUMMARY

This chapter has talked about improving your learning to improve practice. It has particularly looked at ideas to do with the nature of influence, and how you can exercise your own educative influence to improve practice. Doing action research emphasizes the need to exercise influence in a way that is educational. The case story of Liu Xia shows how this can be done.

This chapter has talked about improving learning. The next chapter deals with contributing to theory.

7

Contributing To New Theory

While you remain a practitioner, your main concern is to improve practice. As soon as you become a researcher, your main concern is to generate new ideas, knowledge and theory. As a practitioner-researcher, your concern is to show how you are connecting both your educational theorizing and your practice in the process of working to improve your practice.

In Chapter 5 we began to make the case that practitioners need to become involved in theory generation. This chapter develops ideas about why you should, and how you can do so.

The chapter is in two sections.

1   The need to contribute to new theory
2   How to contribute to new theory

1   THE NEED TO CONTRIBUTE TO NEW THEORY

Most literatures on professional education tell you how to be good at your job. Important though this aspect is, being good at your job does not get you recognized as competent to make decisions about your job, or, further, about directions your profession should take and what to attend to as its matters of professional concern. An otherwise excellent book *Learning to Teach in an Age of Accountability* (Costigan and Crocco 2004) offers plentiful advice about how teachers can survive during their first few years of service, and go on to become mature, experienced teachers. The book offers advice about coping strategies, including strategies akin to what Barry MacDonald (1987) called 'creative compliance' (see page 179 of this book). Nowhere, however, is the case made that teachers should actually begin to investigate how they can acquire the power to make decisions about the nature and purpose of their own profession, and how this can contribute to wider debates about the nature and direction of the society we wish to live in. This idea seems not even to have occurred to anyone. Instead, we are told how to survive within an oppressive bureaucratic system. By colluding in the oppression, by not seeing the need to challenge, or even entertaining the idea that it is possible to challenge, practitioners agree to continue to be seen as worthy practitioners who can talk about practice, but not as highly competent theorists who can talk about the need to explain practice and specify what practice is for and whose interests it should serve. Nor does this process happen by accident. Practitioners are systematically persuaded to believe that they are not capable of thinking for themselves or contributing to theory.

This is how it works.

Manufacturing consent

Throughout his political writings, and especially in a wonderfully accessible little text called *Media Control: the Spectacular Achievements of Propaganda* (1991), Noam Chomsky explains that ordinary people are persuaded to believe that they are not capable of thinking for themselves. This is achieved via a sophisticated propaganda system. At the root of it all is the desire on the part of privileged minorities within the corporate business community to keep ordinary people from questioning the messages they are given, and not to aspire to get involved in debates about how countries should be run or what kinds of societies are worth living in.

Chomksy speaks of two models of democracy. The first is participative democracy, where people take an active part in running their own affairs. The second, which is the current orthodoxy, is what he calls spectator democracy, where people elect representatives to run their affairs for them, and then stand back and watch. Those who represent are seen as aristocrats, both by themselves and by the people who elect them. The rest are seen as serfs, whose job is to get the representatives into power and then let them get on with it without question. To keep ordinary people under control, the privileged elites use various strategies to frighten them. One such strategy is to produce bogey-men. A recent bogey-man may have been Saddam Hussein. Another is to persuade people of their own inadequacy in the shadow of more intelligent others, to instil the proper subservience.

This system works well in professional education. One strategy is to present theory as an esoteric discipline that is conducted only by a privileged group with specialized skills, which it is not. Another is to persuade practitioners to see themselves as not capable, which they are. These mythologies are made real by aristocrats, and also practitioners themselves, who are persuaded to collude in their own subjugation. Privileged persons in elite institutions produce books and papers that present theory as an abstract discipline

(Pring 2000). They also communicate messages that practitioners are not able to do research (McIntyre 1997). Practitioners come to believe these messages, and so develop informal discourses, that enter into professional discourses, about how they are not interested in theory because it is irrelevant and above their heads. You can hear these discourses everywhere, and they are reinforced by the fact that most books on professional education simply do not mention the idea of theory generation, or that practitioners should get involved in it. The subject rarely exists as a subject for discussion. Which is where we came in.

We are saying in this book that you do need to get involved in it. You are not a spectator democrat who is content to have other people run your life for you, but an activist democrat who is prepared to take control of your own life and make statements about what your work is about and how it can best serve the interests of others. Your job is to generate your own educational theories of your own learning as a way of accounting to yourself and others for the life you are living in relation to your values.

Here is how you do it.

2 HOW TO CONTRIBUTE TO NEW THEORY

- First, consider what inspires your life. According to Fromm (1956), what gives our lives meaning is our ability to enjoy loving relationships and productive work. What are the values that give your life meaning? Articulating values can be difficult, but it is important to do so.
- Second, consider whether you are living in a way that is consistent with your values. If you are, how can you show it? If you are not, what can you do about it? Again, articulate this in some way so that people can access the descriptions you give for what is happening, and your explanations for why it is happening.
- Now show how you address this issue, again offering descriptions of what you are doing and explanations for why you are doing it. This will involve you in gathering data, and later generating evidence from the data to support your claim that you have addressed the issue. You will also have to validate your evidence by testing it against other people's opinions.
- Finally, write a report of what you have done and give it to someone to read. Or produce a multimedia presentation and show it to colleagues in your workplace.

Although this process has been disciplined and systematic, it has been entirely achievable and not too difficult. It has in fact been a process of generating theory. Your descriptions and explanations of your learning as you work to improve your practice are your theory. There is nothing esoteric about this.

It is a systematic procedure for accounting for your practice, why you do what you do. Furthermore it shows that you are not just doing it in a haphazard way, but you are thinking carefully and responsibly about your actions and their influence in other people's lives. Further detailed advice is given in Part III, which takes you through action enquiry processes.

Now let's tie this in with ideas about the need for you to believe in yourself, and not be persuaded that generating theory is difficult or that you are incapable of doing it.

- Be aware of what is going on. Be aware of the messages you are hearing. Which ones are true?
- Be aware that you are more likely to believe false messages and retain existing biases when you are on your own. Access some of the work already in existence and you will soon see that you are not alone and that other people also wish to overcome inappropriate biases and do not want to believe false messages. Plenty of practitioners are putting their theories of practice into the public domain, and other people are learning from them.
- Be aware that other people need to hear that they are not alone either, and should take courage, perhaps from accessing your work. You have something important to say.

So how are you contributing to new theory? You are contributing in the following ways.

- You are empowering yourself as a researcher. You are constantly generating valuable theories, and modifying them to keep up to date with your developing practice.
- You are reconceptualizing yourself as a researcher, not only as a shopkeeper, steel worker or secretary. Your practice is a form of research, and your research is a form of practice. Other people can learn from your example and empower themselves.
- You are refusing to be relegated as 'just a shopkeeper', 'just a steel worker', 'just a secretary'. You are creating a new professional identity as a practitioner-researcher, and you are developing new professional discourses with others who also regard themselves as practitioner-researchers.
- You are getting involved in debates about the nature of practice and its uses. You are not prepared to accept other messages that your work is to deliver a service, or a curriculum. Your work is to influence learning for improving practice.
- You are contributing to the wider body of knowledge, within a tradition called the new scholarship.

The new scholarship

This idea began within the field of education, specifically teaching and learning. In this book we are saying that the idea needs to be expanded to include all practitioners who are involved in educational and development work, and should be redefined as a new scholarship of educational enquiry (Whitehead 1999) for the advancement of practice. It is now the task of other professions also to promote the idea of the new scholarship in their own contexts. First, let's look at what the new scholarship involves.

In 1990 Ernest Boyer, then President of the Carnegie Foundation for the Advancement of Teaching, spoke about the need to develop a scholarship of teaching, that is, the systematic, high-level study of teaching practices. This would not simply be study of the actions of teaching, which could be understood by asking questions of the kind, 'What skills and techniques is the teacher demonstrating?', but study of practice from within the practice, that could be understood by asking questions of the kind, 'What am I doing to encourage learning? How am I evaluating my work?' A scholarship of teaching in this sense would be undertaken by those who regarded themselves as research-active teachers as well as teaching-active researchers. Professional education would no longer be 'tips for teachers', offered on one-off in-service days and only in school settings, but an ongoing discussion across sectors, phases and disciplines about how practitioners can study and theorize their teaching and pedagogies.

This idea has profound implications for all practitioners, including teachers, in terms of how they understand their work and their professional identities, and what they see as the object of educational research. Like other practitioners, teachers in schools usually have no difficulty in seeing themselves as practitioners but are often reluctant to see themselves as scholars, whereas many higher education people tend to see themselves as scholars rather than practitioners. For all parties, the issue of what is studied is of key significance. Dominant traditions say that people should study their subject matter, rather than their practice (Lawlor 1990). Boyer's (1990) idea of a scholarship of teaching was grounded in the idea that teaching itself is a form of scholarship, whose findings need to be made public so that other people can learn from them. The findings that teachers generate from studying their practice can contribute to a knowledge base that is created by teachers for teachers, or, in the wider sense, by practitioners for practitioners. The fact that this development work is going on in the teaching profession signals to other professions that they also need to develop a new scholarship of practice.

It may be helpful briefly to outline how the new scholarship differs from traditional scholarship. (Some researchers refer to 'new paradigm' and 'old paradigm' research. Reason and Rowan's *Human Inquiry* 1981 is a classic that explains the origins of some of the different perspectives.)

CHARACTERISTICS OF TRADITIONAL SCHOLARSHIP

In general terms, and regardless of subject matter, scholarship refers to a process of enquiry that involves study, generating evidence to support findings, and testing one's findings in the public domain. Traditional scholarship is a process of study of a particular subject matter. The usual aim is to support or refute a hypothesis, by conducting experiments, and manipulating variables to test the relationship between them. Knowledge tends to be regarded as an object, and findings are disseminated through written accounts. In professional learning contexts, the assumption is that theory can be applied to other people's practices.

CHARACTERISTICS OF THE NEW SCHOLARSHIP

The new scholarship refers to newer holistic forms of enquiry, where a practitioner investigates their own work in order to generate theory from within the practice. Practice itself becomes the context for research, and contains its own theory. Knowledge is developed through the exercise of creative imagination and critical engagement. In professional learning contexts the assumption is that theory is always in process, and can contribute to new thinking about new forms of practice.

You are contributing to a new scholarship of educational enquiry by showing how your practice stands as a process of rigorous theorizing. It simply does not matter that your context of practice is a shop or a factory. You are potentially a valuable practitioner–researcher wherever you are. It is up to you to show it, and to stake your claim to your rightful place among the community of scholars.

SUMMARY

This chapter has continued to emphasize the idea that you are a theorist as well as a practitioner, a knowledge creator in your own right. This involves challenging dominant messages that you should keep your station as a practitioner and not aspire to engage with theory. Advice has been given about how to contribute to new theory in terms of engaging with the new scholarship. The task now becomes how to show the value of what you are doing. This is the focus of the next chapter.

8

Evaluating Your Research

Evaluation is about establishing the value of something, its worth and usefulness. In educational research this means demonstrating its validity and trustworthiness, both methodological and epistemological, and also in personal and social terms. These issues will be dealt with further in Chapter 16. This present chapter focuses on the generic issues of what evaluation involves and how and why you should evaluate your own work. The chapter is organized to address these two questions:

1   What does evaluation involve?
2   Evaluating your own work

1   WHAT DOES EVALUATION INVOLVE?

We said earlier that when you make a claim to knowledge someone is bound to say, 'Prove it.' You cannot 'prove it'. The language of 'proof' is disappearing, as even the natural and physical sciences recognize that the natural world works not so much through cause and effect as through relationships and connections. We are only now emerging from the grip of a powerful empiricist tradition, and gradually developing a new language that includes the idea of reasonable evidence. This can be seen even in many legal systems.

Doing evaluation is never a neutral process. While evaluation is generally understood as establishing the value of something, different people prioritize different values, and use those values to inform their approaches to evaluation. Evaluation processes are always politically constituted and involve the exercise of power. Action research is about developing social justice, so evaluation in action research, like all its other processes, needs to demonstrate egalitarian values. This immediately raises questions:

- Who evaluates?
- What is evaluated?
- How is it evaluated?

Although the questions are discussed here as separate issues for analysis, they should be seen as interdependent with much overlap.

Who evaluates?

In the 1920s, Frederick Taylor introduced the idea of scientific management, an idea that was going to be influential for the entire century. The idea was that people's work could be judged by a manager carrying a stopwatch. A worker could achieve so many units of work in so much time. The prevailing attitude was that people were automata, whose output could be judged in terms of designated targets. This idea has filtered into many social systems. Its influence is evident today, in places such as the UK and US, in fields like education, where people's capabilities and learning are judged in terms of how many targets they achieve in how much time. The quality of people's lives in many ways has become standardized. Apart from the obvious implications of deskilling and deprofessionalization, more insidious elements of centralized control are evident.

When this view enters evaluation, implications include the idea that an external evaluator makes judgements about other people's practices. In some places, the stopwatch has been exchanged for a checklist, but it is still visible in target setting practices, achievement tests and appraisal systems.

In many professional contexts, evaluation takes the form of inspection. In the UK, schools are regularly inspected, as are teachers. Most professions operate regulatory appraisal schemes, many of which take the form of inspection rather than consultation. In work that is submitted for higher degree accreditation, there is still a view that the examiner's decision is final and not open to question or negotiation.

New paradigm work has introduced new systems, which work from a different values base. Because of the underpinning values of justice and democracy, practitioners are able to exercise their own voices about who should evaluate, and on whose terms this should be done. This raises further questions about whether a practitioner is competent to judge their own work, how they will demonstrate its validity, and how they will assure the watching public that their findings are credible and trustworthy. These issues are especially important in current times of increasing calls for accountability and attempts to steer education processes through bureaucratic control to meet centralist political agendas.

Therefore if practitioners want to establish and retain the right to self-evaluate, they need to demonstrate publicly that they know what they are doing and that their own judgement can be trusted. This means that practitioners have to make their evaluation processes visible, show that these are rigorous and robust, and produce strong evidence to show that they as practitioner-researchers are competent and capable.

What is evaluated?

It becomes clear that evaluation is about demonstrating not only the researcher's claims about the validity of the work, but also the validity of the researcher's claims that they are capable of doing the job.

In recent years shifts have been taking place in evaluation practices. In his *Personalizing Evaluation*, Kushner (2000) explains how the emphasis has moved from programmes to people. Many problematics remain, however, especially in assumptions about how practitioners are viewed, and what is evaluated.

Practitioners still tend to be viewed as peripheral. This is demonstrated in books such as MacBeath (1999) and Cousins and Earl (1995), where arguments are made for including practitioners in evaluation processes, on the assumption, however, that, although a professional evaluator seeks their valued opinion, the evaluator is still in charge and practitioners are subordinate. The view is reinforced by influential books such as those by Lave and Wenger (1991) and Wenger (1998), who speak about central and peripheral voices. Practitioners' participation is seen as 'legitimate peripheral participation' (Lave and Wenger 1991), and Wenger's (1998) 'communities of practice' seem to be organized in terms of hierarchies of voices, and, implicitly, hierarchies of knowers. There is nothing peripheral about practitioners. They are central. They are doing the work and they should be held accountable for the work, but this should be done by themselves, not by external judges who operate from their own sets of standards that are often unrelated to the work in hand.

So the question remains: if personalizing evaluation means shifting from an emphasis on evaluating programmes, does this mean that it shifts to evaluating people? This returns us to the issue of who evaluates, how competent they are to make judgements, and whether this can be seen as a practice that realizes the values underpinning the celebration of human capabilities.

How is it evaluated?

Most contemporary evaluation practices work on an apprenticeship model. This calls into question what kind of pedagogies are used and what form a curriculum takes. The experience of many professionals is that they listen to an expert, take notes, and write an essay (or do something equivalent), which is assessed by the expert in terms of what the expert expects to see, often a regurgitation and reinforcement of their own ideas. This can be seen as a closed shop mentality that perpetuates what Popper (1966) calls a closed society. To test out this perception, check with a school student how many times they have been asked in their entire school career what they know and what they think they should learn. Furthermore, pedagogies tend to be didactic, or at least delivery oriented. Many practitioners in organized education settings are heard to complain that they have to cover the syllabus, finish the textbook, or deliver the curriculum. The emphasis is on getting a functional job of work done, and delivering an artefact, rather than about working with people with real lives. Callahan's book *Education and the Cult of Efficiency* was written in 1962, but it represents the reality of practitioners' experiences in many quarters today.

Pedagogies are rightly related to how curriculum is perceived. Bernstein (2000) speaks about how knowledge is pedagogized, that is, formed as specific pedagogic structures that often work as symbolic forms of the control of knowledge and identity. Technicist approaches view curriculum as an accumulation of information. The task of the educator is to get this information across to trainees. Pedagogies that emphasize delivery to the passive masses reinforce the perception of the differing status of experts and apprentices, them and us. Pedagogies control identities.

Action researchers see limitations in these technicist views. Like Habermas (1987), action researchers believe that all are participants in communicative action. Like Senge (1990: 4) they believe that 'The organizations that will truly excel in the future will be the organizations that discover how to tap people's commitment and capacity to learn at *all* levels in an organization' (emphasis in the original). This means that all should be prepared to evaluate their own practice, in relation to what they are doing with other people, and test their findings against the critical scrutiny of the public world. This can be uncomfortable for those who like to be positioned as experts and managers. It can, however, be liberating for others who do not wish to be so positioned, and who wish to remove the constraining identity of an aristocrat and be seen as a person doing a worthwhile job of work in company with others who are doing the same. To make this shift demonstrates considerable courage and vision, and frequently involves engaging with institutional politics, but it is essential if the values underpinning a view of human capabilities are to shift out of the rhetoric and become reality.

2   EVALUATING YOUR OWN WORK

If you want to be seen as capable and competent to evaluate your own work (which you are), you have to fulfil certain conditions. Here is a summary of the conditions.

Explaining how you see your work as a rigorous research process, and what this implies

Research is a matter of identifying an issue of practice, formulating a research question, and then systematically addressing that question by generating evidence from the data to show that you are answering the question (see page 74). The question for most action researchers is, 'How do I improve my practice?'

You are required to show how you are improving practice in relation to a specific area of your work with others, and to show the significance of what you have learned from the research (your findings). This can be how your learning from the specific research area can inform other areas of your work, and also how others can learn from what you are doing. In other words, you show how your work has improved through learning from your research, and also how other people's learning can be improved by accessing your research. It is important to recognize, however, that actions may not go as planned and that sometimes we have to accept that we have made a mistake. Our actions do not always lead to improvement, but even when they don't, we can still produce a good quality action research report by showing that we have learnt from our mistakes.

Explaining that you are offering both descriptions of practice and also explanations for practice, and what this implies

Your accounts contain both descriptions of what you did, and also explanations for why you did it and what you hoped to achieve. This means articulating the values that inspired your work, and how you are hoping to realize those values in your practice. It also means engaging in some discussion around why you have identified those values and not others. It may involve explaining how your personal or work contexts promote or deny the realization of your values, and what you have done to celebrate or compensate.

Linking these ideas to the ontological values base of your work and what this implies in terms of your epistemological standards of judgement and their transformation into pedagogical practices

Your ontological values are what give your life meaning and purpose. These values are embodied: they are within your living body. Your epistemological standards of judgement are the critical judgements you use to test the validity of a claim to knowledge. In the action–reflection process, your embodied values become clear as they emerge through your enquiry. As you live in a just way, your embodied value of justice becomes visible through the way you act. As you communicate your embodied values to others, you transform them into your living epistemological standards of judgement. When you say, 'I believe in justice, and I am trying to live in a way that is just,' you explain how you use justice as a standard by which you can judge your actions. Action researchers who believe in the values of justice, freedom, democracy and entitlement try to live their embodied values as fully as they can. You transform your values and commitments into pedagogical practices that show how you value the capacity of all to think for themselves, and how you ask critical questions to promote and sustain your own and others' critical thinking. You show how you do not supply answers, but demand of people that they come up with their own answers, while also providing justification for those answers. You also show how you test your own ideas against those of others, to ensure that you are not slipping into complacency or seeking to justify your own prejudices.

Validating your claims to knowledge through the production of authenticated evidence, and relating these to identified criteria and standards of judgement

You make clear the processes you have gone through to monitor practice, gather data and generate evidence from within the data. You explain how you relate your evidence to specific criteria, and use standards of judgement that are related to your values. If your values include the ideas of freedom and participation, you need to show how your evidence contains instances from practice of you encouraging freedom and participation. You need both to produce such evidence, and also to state why the evidence should be seen as evidence and not simply illustration. This means articulating the standards you use, and saying why you are using these standards and not others.

Testing your claims by making them and their evidence base available to public scrutiny

Producing authenticated evidence is still not enough to have your claims pronounced valid. You also have to subject your claims and their evidence base to the public scrutiny of others, such as your critical friends and your validation group. If these groupings say your claims are reasonable, you can proceed with some confidence to put your claims into the public domain for further testing (but see also next paragraph).

Being open to requests to modify claims if they are shown to be wanting by justified critique, or standing firm if the critique itself appears to be unjustified

You need to state that you know your claims are always provisional, and open to further testing, critique and modification. When you make your claim you do not present it as a final answer. It is always a temporary position, your present best thinking, that will probably change in light of further reflection, evaluation and feedback. In traditional scholarships, uncertainty tended to be taken as a sign of weakness. In new scholarships, it is a sign of strength, a statement that you are always open to learning and modification of your own ideas. Traditional scholarships aim for certainty and closure. New scholarships aim for creativity and transformation.

What happens if people's feedback tells you to rethink your position, while you believe your position is justified? In this case you go back and check. Check the accuracy of your data. Check that you have produced authenticated evidence to support your claims to know. Check that you have tested your own stance. Are you reinforcing a prejudice? Is your thinking clear? If you feel that your position is justified, go ahead in spite of the feedback, but be very aware of the critique, and take it as an indication that you need to be even more rigorous about demonstrating the validity of your position. Be aware that in a process of democratic evaluation it is possible for the majority to be mistaken in their beliefs, so be undaunted, but be cautious.

Self-evaluation is not a simple option. It is not a question only of reflecting on what you have done in practice and writing a report. It is an extremely rigorous and scholarly process. However, although it appears rather intimidating, in terms of what is written here, it is actually straightforward and achievable.

The potential rewards are high. By producing your own self-evaluation report you are contributing to a public body of knowledge on evaluation practices, and reinforcing the legitimacy of practitioners as capable and competent. Your hard work sets important precedents. The stronger the evidence base, the easier it will be for others to achieve what you have done, and public perceptions will be strengthened about the rightness of practitioners judging their own work.

SUMMARY

This chapter has set out the need for you to evaluate your own work. Self-evaluation raises political questions about who does evaluation, what is evaluated, and how. Evaluating your own work is a rigorous process that involves the testing of any claims that you put into the public domain.

Now, in the next part, we deal with the practicalities of doing action research.

Part III

How Do I Find Out?

This part deals with the practicalities of doing action research. It contains the following chapters.

The chapters contain practical advice about how you can set about doing action research. They are meant not as definitive guides, but as useful ideas that can get you started. At all times, you are encouraged to develop your own ways of doing things.

At this point in your enquiry into how and why to do action research you are asking, 'How do I address my concern?' In asking, 'How do I find out?' you signal your intent to take action by learning and using the learning to inform your practice.

The case studies in Chapter 12 show how two practitioners worked their way through the action plans they drew up.

9

Feasibility Planning: What Do You Need To Think About First?

Previous chapters have spelt out how action research can support personal and social improvement, and why you should do it. However, there are hidden pitfalls, which you need to be aware of before you commit yourself. Therefore, even before you begin planning, do a small preliminary feasibility study, that is, identify some of the opportunities and constraints, and do an audit around what resources you may need. This will help you decide whether it makes sense to go ahead with your planning. Also bear in mind that problematics are bound to arise, and part of the process is learning how to negotiate difficulties and transform them into new possibilities.

Link your feasibility study to your proposed action plan, which will look something like this (see next chapter for details).

- What is my concern?
- Why am I concerned?
- What experiences can I describe to show why I am concerned?
- What can I do about it?
- What will I do about it?
- What kind of data will I gather to show the situation as it unfolds?
- How will I explain my educational influences in learning?
- How will I ensure that any conclusions I come to are reasonably fair and accurate?
- How will I evaluate the validity of the evidence-based account of my learning?
- How will I modify my concerns, ideas and practice in the light of my evaluations?

Now, assess realistically whether you can address the questions, in terms of your current circumstances and contexts, and the resources you need. You also need to consider ethical issues, about how you are going to involve others in your research.

This chapter is in three sections.

1   Thinking about the practical aspects of each step
2   Thinking about resources
3   Thinking about ethical issues

1   THINKING ABOUT THE PRACTICAL ASPECTS OF EACH STEP

Work your way through the questions in your action plan, asking whether you will be able to address each one in relation to your current circumstances.

What is my concern?

You have a concern about an aspect of practice, but is it realistic to focus on this aspect? Can you actually do something about it? Will you be allowed to? What would happen if, say, you wanted to investigate how you could improve relationships among different religious groupings in your workplace? This would involve you establishing to what extent your workplace already encouraged good relationships, or whether prejudice was possibly structured into practices. Or perhaps you want to find ways of encouraging greater staff participation in decision-making. This may upset some managers, who may try to block your enquiry. Will you be able to counter these obstructions? Will you personally be able to cope with the fallout? What if you are a teacher working in situations that consistently deny access to educational opportunity to some students? You can't change the system. What do you do?

Common-sense advice in such circumstances is to keep the project small, manageable and focused on your own practice and learning, and then plan accordingly. If you work on a part-time basis, do not enquire into how you can develop quality relationships with an entire departmental staff, but focus instead on your relationships with only one or two persons. If you want to encourage religious understanding, focus on how you do that with one or two colleagues or students. If you want to increase participation, find ways of participating more yourself, or encourage one or two colleagues to get more involved. Keeping it small gives you a greater chance of having some influence, and also showing how organizational change works.

Why am I concerned?

We said on page 46 that many action researchers begin their research out of a sense of frustration that they are not living their values in their practice. Sometimes they themselves are doing something contrary to what they believe in.

They may say they want to put it right, but the cost is often too high. You can check this out for yourself, by, for example, setting up a role-play situation and inviting someone to play you. Or you could videotape yourself in action and see yourself as others see you. These are risky strategies, and can lead to some destabilization, so be careful. They can also be powerful in helping you to see where you need to take action and resolve to do so.

More often, however, institutional circumstances are the obstruction. Many institutions, for example, engage with the rhetoric of participation, but when it comes down to it, they do their best to prevent participation. Is yours an institution that is open to learning, and that will allow you to investigate how to put an unsatisfactory situation right? Too often sad stories are told about whistleblowers and broken lives (Alford 2001). If doing your action research requires you to blow a whistle, will you do it? Again, common-sense advice would be to focus on your own self-study, which no one can prevent you from doing.

What experiences can I describe to show why I am concerned?

Producing evidence means gathering data and generating evidence from the data to support (or refute) a claim that you have learned something new. Gathering data means observing yourself in relation with other people. Will you be able to do this? Will you have access to the people you need? Will you be able to negotiate with people to help you in your enquiry? (See below under 'participants' for further discussion.)

What can I do about it?

Asking this question means that you intend looking at your options for action. Will you have options? Do you need to ask someone's opinion, or get clearance, or go through a permissions process? Will you meet with opposition? Geoff Suderman's classroom research was blocked by a university's ethics committee, an experience that has been shared by others. He demonstrated what Barry MacDonald (1987) calls 'creative compliance', that is, finding other ways through without compromising the original research intent, and studied his own learning in the process of seeking ethical approval (Suderman-Gladwell 2001).

What will I do about it?

This question implies that you will take action with intent. Will you be able to implement your decision? Will you be able to carry through a project in a systematic way? Will you have the stamina, and time, and resources, and support of family? What will you give up in order to put your research in? Will you maintain the moral conviction that you are doing something worthwhile when you have to miss the match on Saturday to go to a validation meeting?

What kind of data will I gather to show the situation as it unfolds?

This means gathering more data to show how people are learning in response to your influence. Will you be able to gather data on this ongoing basis? Will you have sufficient time and equipment? Sometimes people get the impression that you are researching them, rather than researching yourself. How do you prepare for this and cope with it? Sometimes key participants leave, or withdraw from the research. Parents refuse to sign permissions slips, and managers want evidence of progress. Sometimes principals want you to show how your research is changing students' attitudes and behaviours, which is often impossible. How do you persuade them that your learning is a vital piece of improving others' learning?

How will I explain my educational influences in learning?

Furthermore, how will you show that your own learning is influencing further learning? For example, you can influence your own learning by deciding to question your own assumptions and change them where necessary. You can influence the learning of others with whom you work, and you can influence what we term in this book the education of social formations, that is, you can influence groups of people to learn new ways of working together. How will you gather data and generate evidence to show these things?

How will I ensure that any conclusions I come to are reasonably fair and accurate?

You will need to find critical friends and convene a dedicated validation group who are prepared to offer you constructive critique about your evidence and claims to knowledge. Will you be able to find such a group, and will they be willing to meet with you on several occasions? Organizing meetings takes enormous amounts of time and energy. Are you up for it? Will you have the personal resources to deal with any adverse critique? Will you have the courage to rethink your position and challenge your own prejudices in light of their feedback?

How will I evaluate the validity of the evidence-based account of my learning?

When you produce your accounts, such as your progress and final research reports, you will make a claim to knowledge, that is, you will say that you know something now that you didn't know before. You have learned something new, both about practice and about your own learning. Making a claim to knowledge includes different aspects: making the claim, establishing criteria and standards of judgement, and generating evidence from the data in relation to the criteria and standards of judgement. Will you take every care in the detail of these procedural aspects, recognizing that they are essential for demonstrating the validity of your evidence-based account of learning? Will you develop your own understanding of these issues to the extent that you can make clear what you have done and why you have done it?

How will I modify my concerns, ideas and practice in the light of my evaluations?

Will you be open to new learning according to what the data reveal? Sometimes data show us things we would rather not see. Are you prepared for this, and to modify your own behaviour in light of the evidence?

The chapter so far could easily read as 'The perils and pitfalls of action research'. However, while it is true to say that you need to be aware of some of the possible difficulties, this must not deter you from undertaking your study. Although there is sometimes resistance to people who challenge existing systems and want to introduce new thinking, those people are the ones who influence social change. Your new insights are essential to helping others to learn, and you develop those insights by studying your own practice and improving your capacity to learn.

2   THINKING ABOUT RESOURCES

Resources can be understood as time, equipment and people.

Time

Will you be able to make time for your project? Some organizations encourage practitioner action enquiry and make time for it within the working day. Most higher education institutions expect their personnel to undertake research. Some allocate research time, but not all. Many schools and organizations also give study time or meeting time to practitioners. Be aware that doing your project will probably take more time than you are granted. Regardless of the depth of your research, it will involve some amount of reading and reflecting, meeting with people to negotiate access, gathering data, validating the evidence, producing progress reports, and writing the final report. Putting your research into your life means putting something out. Do you need to negotiate this with family, friends and colleagues? What is negotiable in your life and what is non-negotiable? Do not underestimate the extra time and effort you are going to commit, but at the same time be aware that it will be most worthwhile. Sometimes people become obsessed with their research so that it takes over their lives. Avoid this wherever possible. Time out for recreation and relaxation is essential, and you must keep family and friends in clear focus. Whatever you decide about these things, be aware that you will need to dip into your private time, and don't complain later.

Equipment

Equipment means money, so check beforehand whether you can use your organization's equipment or have to buy it yourself. What data gathering equipment will you need? Stationery, camera, video? You will definitely need a computer. Will you use the organization's, or your own? What about reprographics and photocopying? Draw up a list of what you may need and check availability in advance. Also be aware that the ideas of others can be accessed through many influential texts online, and many research journals are now available in e-forums. A Google search on the topic of your enquiry is often a good way to see what others are thinking about it.

You will need four or five key books, perhaps more, depending on how deeply you want to get involved in developing the scholarly aspects of your work. Be prepared to buy these yourself, unless your organization has a policy of supporting professional learning. Perhaps you can suggest to a manager that they decide – or decide yourself, if you are the one with the money – to develop a staff library, which could include subscriptions to journals such as *Educational Action Research* and *Reflective Practice*. This would be a good investment for the future.

People

Although the centre of your research is you as you investigate your individual 'I', you are never alone. You are always in company with others who are also studying their individual 'I's'.

The people you need to involve are those who will work with you as participants, critical friends and validators, and interested observers.

Participants

Remember that your research participants have the same status in your research as you. They are not objects of enquiry, or somehow subordinate. They are research equals. Your research is about studying you, not them, and investigating the quality of your influence in their learning. This means that you have to check how they are responding to you as you interact with them. You ask, 'What am I doing in relation to you? What am I learning with and from you? What are you learning with and from me?' Your participants mirror yourself back.

Critical friends and validators

The aim of your research is to make a claim to knowledge, in your case that, in your enquiry into improving practice, you actually have learned how to improve practice. This claim has to be justified, otherwise it could be seen as your opinion. If you say, 'I have influenced the quality of relationships in my business,' or 'I have helped students improve their motivation,' you need to produce evidence to show that this really is the case and you are not making it up. This public testing is a core feature of all research, and is especially important in educational action research, where claims to knowledge are grounded in subjective experience. You need to submit your data and findings to rigorous critique at all stages.

One of the ways to do this is to get critical friends to give you feedback on your data and your ideas. These persons can be drawn from your circle of professional colleagues and can include other colleagues, parents, clients, students or anyone else who is going to give you a sympathetic but critical hearing. You may have one or several critical friends, depending on your needs.

Validation groups

You will also form a validation group for the duration of your project. This group will number about three to ten, depending on your own circumstances. Their job is to meet at crucial stages of your project, especially at the reporting stage, to scrutinize your evidence and to listen to your claims to knowledge, and agree or not whether your claims and their evidence base are coherent and believable. Researchers are of course looking for positive feedback at these events, but should be prepared for people to raise questions about taken for granted aspects, which means going back and thinking again.

Validation groups meet with you of their own free will, so never abuse their goodness of heart. Thank them properly, and acknowledge them in your report.

Interested observers

These are people who are interested in your work, but not directly involved, such as your manager or the parents of the students who are your research participants. Treat them with the greatest consideration. Again, they don't have to put their time and energy into being involved with you, so thank them properly and let them know they are valued.

3   THINKING ABOUT ETHICAL ISSUES

Involving other people in research demands a consideration of ethical issues. In our current climate of sensitivity to abuse, this is a matter not just of courtesy but also of the law. Involving children and vulnerable people is especially important. If you involve children in your research without getting prior permission or clearance, it could cost you dear.

Ethical considerations involve three aspects:

- negotiating and securing access
- protecting your participants
- assuring good faith.

Negotiating and securing access

You must negotiate and get permission to do your research before you begin. This means formally seeking permission in writing. You should organize letters for all participants. For those persons who cannot read, still give them a letter and read through its contents with them. In the case of children or vulnerable people, seek and get permission from parents or legal caregivers, as well as from the children themselves. Keep permissions letters carefully for reference. Place a copy of your letters to participants as an appendix in your report, and have your original permissions letters available if your readers want to see them. Producing these permissions letters is a matter of sensible negotiation in research projects that deal with sensitive issues, where you may decide on limited disclosure. To repeat, this is not just an issue of courtesy. It is a matter of avoiding potential litigation.

An example of a letter of permission is on page 87. You can modify this for your own purposes.

Protecting your participants

Make sure that you do not name or otherwise identify your participants, unless they wish. Many participants in action enquiries wish to be named and often to contribute their own accounts of their own learning. When participants do not wish to be identified, give them numbers or initials such as 'Student 3' or 'Colleague M'. This is an issue when using video data, when people are easily identifiable. Difficulties can be anticipated by being open about what you are doing from the start and seeking and obtaining permission, and also by making clear throughout that you are monitoring your own practice and not theirs. Also be careful about naming your location. Check with your manager or principal about this. Often people are only too glad to be identified and to celebrate their work. In this case, go ahead and identify them, but make sure you have their written permission before you do.

Assure your participants that you will put their interests first, and that you will maintain confidentiality at all times for those who wish it. Never break this promise. It could be expensive if you do. Also promise that participants may withdraw from the research at any time if they wish, and that all data about them will be destroyed.

Let your participants know that you are to be trusted. Draw up and give an ethics statement to each person involved. Include a tear-off slip for their signature to show that they have received it, and keep these carefully (see the example on page 88).

Assuring good faith

Always do what you say you are going to do. This means maintaining good faith at all times. Aim to create a reputation for integrity, and protect it. People are more willing to work with someone they trust.

Having observed all ethical aspects, you can now exercise your duty to yourself, and go ahead and do your project. Ensure that you protect and exercise your own academic freedom, to speak from your own perspective as a person claiming originality of mind and telling your truth with universal intent (Polanyi 1958). Your work is important, and you have a duty of care to others to publish your findings so that they can learn with you and from you, with the intent that they should do the same for others.

A LETTER REQUESTING PERMISSION

```
                                    Your institutional address
                                    Date

Name of recipient

Address of recipient


Dear [Name]
```

I am hoping to undertake an action research study into how
I can improve lines of communication in my department. I
would be grateful if you would grant permission for my
research to proceed.

Two copies of this letter are enclosed. Please sign and
date both. Keep one copy for your files and return one
copy to me.

With thanks.

Your name ....   Date ....

✂--

I hereby give permission for [your name] to undertake
her/his research in [name of organization].

Signed ....   Date ....

AN ETHICS STATEMENT

To whom it may concern (or Dear colleague, or Dear [Name])

I am undertaking an action enquiry into how I can improve
lines of communication in the department, and am asking you
to be a participant in my research.

I will give priority to your interests at all times.
I promise the following.

- Your identity will be protected at all times unless
  you give me specific permission to name you.
- You are free at all times to withdraw from the
  research, whereupon I will destroy all data relating
  to you.
- I will check all data relating to you before I make
  it public.
- I will make a copy of my research report available
  to you prior to its publication.

Two copies of this statement are enclosed. Please sign and date both. Keep one copy for your files and return one copy to me.

Your name .... Date ....

✂--

I have received an ethics statement from [your name].

Signed .... Date ....

SUMMARY

This chapter has given practical advice about planning to do an action research study. It has set out a possible action plan, and suggested what you need to think about in terms of the practical aspects of each step, the resources you may need, and which ethical issues you need to consider. Examples have been given of ethics statements and letters requesting permission.

Having considered some of the problematics of doing a study, we now move into developing an action plan, so that you can organize your ideas about how to take action.

10

Action Planning: How Do You Develop an Action Plan?

Before launching into your research, draw up an action plan. This chapter offers advice about how to do this. You can easily adapt the advice to many other areas of your work. The next chapter gives advice on how to implement your action plan, that is, how to conduct your research, followed by examples.

This chapter is in three sections.

1 What does action planning involve?
2 The action plan in detail
3 Examples of action plans

1 WHAT DOES ACTION PLANNING INVOLVE?

Your action plan should guide you through the process of asking and answering the question, 'How do I improve what I am doing?' (Whitehead 1989), and explaining why this is an important question and the possible significance of an answer. A difficulty with action planning is that sometimes people assume that life will go according to plan, which is seldom the case, so they get agitated when the unexpected happens. Try to regard your action plan as a set of prompts to guide you, rather than a fixed sequence of steps. Do not be surprised if things don't turn out as expected. Also remember that the word 'improve' does not imply that something is wrong. It communicates the idea that you want to evaluate your work at any point and check whether it is as you wish it to be. Any improvement is still improvement, no matter how small.

The question 'How do I improve what I am doing?' often arises from a situation where you experience yourself as a living contradiction when your values are denied in your practice (Whitehead 1989). As an educational leader, for example, you say you believe in democratic leadership but then find yourself behaving autocratically towards a particular colleague. As a parent you want to allow your children freedom of choice yet lay down the law about what kind of friends they can have. How do you resolve the tension? Should you try to do so? How do you justify your decisions?

Jack Whitehead (1989; 2003) expresses these ideas as follows:

- I experience a concern when some of my educational values are denied in my practice.
- I imagine a solution to the concern.
- I act in the direction of the imagined solution.
- I evaluate the outcome of the solution.
- I modify my practice, plans and ideas in the light of the evaluation.

Although the starting point of an action enquiry is often a situation in which you may experience yourself as a living contradiction, you may also want to celebrate an existing situation. Whatever may be the starting point, this set of ideas can transform into an understanding of what action research involves:

- We review our current practice,
- identify an aspect that we want to investigate,
- imagine a way forward,
- try it out, and
- take stock of what happens.
- We modify what we are doing in the light of what we have found, and continue working in this new way (try another option if the new way is not right),
- monitor what we do,
- review and evaluate the modified action,
- evaluate the validity of the account of learning, and
- develop new practices in the light of the evaluation.

(This is an updated version of McNiff et al. 2003.)

You can then transform these points into a series of questions that can act as your action plan.

- What is my concern?
- Why am I concerned?
- What kinds of experience can I describe to show why I am concerned?
- What can I do about it?
- What will I do about it?
- What kind of data will I gather to show the situation as it unfolds?
- How will I explain my educational influences in learning?
- How will I ensure that any conclusions I reach are reasonably fair and accurate?
- How will I evaluate the validity of the evidence-based account of my learning?
- How will I modify my concerns, ideas and practice in the light of my evaluations?

This is a generic action plan that can be modified to suit your own circumstances. The need for evaluating the validity of accounts of learning was made explicit in *Action Research for Teachers* (McNiff and Whitehead 2005), and is now fully articulated in this book.

The dual nature of action research

Be aware when planning that action research involves two interrelated processes. First, you take action in the social world, by doing things differently in relation to the people you are working with. You carry out certain actions and monitor what happens. This can be seen as action in the social world 'out there'. At the same time, you think about what you are doing as you carry out the actions, and reflect on what you are learning. You are learning not only *about* the action, but also *through* the action. This can be seen as action in the mental world 'in here'. The two sets of 'out there' and 'in here' actions go on during action research, and are both intertwined and of equal importance.

Most of the action research literature focuses on social action 'out there', and not too much on the learning 'in here', especially in terms of how learning arises from the action and feeds back into the action. The best action enquiries show the interrelated nature of learning and social action, and how one interpenetrates the other. Here are some examples.

Timothy Glavin (1998) undertook his action enquiry for his masters degree into, 'How can I improve my evaluative and advisory role in a primary school in Cork City?' The enquiry took place in the Republic of Ireland where, as a school inspector, Tim studied his own assessment and advisory practice in relation to a primary school. His choice of topic arose from his belief that he could not influence others unless he was prepared to change his own practice. Doing his research enabled him to produce his living educational theory in relation to how he reconceptualized his role and his practice. He now uses his workplace as a resource for thinking and learning, and understands his own professional development as a continuous and changing process in relation with others who are also engaged in their professional development.

Beatriz Egues de Grandi (2004) carried out her action enquiry for her masters degree into, 'How can I influence my students in developing their creativity and critical thinking? A self study'. The enquiry took place within a school in Argentina, and Beatriz describes the birth of her pedagogical concern in children-centred education that transformed her from being a source of knowledge to being a facilitator in encouraging skills that allow the practice of discernment in learning. Beatriz shows how the voices of her students guided her journey through her practice, and she presents evidence of conflicts when she failed to live up to her values. Her living educational theory emerged from her reflections on the values that gave purpose to her life and practice. In clarifying those values in the course of their emergence in practice, Beatriz transformed them into the standards of judgement that could be used to test the validity of her living educational theory. Beatriz's account of her learning is fully contextualized within the political and economic context of her life and work in Argentina.

Daisy Walsh (2004) carried out her masters enquiry into, 'How do I Improve my Leadership as a Team Leader in Vocational Education in Further Education?' The enquiry was carried out in the context of Daisy's work as a programme area team leader, for vocational 'A' level, GNVQ and GCSE ICT, at a further education college in the United Kingdom. Using a reflective journal, Daisy recorded her thoughts on significant events throughout her practice. One of these included her responses to a racist incident. Using narratives, she constructed representations from the data gathered. She traced and explored her journey as a team leader in further education from a concern to improve her leadership practice for the benefit of her team and her students.

2   THE ACTION PLAN IN DETAIL

Here are some ideas about how you can draw up an action plan of your own. It can be helpful when planning to write ideas down in note form. At this point we want to offer ideas about how to organize your ideas as notes, and some ways in which you can do this. You could use columns, straight text, spider diagrams, and also pictures and cartoons. We are not adventuring into pictorial forms here, because of limited space, but we encourage you to do so. The best forms are those that you create yourself. After each set of ideas here, you are invited to do a similar task for yourself. Remember that your action plan is not a fixed schedule, but a guide to your thinking and action. Any action plan you draw up is notional only, and subject to change at all times.

Here is the action plan in detail.

What is my concern?

Identify what you want to research, keeping your issue small, focused and manageable. For example, you may want to find ways of managing your time more successfully, or how to improve the quality of your educational leadership, or how to encourage good staff relations.

Turn your research issue into an action research question, beginning with 'How do I ...?'

Research issue	'How do I ...?' action research question
I need to manage my time better	How do I manage my time better?
Improving the quality of my educational leadership	How do I improve the quality of my educational leadership?
Encouraging good staff relations	How do I encourage good staff relations?

Task

Write down your research issue and turn it into a research question. This kind of layout is especially helpful for letting you see the immediate transformation of an issue into a question.

Why am I concerned?

Say why this is an issue for you. Perhaps it is simply bothering you, or has implications for your work. Perhaps it is something related to your values, such as justice or freedom, but you are not living in the direction of your values. Write down what value underpins your practice, and say whether you are or are not living towards it. Give some examples of situations which would show whether or not you were living towards your value. For example, you could write:

Value   Participation
Am I living towards it?   Yes
How can I see that?   Everyone participates in meetings

Value   Freedom
Am I living towards it?   No
How can I see that?   People are not able to express what they think in meetings

Value   Empathy
Am I living towards it?   No
How can I see that?   People do not relate well to one another

You could also use the same layout as above, for example:

Value	Am I living towards it?	How? How not?
Participation	Yes	Everyone participates in meetings

Task

Using your preferred kind of layout, write down the value that is important in your situation, say whether you are or are not living towards it, and how that can be seen.

What kinds of experience can I describe to show why I am concerned?

How will you gather data and generate evidence to show the situation in reality? On page 148 we explain the differences between data and evidence. Briefly, 'data' refers to all the information you gather in relation to a particular issue. 'Evidence' refers to those special pieces of data that show the issue in action. Evidence is therefore found in, and extracted from, data, which are usually contained in artefacts such as books, records, memos, transcripts, computer files, videos, pictures and so on. Your task is to imagine where you could find evidence, that is, what sources of data you would look at to find instances of what you are looking for. In your notes, write down the value at the heart of your research, and then think of which sources of data, or artefacts, you would look in to find it being shown in action.

For example, if you were looking for a manifestation of kindness, think of where you might find examples of kindness in action. You could write:

Kindness	Yes, apparent in a letter from a friend saying she is experiencing understanding from her colleagues following an illness
	No, not apparent in the minutes of a staff meeting when one colleague asks when Ms X is going to resume normal duties
Good relationships	Yes, apparent in a photograph of colleagues laughing together at a party
	No, not apparent in an e-mail to all staff sending New Year good wishes from the manager via their secretary
Justice	Yes, apparent in field notes from your conversation with a colleague where they say they have negotiated a good pension plan
	No, not apparent in a memo from a colleague saying he is being bullied

You could also use the same form as above if that is easier.

Value	Artefact/source of data
Kindness: is kindness evident in your situation?	• Letter from friend saying that she is experiencing understanding from colleagues following an illness • Minutes from staff meeting asking when Ms X will resume normal duties

Task

Using whatever kind of notes suits you, write down the value that is (or is not) being shown in practice, and what kind of evidence you could find in the data to show the situation as it is, that is, which artefacts you could look at for data that show the value in action, or not. If the value is not evident in action, you could say that the value is being denied.

What can I do about it?

Think about what you could do to improve the situation. Remember that you are not going to force a decision on anyone. You are going to try to exercise your influence so that they will think again and perhaps do things differently. In your notes, write down what you might do in response to your concern. For example, and taking the same situations as above, you could write the following.

Issue 1

My concern
My colleague has written me a letter saying that she is not experiencing understanding from others following her illness. This denies my values of care and compassion. What can I do?

My options
I can do the following:

* Explain her situation to management and encourage their understanding.
* Encourage her to approach peers and senior colleagues and explain her position.
* Tell her to buck up.
* Encourage peers to be more understanding.

Issue 2

My concern
I see a photograph of colleagues laughing together at a party. I wonder what I can do to maintain good relationships.

My options
I could

* actively think about ways of maintaining staff relationships
* produce reports to say why staff relationships are so good
* organize a small social committee.

Issue 3

My concern

I receive a memo from a colleague saying he is being bullied. This causes me deep concern and denies my values of justice and kindness.

My options

I could

- talk with my colleague and find out more
- encourage him to stand up for himself
- arrange a meeting between him and his persecutors with me as mediator to talk it through.

Task

Using whichever kind of notes suits you (you could use the same kind of lay-out as above), or a spider diagram, write down how you might deal with the situation, as represented in the evidence.

What will I do about it?

This is where you think of a possible way forward. Choose one option only and follow it through in action. You will keep track of whether or not it works. If it seems to be working, you will probably continue working in this way. If it isn't working, you will try another option. Using the same examples as above, you could write the following.

Issue 1

Chosen option

I will encourage peers to be more understanding of M.

Follow-up plan

I will speak with individuals and small groups, suggesting how they can be more supportive of M. I will arrange for someone to sit with her at coffee breaks. I will arrange for the office to send her a bouquet and a good wishes card.

Issue 2

Chosen option

I will find ways of encouraging staff to maintain their good relationships.

Follow-up plan

I will invite three members of staff to form a social events committee. I will find some money to pay for a group dinner. I will initiate a task group on how to maintain good relationships.

Issue 3

Chosen option

I will encourage my colleague to stand up for himself.

Follow-up plan

I will invite him to imagine what he can do for himself. I will urge him to have confidence. I will role play a situation with him to let him see other options.

Task

Using a framework like this, or anything that suits, map out a possible course of action.

What kind of data will I gather to show the situation as it unfolds?

How do you anticipate that you will have an influence in people's learning? Will others come to think differently, and so act differently? What do you think will happen?

You are now into your second round of data gathering. What kind of data will you gather to show the evidence of your influence in other people's thinking and action? Will you use the same data gathering techniques as before, or different ones? What kind of artefacts, such as journals and memos, will you expect to find the data in? Here are some ideas, using different examples.

Artefact/data source	Evidence of my influence
Diary entry	Colleague writes a diary entry to say that you have helped them to rethink their position and act differently
Photograph	Photograph of colleagues enjoying a joke together, when before they wouldn't speak. Note on the back of the photograph saying thank you for bringing them together
Examinations result	Results of so-called 'learning disabled' student whom you especially encouraged and who has now passed an exam. Letter from student saying it was because of your influence that they passed

Task

Using a framework like this, or another form, say where you may find evidence to show your influence. Say what kind of artefacts you may look for. These may be the same as or different from your previous set of data gathering.

How will I explain my educational influences in learning?

How do you make judgements about your influence, and whether you are achieving what you hoped to achieve? Write down the original value that inspired your work, and then say whether or not you feel you are living towards it, at least in some instances. Where could you find examples of this realization of your value?

For example:

My value	Fairness
Where would I look for evidence?	I would look in assignments I have returned to my students. I anticipate that my comments to them would show me offering fair critique. My comments would be written in pencil, which is less violent than traditional red pen
My value	Freedom
Where would I look for evidence?	I would look at the minutes of staff meetings, and search for instances that show me encouraging others to speak their minds, and to challenge my own ideas
My value	Inclusiveness
Where would I look for evidence?	I would look in the records of the peace talks to find instances of me honouring others' rights to live according to their own traditions

Task

Using whichever form suits you, write down your value and what kind of evidence you would aim to produce to show you living in the direction of your value.

How will I ensure that any conclusions I reach are reasonably fair and accurate?

How will you ensure that people will see your claim as unprejudiced, authentic, and not simply you expressing an opinion or wishful thinking? How do you get critical feedback? How do you authenticate your evidence? The procedures of action research involve inviting critical friends and validation groups to endorse, or refute, your claims to knowledge by scrutinizing your evidence, and agreeing, or not, that your case will withstand rigorous critique. Write down what you are hoping to claim and what you hope your validation group will see as your evidence. For example:

My anticipated claim	What I hope my validation group will see
I hope to claim that I have improved my teaching of geography	I hope they will see my well-kept records and lesson plans. I hope they will see an improvement of exam results this year
I hope to claim that I have encouraged students to be more responsive	I hope they will see videos of my students taking an active part in lessons. I hope they will see students taking a teaching role
I hope to claim that I have exercised my academic leadership	I hope they will see more faculty enrolling for academic study. I hope they will see a greater publications output

Task

Using whatever kind of notes suit you, write down what you are hoping to claim through your research, and what kind of evidence will help your validation group and critical friends to make judgements about what you have done.

How will I evaluate the validity of the evidenced-based account of my learning?

Your critical friends and validation group not only consider your conclusions, but also scrutinize carefully whether or not you have fulfilled all the methodological procedures for supporting a claim to knowledge. This means that you have to be clear yourself about the differences between data and evidence, and between criteria and standards of judgement. These issues are explained fully in Chapter 15. Briefly, criteria refer to the general aspects or indicators we look for, such as 'participative working' or 'listening carefully', whereas standards of judgement refer to the process of making judgements about whether or not the values underpinning these aspects are realized, such as 'Did I realize my value of democracy?' or 'Did I fulfil my value of attending to the other?'

Task

Go back to your notes where you wrote down the values at the heart of your research and think about how these could be construed as criteria and standards of judgement. You could write:

Value   Kindness
Criterion   Demonstration of kindness
Standard of judgement Am I practising in a kind way?

Value   Fairness
Criterion   Demonstrating fairness
Standard of judgement Am I practising in a way that treats everyone fairly?

Using a framework like this, or another form, write down your core values and how these can be transformed into criteria and standards of judgement.

How will I modify my concerns, ideas and practice in the light of my evaluations?

What do you think you may do differently, in light of what you will learn? It is probably not realistic at this stage to plan for this, because you will not know until you get there. However, the fact that you are prepared to ask these kinds of critical questions is an indication that you are determined not to take no for an answer, and to keep raising new problematics to ensure that your value of non-complacent participation is always held as a guiding principle to action.

3   EXAMPLES OF ACTION PLANS

Now, draw up some action plans of your own. Here are some expanded examples of how some people went about it and the thinking involved. The plans are written out like this to give a sense of overall coherence. You don't need to write out such extended plans, but you do need to produce some kind of plan of your own.

HOW DO I ENCOURAGE GREATER PARTICIPATION AMONG STAFF?

My context

I am the newly appointed principal of a sixth-form college, which so far has been run in a fairly autocratic way. I believe that sustainable growth comes from participative working towards democratically negotiated goals. I was appointed on the basis that I could exercise my influence in such a way that attitudes and practices could change into a new culture. How do I do this?

Why am I concerned?

I am concerned because I hold values around democratic ways of working that expect all to participate in public decision-making processes. I believe that all colleagues are able to speak for themselves, but they are silent. The situation denies my values of social justice and the exercise of individual accountability. I also want to encourage greater student participation in college affairs, in order to develop their confidence and possibly their academic standards, but I cannot hope for that when the staff do not feel engaged.

What experiences can I describe to show the situation as it is?

I will gather data to show the realities of a non-participating staff and the possible influence on the college culture. I would like to videotape a whole staff meeting but this would possibly be too threatening at this stage of my enquiry. I can instead interview some key members of staff, such as heads of department, and two junior members of staff. I can also interview four or five students. This means that I need to draw up my ethics statements, and my letters requesting permission to do my research, which need to be given to those whom I would like to invite as research participants, as well as to parents and caregivers. I also need to explain my plan at the next staff meeting, and at the next meeting of the board of governors, and get permission. I need to reassure people that I am investigating how I develop my work, and not inspecting theirs.

What can I do?

As noted, I could ask some key members of staff if they will act as my research participants. I could invite my other senior management colleagues to act as critical friends throughout. I could conduct short interviews with the identified members of staff to check whether they share my educational goals of maximum participation. Should I involve administrative staff at this stage too?

(Continued)

What will I do?

I will do all of the above but I will not invite administrative staff yet. First I have to encourage greater confidence in participation from academic staff. Over time I hope to build stronger relationships between the academic staff and the administrative staff. I will also share the data I gather with my senior management critical colleagues, and invite their feedback on whether I am achieving my goals of encouraging staff or simply putting pressure on them.

How will I gather data to show the situation as it unfolds?

I will continue to gather data with my research participants. I will especially ask them if they feel more involved, and whether other staff appear to be more positive. I will invite them to develop with me a new approach to staff meetings that will invite greater participation, and ask them to write down their ideas with a view to discussing these with the full staff. These reports, and the minutes of staff meetings, will stand as important data.

How do I evaluate my potential influence?

I need to outline the standards of judgement I am using to judge whether or not I can claim to be realizing my goals in my practice. These goals can be understood in terms of my values of social justice and personal accountability. Do these values come to life in my own and others' practices? Are people participating more? Are they beginning to accept their own responsibility for making our workplace a more democratic place to be? Can I show how my values act as my living standards of practice and judgement?

How do I ensure that any conclusions I reach are reasonably fair and accurate?

I will invite my senior management critical colleagues to meet with me and look at the initial data, and also at later data as they emerge. I will ask them whether they agree that the initial data show a situation in which there was minimal participation by the staff, to a situation where there is more participation. Of course we still have a long way to go, but even the smallest amount of improvement is still improvement. I will ask them whether I am justified in claiming that people are accepting my influence, or whether these things are perhaps an outcome of the departure of the old regime. Perhaps they will not be able to say at this moment, and we will need more time for the issue to become clear. I also recognize that this is a sensitive situation, and that we all have to tread with care. I hope they will give me feedback that confirms my intuitions, but you never know.

(Continued)

How do I evaluate the validity of my account of learning?

In presenting my account of learning to my critical friends and validation groups, I will take care in all methodological features. I will draw their attention to my articulated criteria and standards of judgement, and I will ask them to focus on the explanations I give for my learning as well as my conclusions. I will take careful note of what they say in my constant attempts to demonstrate the methodological rigour of my claim to knowledge.

How will I modify my concerns, ideas and practice in the light of my evaluation?

I will develop my action enquiry into a new cycle that focuses on involving the more junior members of staff and helping them to build their confidence to become active participants. My overall plan is to work with people individually and in small groups, and so build up local relationships that may influence the formation of wider relationships.

HOW DO I ENABLE VISUALLY IMPAIRED STUDENTS TO GAIN EASIER ACCESS TO CONTINUING EDUCATION?

My context

I am a learning support tutor for visually impaired students who wish to access continuing learning opportunities in further education. I want to find ways of helping them gain easier access.

What is my concern?

My concern is that the students I teach, who are all visually impaired, are not getting the opportunities they should to go on to further education. Although legally they have right of access, practically they are disadvantaged in that they don't know systems and find it difficult to negotiate information.

Why am I concerned?

I have strong values around the worth of each individual person, and that no one should be disadvantaged because of physical, mental, or emotional impairment. I do what I can to ensure that all have equal opportunity of access and outcome. I am not sure, however, whether my students are being disadvantaged at a systemic level because of their visual impairment.

(Continued)

What experiences can I describe to show the situation as it is?

I can produce statistical analysis of fully sighted students who do gain access to further education, and compare it with an analysis of the rate of access of visually impaired students. If both sets of statistics appear commensurable, I do not have grounds for concern. However, from conversations with visually impaired students, I know how much of a struggle it is for them to gain access. I can make some tape recordings of their stories to show that there are grounds for concern. I will ask two students to become research participants, so that I can see whether listening to the tapes does help them gain confidence around knowing what to do.

What can I do about it?

I can make greater use of resources that appeal to their fully operational senses, in this case, audiotapes. I aim to make audiotapes of the information they need to gain access to further education, as well as the stories of students who have already successfully enrolled and are pursuing their studies. I am hoping that my current students will gain confidence and inspiration from listening to the stories of successful students. I will give my students my letters asking their permission to be research participants. Because they cannot see well, I will ask a trusted colleague to act on their behalf and sign. I will also conduct audiotaped conversations with them, explaining my request for their permission, and getting their agreement on tape. One copy of the tape stays with them and one with me.

What will I do about it?

I will ask my principal for funding so that I can make these tape recordings. I will contact a local drama group so that I can get speakers with clear speaking voices. I will ask them to read the college prospectus, and explain to listeners what they have to do. I will invite three students in particular to give me regular feedback on how they respond to these initiatives.

How will I gather data to show the situation as it unfolds?

I will gather responses from the three students, and any others who wish to be involved, to see whether they feel they have the information they need, and what further resources may be useful. I will ask them to tape record their experiences as they go for interviews or fill out forms. I will later incorporate these ideas into a handbook for wider college use.

How will I evaluate my potential influence?

I will take my values as my living standards of judgement. Are the audiotapes enabling greater ease of access to further education? Have I learned how to counterbalance disadvantage by introducing new systems?

(Continued)

How will I ensure that any conclusions are reasonably fair and accurate?

I will present my provisional findings to critical friends and a small validation group, and I will think carefully and act on their feedback. I will later present my findings to a staff seminar. When I produce the handbook I will create it as a living document which regularly incorporates feedback and good ideas.

How will I evaluate the validity of the evidence-based account of my learning?

I will ask my critical friends and validation groups to focus on the explanations I offer for my learning. I will ask them to comment on whether I explain how I make my own validation processes clear so that readers can see how I am aiming for transparency in my attempt to establish the validity of my account.

How will I modify my concerns, ideas and practice in the light of my evaluation?

Provided the initial feedback is reasonably positive, I will continue to develop audiotapes as resources. Perhaps I will build up a resource bank. I will definitely let people in other colleges know what I am doing, and perhaps write a paper for wider dissemination. It would be helpful if I could liaise with other colleagues in similar situations to find new ideas and test existing strategies.

SUMMARY

This chapter has given practical advice about planning for an action enquiry. It has considered what action planning involves, and set out the details of what you need to think about at each point. Examples of action plans have been given to help you see what planning involves and how it can be done.

The next chapter gives advice on how to implement your action plans.

11

Doing Action Research:
Carrying Out Your Action Plan

Now you are ready to begin doing your action research. Here are some ideas about how you can carry out your action plan, in relation both to social action and to learning. The chapter sets out the different questions in your action plan, and offers ideas about each one. Chapter 12 contains examples of how people carried out their action plans.

Here is your action plan again. Remember that you can change these questions to suit your own circumstances. It is important, however, that you do ask questions.

- What is my concern?
- Why am I concerned?
- What experiences can I describe to show why I am concerned?
- What can I do about it?
- What will I do about it?
- What kind of data will I gather to show the situation as it unfolds?
- How will I explain my educational influences in learning?
- How will I ensure that any conclusions I reach are reasonably fair and accurate?
- How will I evaluate the validity of the evidence-based account of my learning?
- How will I modify my concerns, ideas and practice in the light of my evaluations?

Now, here is your action plan in action.

What is my concern?

Go back to the issue you identified in your action plan, or identify another issue that has arisen in the meantime. Make sure it is something you can do something about. You cannot change the organizational system you work in, but you can change your immediate work situation. You cannot change the policy around inclusion of patients or unemployed people in organizational decision-making practices, but you can include those people in your own practice.

Keep the bigger picture in sight as a goal to be worked towards, and walk backwards to basics and ask what you can do to address the issue in your immediate practice context.

Having identified your research issue, turn it into a 'How do I ...?' action research question. Here are some examples.

Research issue	'How do I ...?' action research question
I need to manage my time better	How do I manage my time better?
I want to negotiate a more productive relationship with colleague M	How do I negotiate a more productive relationship with colleague M?
I want to find ways of supporting my mature students more effectively	How do I support my mature students more effectively?

Your question may change over time, and so may your issue. This happens in action research, because it is a developmental process where nothing stands still. Your question, 'How do I manage my time better?' may transform into 'How do I find protected time for my research?', and 'How do I support my mature students more effectively?' may transform into 'How do I ensure that my mature students have access to distance learning facilities?' Parlett and Hamilton (1977) describe these kinds of processes as progressive focusing.

Now, relate your issue and your question to a value. Here are some examples.

Research issue	I need to manage my time better
Research question	How do I manage my time better?
Underpinning value	Integrity in professional practice; responsible practice

Research issue	I want to negotiate a more productive relationship with colleague M
Research question	How do I negotiate a more productive relationship with colleague M?
Underpinning value	Care as the basis of quality relationships; inclusion and respect

You could set this out as follows:

Research issue	Research question	Values
I need to manage my time better	How do I manage my time better?	Integrity in professional practice; responsible practice

Doing this gives you your explanatory framework, which shows the overall scope of your project, its direction and purpose. You can show clearly why you are doing your research and what you hope to achieve, in relation to your values.

You may focus on your social action 'out there', or on your learning 'in here'. The best projects show both. An initial focus on learning may also transform into a later focus on action, informed by the learning, and which informs future learning. These two foci may give rise to different action–reflection cycles. Here are some examples that show this possible transformation.

Example 1

First research cycle, with a focus on learning

Research issue	Am I working according to my own values, or according to what others lead me to believe? I want to find ways of ensuring equal access to continuing provision for learning-impaired students, within a system that denies this access
Research question	How do I check that I am thinking for myself, and not giving in to bureaucracy?
Value	Integrity of self; shaping one's own identity; honesty

Second research cycle, with a focus on action informed by the learning

Research issue	I want to ensure access to further continuing provision for my learning-impaired students. I am concerned that the current system is denying them access
Research question	How do I ensure access to further continuing provision for my learning-impaired students?
Value	Personal and social justice; entitlement; democratic forms of living

Example 2

First research cycle, with a focus on learning

Research issue	I want to understand the power relationships in my workplace, so I'd like to learn more about the ideas of Foucault. I am working in a context where power relationships are getting in the way of participative working
Research question	How do I learn more about the ideas of Foucault?
Underpinning value	Freedom; personal and social integrity; need not to be colonized by dominant discourses

Second research cycle, with a focus on action informed by the learning

Research issue	We need to develop a coherent staff development plan, to encourage new thinking about participative working
Research question	How do we develop a coherent staff development plan?
Underpinning value	Relational and inclusional ways of working; morally committed and socially oriented planning as the basis for action

Example 3

First research cycle, with a focus on learning

Research issue	Why am I teaching in the way that I am? I want to ensure that I am presenting issues fairly and not communicating my own prejudices as truth
Research question	How do I evaluate my teaching and my influence?
Underpinning value	Honesty; personal and social integrity; social justice

Second research cycle, with a focus on action informed by the learning

Research issue	We need to evaluate our work
Research question	How do we evaluate our work?
Underpinning value	Personal and social accountability; integrity; truth, justice and honesty

Why am I concerned?

Setting out your research issues, questions and underpinning values like this can help you to think of your work as attempting to realize your values in your practice. Now you need to think about how your 'How do I …?' question can transform into the articulation of your research purpose, so that, when you come to make a claim to knowledge, you can show how you transformed your practice in such a way that you were living out your values, and how you transformed your question into a claim to knowledge.

Remember that practices are informed by values. Actions are not necessarily practices. You can smile, or trip over, which are actions but not practices. Practices are purposeful, value laden and socially oriented. You need to show that your practice is not simply action, but is a considered, purposeful practice. It is praxis, that is, committed and morally oriented.

Write down the values that inspire your work, and show the relationship between your values and other aspects of your research and ultimately your claim to knowledge. You may identify several values. Here are some ideas.

Research issue	Research question	Values	Anticipated claim to knowledge
Improving the quality of my relationship with colleague M	How do I improve the quality of my relationship with colleague M?	Relational and inclusional relationships; recognizing the other	I have improved the quality of my relationship with colleague M for the purposes of better working practices
Encouraging students' interest in history	How do I encourage my students' interest in history?	Importance of understanding the basis of social actions; need to transform the past into a better present	I have encouraged my students' interest in history for the creation of a more sustainable world
We need to create a resources centre that will benefit our community	How do we create a resources centre that will benefit our community?	Need for knowledge; learning; access to information; sustainability of community	We have created a resources centre that is benefiting our community

Doing this will help you justify your work by showing how your values came to act both as the living standards that guided your practice and also as the living standards by which you made judgements about your work.

What experiences can I describe to show why I am concerned?

You need to gather data throughout your project, using any of the techniques described in Chapter 13. Aim to gather your data with an eye to your research question. If you ask, 'How do I stop the bullying?' look out for data that show bullying in action, or possibly what could be the reasons for the bullying. Watch out for really key pieces that may get turned into evidence. In your enquiry about how you can improve the quality of relationships in your organization, you may receive a letter from a colleague, which shows how caring relationships are not prioritized. You could highlight an entry from your diary, saying that you needed to take action in relation to the bullying or developing better relationships. You should gather data that are representative both of the social situation and also of how you responded to the situation. You are hoping to understand better, as the basis of action aimed at improvement. Here are some examples of how this can be done.

Reason for my concern	Bullying of one colleague by another
What evidence can I produce?	Letter from victim to you, asking for help. How do I help?

Reason for my concern	Need to maintain caring relationships
What evidence can I produce?	Videotape of staff party showing some people not talking with one another. How do I intervene?

Reason for my concern	Need to maintain full participation in staff meetings
What evidence can I produce?	Minutes of staff meeting recording affirming comments. How do we keep it this way?

Store your data carefully. Check out ideas about your data with your critical friends, and keep records of these meetings, perhaps by tape recording. This recording can itself stand as evidence when you come to write your report. Note especially whether you are beginning to question your own assumptions about how you are interpreting data. How did you react when you got the letter from your colleague? What did you think when you saw the video of the staff party?

What can I do about it?

What options are open? What can you do in relation to others? What do you need to learn? How are you going to find out?

Now is a good time to consult with others who may or may not be involved in your research. Get insiders' perspectives, and also get more distanced opinions. Getting others' reactions helps you to check out your own perceptions and possible prejudices. Are the difficult relationships real or do you perceive them as such because you are personally feeling under pressure? Is dealing with the bullying perhaps a matter of firm encouragement? Getting others' opinions on possible courses of action can help you to avoid taking inappropriate action. Other people can also suggest other options that you may not have thought of. Here are some examples of how this can be done.

What do I need to find out?	Who do I consult?
What can I do to stop the bullying?	Trusted colleague who has also experienced bullying
How do I improve/maintain good staff relationships?	Small group of experienced staff, who could later form a committee
How do I keep staff meetings enjoyable?	All staff at staff meeting, requesting feedback about possible strategies

What will I do about it?

Having considered all your options, try one out. If that one doesn't seem to work, try something else. Don't get discouraged if things do not go as you wish, or if you make mistakes. Mistakes can be valuable sources of learning. You may develop a new project from how you learned from mistakes.

Be aware that this can be uncomfortable. It is much easier to stay as we are and not try something new, but if the way we are is not right, we have to do something about it. No one else will. It is our responsibility. We are the responsible creators of our own lives, individually and collectively, and we are potentially influencing others all the time, so we have to ensure that our influence is as life-affirming as possible.

Keep careful records as you go. Keep records of action in your research diary, and records of learning in your reflective journal. These can be different journals or the same. For example, using just one book, you could write in one column, 'What did I do?', and in a second column, 'What did I learn?' Leave a space after entries, or a blank third column, so that later you can ask, 'What is the significance of my action and my learning?' Here is an example of how this can be done.

What did I do?	What did I learn?	What is the significance of my learning?
I spoke to the bully. She told me to mind my own business	Perhaps I should have concentrated on encouraging the victim	Externally imposed solutions do not always work. Solutions developed by those involved lead to more sustainable scenarios
I asked a small group of experienced staff to help	They were pleased at my approach	Relationships are in people's practices. People themselves need to decide how to manage their own affairs
I consulted with all staff and requested feedback	They appreciated being involved and gave me positive feedback on my actions	Good leadership involves enabling other people to take control

What kind of data will I gather to show the situation as it unfolds?

Throughout you will be gathering data at intervals whose frequency you decide. It you are doing a three-week project, you may need to gather data every two or three days. If it is a three-month project, every week will do. When you gather data, make sure they are relevant to your research question. Asking 'How do I encourage participation?' means you will gather data to show aspects of participation (or non-participation, as the case may be).

Remember that you are not trying to change something in the sense of directly impacting on someone. Change can work like this, when one person forcibly gets someone else to do something. The values underpinning control are usually to do with self-interest, aimed at domination. You are aiming not for control but for sustainable change, rooted in the values of inclusion and relationship, and intended to encourage negotiated forms of living.

Therefore, rather than thinking about changing things, think about exercising your influence. How do you exercise your influence? Do you keep in mind the fact that people can think for themselves, and they decide whether to be influenced or not? Many people are told that they cannot think for themselves, and have to think in a certain way, and they come to believe this. Do you think people should internalize what you think, or come to think for themselves? How do you do this? How do you find ways of freeing your own thinking as well as helping others to come to think for themselves?

Maintain careful records of what you are doing in relation to your social action and your learning. You can use the same data gathering methods throughout, or you can vary them. Be imaginative. Do not instantly opt for a questionnaire. Think creatively. Go for an interview, or artwork, or role play and performance, or video. Keep your ethical considerations in mind, and get permission from the author for any piece of work they produce that you would like to use as data. If you are using other people's work, ask them to sign and date the piece of work, and sign and date it yourself. This is an important form of authentication.

Sort your data regularly and consolidate them at intervals. Bear in mind that you are showing development, where people, including yourself, came to do things differently. You need to show how processes unfolded, and what influences were at work. In your report you will comment explicitly on these processes.

Here are some ideas about which data sources may possibly contain evidence of your influence.

Where will I find evidence?	What kind of evidence might I find?
A participant's research diary	Diary entry saying that she found your support invaluable for helping her settle in at work
Transcript of a tape-recorded conversation with a colleague	Extract from conversation in which colleague says that you have helped her become more confident
Video of workshop you have run to improve self-assertion	Clip of shy person holding her own in a problematic conversation with others

How will I explain my educational influences in learning?

Remember that the centre of your enquiry is you. You are monitoring your actions and learning, as you try to influence further learning, in relation with other people. How do you make judgements about whether or not you are contributing to improved learning?

Go back to your values. Are you living them out? Are you working in ways that are just, truthful and free, both in your social contexts and in your own thinking? If you claim that you are, your claim must be backed up by authenticated evidence. Your claim has to show your values in practice, so these values come to be recognized as your standards of practice and judgement.

Remember that you are not evaluating other people's practices. They can do that for themselves. You are evaluating your practice, that is, you are saying whether or not you feel that you are justified in saying that you are achieving your own high standards.

Here are some examples of claims to knowledge you could make, and the standards of judgement you could use to make judgements about those claims.

My claim	My standards of judgement
I claim that I have encouraged good working relationships	My data archive contains instances of people being courteous and considerate to others. Previously these kinds of relationships were not so much in evidence. My values of care and participative working are being realized as my living standards of judgement
I claim that I have influenced the quality of communication in our department	I can produce instances of practice, such as e-mails and memos, to show that colleagues are communicating well and pleasantly. My values of relationship and inclusion are being realized as my living standards of judgement
I claim that I have encouraged my students to think for themselves	Essays and assignments show the exercise of original thinking and critical judgement. My values of freedom in thinking and the exercise of critical judgement are being realized as my living standards of judgement

How will I ensure that any conclusions I reach are reasonably fair and accurate?

You need to test your claims against the critical judgement of others. This means that at all stages of your research you will make your records available to others, for them to comment on any aspect. They may comment on the quality of your methodology, whether you are observing good ethical practice, whether your data appear to be authentic, whether you have generated valid evidence in relation to clearly articulated standards of judgement, and whether the conduct of the whole research gives people reason to believe you. This process of public critique is essential to all forms of research, and especially in action research where claims to knowledge are rooted in subjective experience.

Your process of critique will involve the regular feedback of your critical friends and validation group as you account for your own learning and your educational influence in the learning of others. Be prepared that throughout they may provide feedback that tells you what you don't want to know, for example, that things are not going as you think they are. This kind of feedback can help as a valuable steer to your project. It can keep you focused, and can prevent you from making unjustified claims. It is up to you whether you act on the advice of critical colleagues, but be prepared to defend your decision and future action if you don't.

Here are some examples of where you may get feedback for your claims, and the kind of feedback you may expect.

When do I present my claims?

- Reporting progress to a critical friend.
- Presenting a progress report to a validation meeting.
- Presenting a final report at a staff colloquium.

What kind of feedback can I expect?

- Feedback to say that the research appears to be addressing the research question.
- Minutes to show what the validating group recommended, especially in relation to aspects of the research that needed rethinking.
- Oral and written feedback from colleagues recording their impressions and suggestions for modification.

How will I evaluate the validity of the evidence-based account of my learning?

A clear task for your critical friends and validation groups is to focus on the validity of your account of learning, and to check whether you are offering explanations as well as descriptions. Your explanations will take the form of clearly articulated claims to knowledge, which are not only believable in relation to the specified goals of your research, but whose organizing methodologies are also procedurally appropriate. This means that you should set out your claims, criteria and standards of judgement, and you should also say specifically that you are doing so. It is a question of doing it, and letting your audience know that you know the importance of why you should do it.

By demonstrating your own awareness of the significance of methodological elements, you also demonstrate your capacity as a disciplined researcher and competent knowledge creator.

How will I modify my concerns, ideas and practice in the light of my evaluations?

How do you change your ideas and practices in the light of what you are finding out? Are you prepared to let go of old ways and head for the future? It takes courage and commitment to do so.

If you feel that your new way of working is reasonably satisfactory, you will probably continue working like this for as long as it remains satisfactory. This may not be for long, however, because people change all the time and their social situations change with them. This is one of the delights of working in an action research way, because you can see how one research question can transform into another, and also how one issue can act as the grounds for new issues to emerge. Nothing is ever static. We are constantly changing ourselves and our contexts.

This kind of transformation of existing issues and questions into new ones can help you organize your ideas and practices as ongoing cycles of action and reflection. Focusing on one issue can lead to new learning. This learning can feed back into action, and the action can act as the grounds for new learning. It is an ongoing spiral of spirals that helps us to realize our potentials for unlimited new ideas and boundless forms of new practices. We create our futures as we live our presents.

Here are some ideas about how you could organize your evolving research questions into cycles, and how the research questions change their focus.

Example 1

Research question in first cycle
How do I manage my timekeeping?

Emerging research questions in subsequent cycles

1   How do I protect research time?
2   How do I negotiate with others about my work schedule?
3   How do I manage the process of writing reports?

Example 2

Research question in first cycle
How do I persuade others to be cooperative?

Emerging research questions in subsequent cycles

1   How do I understand cooperative practices?
2   How do I encourage others to speak for themselves?
3   How do I educate for freedom?

Example 3

Research question in first cycle
How do I exercise my influence?

Emerging research questions in subsequent cycles

1   How do I exercise my influence for good relationships?
2   How do I contribute to the education of social formations?
3   How do I work with others for sustainable good social orders?

This returns us to the idea of why we should hold ourselves accountable for what we do. By using our research projects to evaluate our work, we show how we are ensuring that today is the best we can do, and this gives us hope that tomorrow will be even better.

SUMMARY

This chapter has taken you through an action research plan, step by step, with ideas and examples of how you can do this for yourself. Remember to adapt the suggested questions into questions that suit your own circumstances. Use your imagination about how you do your research.

The next chapter contains two case studies that show how an action plan may be put into practice.

12

Examples of Action Research Projects

This chapter contains two examples of projects that used the suggested frameworks as guidance. The examples are from teacher educators in China, who are working with Moira Laidlaw. Moira went to China in 2001 with Voluntary Services Overseas. The new emphasis on China's Open Door policy means that foreigners are invited to provide support in developing new ideas and practices. In education, this has manifested in the development of the New Curriculum (VSO 2003). Moira's work is to offer ideas about new methodologies that support a more student-centred curriculum. She works in Guyuan Teachers College in the north-west of China, in Ningxia Province, as an adviser to China's Experimental Centre for Educational Action Research in Foreign Languages Teaching at the College. Guyuan is one of the poorest areas in China. Because of her tenacity, her vision, and her capacity to influence practice and policy, she has succeeded in influencing the creation of new forms of educational and social practice. The two stories presented here are examples of how her influence is enabling educators to imagine for themselves how to work. The full reports can be accessed at http://www.bath.ac.uk/~edsajw/moira.shtml

---

HOW CAN I HELP MY STUDENTS TO IMPROVE THEIR MOTIVATION IN SPEAKING?

He Lena

First, He Lena sets out her report in summary form. This kind of summarizing can be helpful in mapping out a report. She then goes on to write the report in full. Here is her summary and an edited version of her full report.

(Continued)

Outline of my report

My context

Action research is important to me because it has helped me begin my teaching career as a learner. I have been able to encourage my students' learning and my own.

What is my concern?

I want to encourage my English majors students to practise speaking. I will focus on Jin Guoliang and Li Fang as key participants.

Why am I concerned?

I believe that speaking is essential to the whole learning process. It is obviously a big problem for my students.

How can I improve the situation?

Make speaking a rule:

- Ask each student to do a morning report.
- Ask different people to be the 'speaker' during group discussions.

Vary speaking activities:

- Individual presentations. The morning speech – change from 'recitation' to 'interviewing' and so to 'impromptu' talk.
- Group work.
- Encourage students to 'show off'.

Who can help me and how?

- Dr Moira Laidlaw and Dean Tian, by giving me advice, listening to my concerns, and encouraging me.
- My students, by participating in the research.
- My colleagues, through discussions and suggestions.
- Reading relevant books and online information.

(Continued)

What have I learned?

- Studying my practice has enabled me to be more confident in teaching.
- It has helped my professional development.
- It has helped my personal life.

My report

My context

I very much enjoy teaching. I enjoy helping my students learn English. I was therefore especially disappointed when my students said that learning English was a headache. I was at a loss to know what to do, until I met Moira Laidlaw and her ideas about action research. I began learning to teach. The project has been going on for a year, and already I feel more confident in teaching and have seen improvements in both my students and myself. Here is a brief account of my research.

What is my concern?

I have a class of 28 English major students. They are my first teaching group. They are meant to be good language learners and users, but unfortunately seem capable of only reading and memorizing rather than speaking. Most don't speak in class. My question became how I could help them improve their motivation in speaking. I aimed to help the whole class, but concentrated on Jin Guoliang and Li Fang, two of the most passive students, as key participants.

Why am I concerned?

I believe that active practice is central to the whole learning process. My students (and I) had got into the habit in school of learning 'mute' English.

From a questionnaire I distributed at the beginning of term, I knew that my students had the same concern. Ninety-five per cent said that their biggest problems were speaking and listening.

How can I improve it?

I tried a range of strategies:

(Continued)

Offering equal and sufficient opportunities for speaking: I negotiated with my students that we would all talk in class. We agreed that each student would give a morning report. *Varying speaking activities*: I encouraged an atmosphere of interested activity by encouraging individual presentations, group work, and 'showing off'. This meant that I made every opportunity for students to shine, and I encouraged them every time they succeeded, even if it was simply a matter of good pronunciation. For the first time ever, Jin Guoliang stood up and asked the speaker a question. I noticed that Li Fang had begun to discuss ideas actively with others. On one occasion, Jin Guoliang told me, 'I was afraid to speak in public, but after I tried once, I felt it was not so difficult. I feel more comfortable in speaking now.'

My efforts paid off. I believe I am justified in claiming that I have achieved my goals of motivating some of my students to speak because

- My students have begun to participate actively in every class.
- Those who never volunteered before, such as Li Fang and Jin Guoliang, began to participate actively. Furthermore, Jin Guoliang took part in the English speaking contest. Prior to the event, several students told me that they were too nervous to go on. Finally, however, they stepped onto the stage, and three of them even got prizes.

Who helped me and how?

Moira Laidlaw and Dean Tian helped most of all. Moira visited my class and offered helpful advice.

My students helped significantly. They gave me feedback and direction.

Other colleagues helped me by visiting my class and inviting me to visit theirs. I learned much from them when attending action research meetings, especially about the need for validating action research reports. The key aspect I learned here was the importance of finding evidence for my claims.

Books, online and television services helped me find further information and ideas.

What have I learned?

Action research has become a way of life.

- I am more confident in teaching in the sense that I have learned more about my students and myself and the relationship between us. I realize how important it is to encourage them to be the centre of class.
- I have developed professionally by coming to reflect on my teaching more systematically and find my own answers.

(Continued)

- I have learned how to generate evidence, which has encouraged me also to become more responsible.
- I have learned to work collaboratively with others. I enjoy the scholarly and open-minded atmosphere at work. Work itself has become a form of research. I have tried to create the same atmosphere in my class. I believe that the warmth and strength of collaboration is beneficial not only to my students' study but to their lives as well.

In summary I can say that I have not only achieved my initial goals, but learned and grown professionally as a teacher, while encouraging my students to do the same.

HOW CAN I ENCOURAGE MY STUDENTS' MOTIVATION SO THAT THEY CAN IMPROVE THEIR LEARNING?

Tao Rui

Introduction

As with many teachers in China, my teaching methods in the classroom were traditional. I used a teacher-centred academic style, characterized by grammatical explanation and translation, which is sometimes known as the 'grammar-translation method'.

In the past I did the following.

- I led my students through the sentences step by step.
- I provided background information concerning certain texts.
- I explained difficult words, focusing on grammatical points.

I prepared my lessons carefully and thoroughly. In class, I did my best to pass on as much knowledge as possible to my students as well as cultural information. Once I had completed the syllabus, I was satisfied. Hence I believed that I was a good and responsible teacher.

Then Dr Moira Laidlaw came to Guyuan Teachers College with her action research theory and practice. This is a branch of Western teaching methodology, influenced by Socrates' dialectical method, and characterized by a logic of question and answer, which concentrated on students' perspectives and learning more than teachers' methodology.

I studied its underpinning philosophy, and, even with a brief understanding, began my journey as a teacher-researcher. My first step was to observe my classroom as well as my students' learning. What I later found is really amazing.

(Continued)

My concern

First, during the fifty-minute long class, I kept talking just like a lecturer, explaining difficult vocabulary, paraphrasing troublesome grammatical points, telling students to do this or that. I was like a nanny doing everything for my 'babies'. Students' talking time was therefore far less than teacher's talking time. Second, students became mere passive listeners. Third, the learning atmosphere itself was controlled and intense. Students were passive instead of active and eager to learn. In other words, my academic teaching style restrained students' motivation for learning. I developed this into my first concern and asked, 'How can I encourage students' motivation so they can improve their learning?'

Why am I concerned about it?

I was concerned because of the following issues.

1   From my own experience, and from studying the literature, I knew that students' learning is more important for education than the teacher's teaching. No matter how excellent a teacher's teaching method may be, it is nothing if it fails to encourage and improve students' learning, which is the aim of education.
2   The students' non-participation and passivity really worried me, and led me to wonder whether or not I was a responsible and good teacher after all. I found the answer was 'not really'. I was experiencing myself as a living contradiction (Whitehead 1989), because I wanted my students to succeed, yet was denying them opportunities to do so.
3   I knew from my own experience that an active, lively learning atmosphere could encourage students' motivation and thus their learning. My own experiences as a student had taught me that the teacher has an influence on her students' motivation as well as their learning. It also makes me believe that I, as an educator, can do something to change my students' passivity and non-participation.
4   The questionnaire I issued to my students showed that 99 per cent of students preferred to learn in an interesting, free, and relaxed atmosphere, rather than in a passive and silent atmosphere.
5   From my own teaching experience, I think an 'academic' style benefits teachers' teaching more than students' learning. The teacher talks while students listen. As a result, the teacher becomes a fluent lecturer, while students remain poor speakers.

How can I encourage students' motivation?

I decided to change my teaching method, to offer students freedom to talk, in order to change the passive, silent atmosphere into an active and interesting one.

(Continued)

I tried the following strategies.

My first imagined solution was to introduce group/pair work. Instead of leading students through a text sentence by sentence as before, I asked them to work in pairs or groups, discussing with each other, and then tell me their result. From the beginning, I found that this worked. I walked around the class and observed them. They were talking animatedly, and I could hear them arguing with each other, could see them smiling. They would stop me to ask questions such as, 'Miss Tao, what does this mean?' or 'I can't understand this.' This kind of contact had been impossible when I stood on the platform before, delivering knowledge to them. They were becoming active in raising questions.

My second strategy was to develop a more questioning method. I divided students into groups/pairs, and asked them to discuss the text and solve problems together. They asked me whenever they did not understand something. Alternatively, I sometimes questioned them. I constantly focused on the question, 'Am I encouraging their motivation?'

I sought feedback. Most of them agreed that questioning really improved their interest in learning. All answers were anonymous. Here are some of their comments:

> 'Your teaching style suits me, especially your questioning. It not only makes me more active, but also makes me learn it by myself.'

> 'I am very appreciative of your changed methods of teaching. We can ask you and you can answer. It is better than before.'

However, a few students were less than happy. Comments included:

> 'I think it is good, but not all students can understand this way.'
> 'Before, we were clear about the structure, content and phrases of the articles we read ... Actually questions have nothing to do with what we learn. This is a waste of our time. I still prefer your teacher-centred method because I can learn more.'

These critical comments made me reflect a good deal. I wondered whether there should be a balance between a questioning and an academic style. I therefore decided to use a range of teaching methods according to different teaching materials as well as students' learning needs. One of these was micro-teaching.

This became my third strategy. I asked students to work in groups of five or six, and to choose a group leader who would be in charge of explaining certain paragraphs. To my surprise, they really did an excellent job. Students' feedback showed that micro-teaching really improved their learning.

> 'Our group thinks that this micro-learning is useful for our self-study and enables us to think of questions by ourselves. It also improves our ability in teaching.'

(Continued)

However, another group wrote:

> 'We don't think this is a useful way to learn. There are many difficult vocabulary items and phrases. You should guide us at every point.'

My fourth strategy was to engage my students in experiential learning. I encouraged them to offer their own responses to stories and emotive writing. This also seemed to encourage them, so much so that, when I drew a picture of a forest to show the meaning of the sentence 'a sliver of brilliant red crests the top of the shadowed forest', some students added eyes and mouths to each tree of my 'forests' during the break. I really don't believe this would have happened with my previous approaches.

I also tried changing the organization of the classroom. I asked students to speak from different places in the classroom. I found that even the smallest change seemed to increase their level of interest.

How did I know that I encouraged students' motivation?

I gathered data using a range of techniques, including questionnaires, interviews, oral and written feedback on each class, tape recording, journals/notes and my own observation.

I developed the following specific standards to evaluate my research:

- whether the learning atmosphere changed
- examination results
- students' attitudes to my teaching
- students' improvements in their self-study ability
- students' improvements in creativity and confidence.

Eighteen months into the project, I designed a questionnaire to elicit feedback, and undertook some statistical analysis of the responses, which showed overwhelming support for my new methodologies. I supplemented this with interviews. Comments included:

> 'Previous teaching methods regarded us as containers, which the teacher tried to fill. Now the teacher and students communicate with each other and interact. It is better than before.'

> 'I can learn now without pressure.'

Further testing revealed that the students' examination scores improved. As to the students' self-study ability, I invited Tasha (my dear foreign colleague) to interview six students of mine. We also tape-recorded the interviews in order to increase validity. An analysis of their interviews helped me draw the following conclusions.

(Continued)

They mainly seemed to prefer student-centred teaching methods, especially questioning which they regarded as a good method to motivate them. Most importantly, they all agreed that their self-study ability had improved during that year, and they were more motivated and interested in the learning atmosphere.

My conclusions

During these one and a half years, I have often experienced myself as a living contradiction. Thanks to Moira Laidlaw's and other colleagues' help – Li Peidong, Zhao Xiaohong, Tasha Bleistein, Ma Jianfu – I have reflected on my own teaching and realized that what I had believed in was actually going against what I wanted to happen. I had believed that a teacher would be a good teacher by delivering morals, knowledge and skills, and that an academic style would be essential for this. Ironically, what I later learned from my students was that I was actually denying my values in my actions (Whitehead 1989). I was spoon-feeding knowledge to my students, which, far from motivating them to learn, constrained their creativity and freedom to communicate, as well as their insight and rights as individuals. Moira and my own critical reflection helped me realize what was happening in my class. During my action enquiry, I have also developed my own living educational theory (Whitehead 1989; 1993) which, because it has mainly emerged through my own practice, is bound to enlarge my horizons, strengthen my insight, and improve my knowledge towards second language teaching as a professional teacher.

SUMMARY

This chapter has set out two case studies from professional educators in China. Both reports have shown the systematic nature of action research. You should bear in mind, however, that action research does not always go this smoothly, and often involves a good deal of imaginative replanning and negotiated action. This is often necessary in situations where people disagree about the purposes of the research, which then means finding a compromise. The main point is to concentrate on your own learning, as the main focus of your self-study.

In the next part we look closely at gathering data and generating evidence, which are key features of doing research.

Part IV

How Do I Generate Evidence To Support My Claim To Knowledge?

All research, including action research, aims to make a claim to knowledge. In action research, you aim to explain that you now know something that you did not know before. This could be about how you have learned about your practice by studying your practice, and you are able to describe and explain what you are doing.

Claims to knowledge need to be supported by validated evidence, so that the claim does not appear as opinion or supposition. Evidence is generated from data, so this means gathering quality data from which you will select pieces to stand as evidence.

This part contains the following chapters.

Chapter 13   **Monitoring practice and looking for data**
Chapter 14   **Gathering, sorting and storing data**
Chapter 15   **Turning the data into evidence**

Each chapter offers practical advice about what you need to do to generate evidence.

In terms of your own action enquiry into understanding the nature and uses of action research, you are asking, 'How do I generate evidence to support any claim to knowledge I hope to make?'

13

Monitoring Practice and Looking for Data

This chapter is about what you need to do and think about in order to gather useful data, and not waste time gathering irrelevant data that will clutter you up and probably be discarded later. At this point you need to decide what you are looking for and where and how you might find it. This will involve decisions about how you are going to monitor what you are doing in order to track developments over time.

In your action research you are looking primarily for two things:

1 Episodes of practice that show the developing educational influence of your own learning
2 Episodes of practice that show your educational influence in the learning of others

The chapter is organized as two sections to address these questions.

1 EPISODES OF PRACTICE THAT SHOW THE DEVELOPING EDUCATIONAL INFLUENCE OF YOUR OWN LEARNING

Three main questions emerge.

- What data am I looking for?
- Where will I look for the data?
- How will I monitor my practice over time?

What data am I looking for?

To decide what you are looking for, remind yourself what your research is about and specifically what your research question is. Whatever you look for will be in relation to your research question.

Asking action research questions is rather complex. First, action research questions involve the generic question, 'How do I improve my work?' Perhaps your specific question uses a different form of words, such as 'How do I help …?' or 'How do I find ways of …?' Whatever form of words they use, action research questions are always linked with the idea of improvement. Second, improvement happens over time, so you will look for episodes of practice that show the development of your own practice over time. Third, practice does not just happen. Actions can 'just happen', such as laughing, but these are actions and not practices. Practices are always informed and intentional. They are informed by learning, and their intent is improvement. So when you look at your practice you are really looking at the influence of your learning. What you are looking for, therefore, when looking for data, are episodes that show initial contexts, when perhaps you did not know something so well, and later episodes when you knew it better, and that show the influence of your own learning.

For example, imagine your research question is, 'How do I help my students to improve their spelling?' Underlying this question is the deeper question, 'How do I learn how to help my students to learn to spell better?' This means that you will look for episodes of practice that turn the question into reality. Bearing in mind that improvement happens over time, you will look for episodes when you did not know so well how to help your students to improve their spelling, and for later episodes when you began to help them more successfully. Bearing in mind also that practice is informed by learning, you will look for episodes when you began to learn about these things, and how your learning developed as you tried things out in practice.

TOWARDS A THEORY OF LEARNING

Caitríona McDonagh

Caitríona McDonagh tried a range of reading programmes for her so-called dyslexic school children. She found that these programmes did not particularly help the children to form their letters correctly or learn how to spell accurately. She began to ask questions about what she could do to help them. Over the course of a two-year masters research programme (McDonagh 2000), she came to the realization that the responsibility lay with her as their teacher to investigate her own pedagogies, and try to find ways of teaching that would enable her children to learn. She found that if she developed pedagogies that made the material relevant and meaningful to children's experience, their motivation would rise and they would attend more to the accurate formation of letters and words. Caitríona's later PhD studies (McDonagh 2003) have focused on issues of justice in relation to the marginalization of children who are labelled 'special educational needs' but who actually think in ways that

(Continued)

are not fully recognized within normative curricula or traditional pedagogies. Caitríona is now having some influence at national level in Irish education, through the dissemination of her ideas and writings. You can access her work at www.jeanmcniff.com and www.actionresearch. net, and you can see how she generates evidence from the data to show episodes when she was struggling to find ways forward, later episodes when she began to test her provisional ideas, and episodes that show how she finally came to the point where she was able to artic-ulate her theory of learning difference. That theory is currently subject to ongoing modifi-cation as she explores new ways of refining it and making it more robust, as for example with the introduction of ideas about metacognition (McDonagh 2004).

Where will I look for the data?

Think about experiences when episodes of learning occurred. Perhaps the time when you began to understand that your students needed help was when two of them were marked down in examinations because of their poor spelling. You were shocked to receive notification of the exam results (source of data). You made a note of this in your record book (source of data). You noted in your journal (source of data) that you would do something about it. You consulted with colleagues through e-mail (source of data) about what you could do, and read books (source of data) about possible strategies. You decided to try some new 'look and say' spelling strategies, and began to keep detailed records (source of data) of what you were learning as you tried them out. You also kept detailed field notes (source of data) about how your students were responding, and you invited them to keep their own journals (source of data) about what they were learning (see also Section 2).

Over time your strategies seemed to be working. You could show examples of poor spelling from the students' written exercises and notebooks (source of data), and how they worked with the exercises you gave them (source of data). You could show how their spelling improved over time from later written exercises (source of data). Finally, you could show how the two students passed their resit exams, and produce notification of results as a possible source of data.

Some points to note in this story:

1   It is unlikely that you would use all the possible sources of data in your account. You would use your own sense about what was sufficient to make your point.

2   When you are monitoring practice it is vital to monitor the learning that informs the practice. This is essential for when you come to explain the significance of your research (see Chapter 23). Then you will say that you have contributed to new practices – you have found ways of helping students to improve their spelling – and you will also say that you have contributed to

new ideas and new knowledge – you know what you did and why you did it, in relation to learning how to help students to develop their own capability.

3   It is also important to remember that you are not claiming to have caused the students to spell better, or even that you were the only influence in their learning. However you can hope to claim that you had an influence somewhere, but this claim would have to be supported by your students' testimony (see Section 2).

How will I monitor my practice over time?

You need to decide the following.

- How are you going to monitor practice? This will involve choosing data gathering techniques that are appropriate for what you want to find out. Chapter 14 gives advice about what techniques are available and what they are appropriate for.
- How often are you going to gather data? You need to make some common-sense decisions about frequency of data gathering. The longer the project, the more you can space out your data gathering.
- Which data gathering techniques will you use? You can use the same techniques throughout your project, or mix and match them. You may use field notes throughout, but use memos and e-mail correspondence as they occur. There are no general guidelines except to remind you that you will be producing a report in which you present your data as evidence, and you need to keep your audience in mind. What will they be able to attend to at any one time? Too many data will confuse. Too few will weaken. Use your own judgement to get a balance.

2   EPISODES OF PRACTICE THAT SHOW YOUR EDUCATIONAL INFLUENCE IN THE LEARNING OF OTHERS

This section asks the same questions as before, but with a different focus.

- What data am I looking for?
- Where will I look for the data?
- How will I monitor my practice over time?

What data am I looking for?

You are now looking for data that show how your practice (informed by your learning) is influencing the learning of others (as is manifested in their practice).

Let's take another example. Imagine you are a principal of an organization. You know that quality work comes from good relationships, so you ask, 'How do I help my staff develop good relationships?' You are of course asking, 'How do I learn to help my staff learn how to develop good relationships?' Asking the question signals your intent to learn.

As in Section 1, you look for episodes of practice that show how your learning is influencing your practice, and you resolve to gather the data in recordable form. You also need to show how your learning is influencing the learning of others, otherwise your later claim that you have improved your practice will not make sense. You can do this in different ways:

- You can produce the testimonies of others who say they have learned because of your influence.
- You can produce examples of people acting in new ways, which you claim have developed through your influence.

The kind of testimonies you are looking for are when people say things such as, 'You have helped me to learn' or 'I feel much more confident now, thanks to you' (see the case story of Tao Rui on page 123). The kinds of actions you are looking for are those about which critical friends and validation groups say things such as, 'That is evidence of lively enquiring minds', or 'You have clearly enabled them to think for themselves.' Pages 163–4 give an extended example.

Remember that you must get permission from your participants to involve them and to use their words. We said earlier that you do not need permission to undertake your own self-study, but you must have permission from others whom your self-study involves.

Where will I look for the data?

As above, look for episodes that occur over time and that show the development of your participants' learning in relation to your own.

SOURCES OF DATA

For example, you decide to put in place a staff development programme. Because you do not think you have the right facilitation skills, you engage the services of a professional facilitator (letter to facilitator is a source of data). You arrange a series of staff development days (the firm agrees to support this), and send out a memo (source of data) inviting all to attend, on a non-compulsory basis. Most do, including a loudly spoken colleague and two new colleagues. You also become a participant.

(Continued)

Over the series of meetings the facilitator introduces different strategies that help people see how they influence others and how they might modify their practice. With the written permission of all, she makes video recordings (source of data) and invites people to comment on what they see (field notes and personal jottings are sources of data of their learning). She makes her own records and personal evaluations available to you (source of data of her learning). She insists that everyone keeps a reflective journal (source of data of their learning), which they may let others see if they wish.

The videos come to be a visual narrative (source of data) that shows the transformation of attitudes and behaviours. Gradually the loud colleague comes to cease forcing her opinion on others. One video (source of data of her learning) shows her listening carefully. The two newcomers begin to speak up. After the series of seminars one of them writes you a thank you note, saying that he has learned much from the experience (source of data of his learning).

Six months later, when the programme has ended, at a staff meeting you ask people's opinions about the seminars. Most say it has been useful for helping to bond the staff. This is recorded in the minutes (source of data). You put out a questionnaire (source of data), the results of which make you feel optimistic. You later receive a written request (source of data) to support the development of a staff social committee.

Bear in mind that this story is primarily in relation to your own learning, but contains episodes of other people's learning. It may be that other people also began to regard their participation as a research project, and your words and actions became sources of data for them. You could have developed the initiative into a collaborative action research project, where everyone monitored what they were doing in relation to others.

Bear in mind also that examples like this are fairy stories, and things often do not go so well or so smoothly. The story is presented to give ideas about where you can look for data. However, most real-life stories contain episodes of forward and backward movement. It is important to record them all, so as not to give the impression that it was an easy ride or a victory story (Lather 1994, cited in MacClure 1996). It is important also to show times when your values were denied in your practice, so that you can show the transformation that you can claim to be a living out of your values.

How will I monitor my practice over time?

Again, remember to look for episodes of learning, such as recordings in journals or statements by people that perhaps they never thought of that, as well as episodes of action that appear to be manifestations of critical learning. Critical episodes of underlying learning are those that show new, clearly changed attitudes and behaviours, such as when a colleague listens carefully for the first time, or a child learns how to spell a word correctly. Perhaps if you interviewed them (a transcript or notes from the conversation would be sources of data), you would hear them say that they had thought carefully about the influence they were exercising on others. Instances like these can be elusive, but they definitely occur. Also remember that your job is not to get people to confess to their shortcomings, but to encourage them to think and learn for themselves. When you come to generate evidence these episodes will be key pieces of data.

Aim to build up your data archive to show the unfolding of the learning and action over time. It is important to label your data and date them, so that you can show the sequencing. Make sure you store and sort your data (Chapter 14) so that you can show the relationship between your own action and learning, between the action and learning of others, and the relationship between the action and learning of all participants. This will also help you to see practice and learning as a web of interconnected relationships and practices. The best action research reports show this complexity, yet present the complexity in such a way that their reader can appreciate how the actions they see represent deeper meanings related to learning.

SUMMARY

This chapter has discussed issues of monitoring practice and gathering data. The main point is to know what kind of data you are looking for and where to look for them.

At this stage in your action enquiry, you are looking for data that you will be able to use as evidence in your account of educational influence, that is, in your own learning and in the learning of others. You will therefore look for episodes of practice that show these elements.

The next chapter deals with how to gather, sort and store data.

14

Gathering, Sorting and Storing Data

This chapter deals with gathering, sorting and storing data. It contains the following sections.

1 Gathering data
2 Sorting and storing the data

1 GATHERING DATA

Gathering data involves several processes: knowing where and when to look for data, observing what is going on, recording, storing and sorting the data, and knowing how to retrieve them later. Many of these processes overlap, so take the following advice as a guide to help you get to grips with the task; not to be interpreted in a linear way.

This section deals with the questions:

- How do I gather data? Which observation and data gathering techniques are available?
- Where do I gather data? When do I look for data?

How do I gather data? Which observation and data gathering techniques are available?

At this point you are observing what is going on and finding ways to record it. Remember that you are not simply looking at action, but trying to see and record how learning enters into action. Many techniques are available, some of which are appropriate for monitoring actions and how these may be indicative of learning, and others that aim to focus on what kind of learning is going on.

Observation and data gathering techniques to observe and record the action

You can use the following techniques to observe and record your own action as well as other people's actions. These are perhaps the most commonly used data gathering techniques, but they are just a selection from a vast array.

Field notes

These are the notes you make as you note actions. You can write them into a special notebook, or on the back of your hand, in which case you would write them up later. You can write in straight notes, or try mind maps, spider diagrams and pictures.

Notes from a PhD supervision session

N (candidate) was unhappy today. Said she wasn't managing writing up. Long conversation. Offered more intensive e-mail support. Said she would have a go.

Notes from the shop floor

Sales of toys going well. 'Magic mouse' seems slow. Wrong location? Better lighting? Talk to display team.

Figure 14.1 shows an example of a mind map.

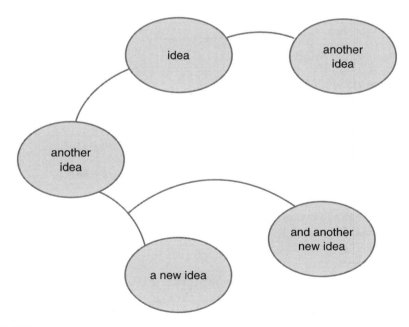

FIGURE 14.1   An example of a mind map

Record sheets and observation schedules

These are the different sheets you produce to gather data and maintain records, such as observation schedules, analyses of actions and pictorial representations of action. The best are the ones you devise yourself, but here are some ideas to get you started.

Here are some examples of record sheets. Note that the tally marks refer to the number of interactions. Also note the use of the 'five-bar gate' to count in multiples of five.

Record sheet to show number of interactions by Mr X during a meeting

Minutes	1	2	3	4
Interactions by Mr X	Ж IIII II	III	Ж IIII Ж II	Ж IIII I

Record sheet to record number of times participants speak at a business meeting

Participant	Number of contributions
Mr Green	Ж Ж II
Ms Black	II
Mrs White	Ж Ж Ж II
Mr Grey	IIII II
Ms Pink	Ж Ж Ж Ж I

Sociometric analysis

Figure 14.2 shows an analysis in graphic form of the interactions among members of a meeting. Note how many times each person talks, and who they talk with.

Observation and data gathering techniques to observe and record learning

You can use the following techniques to observe and record your own learning as well as other people's learning.

Written accounts

You can use prose or poetic or other forms to show your own and other people's experience and learning.

Here is an example from the PhD thesis of Paul Roberts (2003). You can download this for yourself from http://www.bath.ac.uk/~edsajw/roberts.shtml.

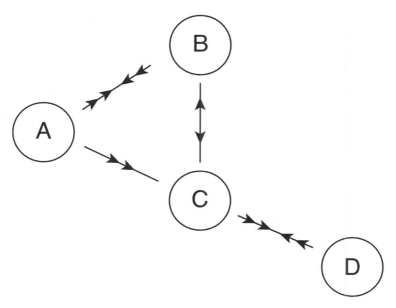

FIGURE 14.2 An example of sociometric analysis

A LEARNING JOURNAL

Paul Roberts

When I began the CARPP [Centre for Action Research in Professional Practice] programme at the University of Bath, my interest was in attaining a PhD in order to pursue an in-depth programme of study in a number of areas that interested me. I wanted further to develop my professional practice to encompass these areas in a way that gave greater satisfaction and purpose to my working life.

After attending the initial workshop on the programme in February 1997, I wrote the following passage as part of the first entry in the learning journal I was to keep for the next three years.

What came across to me most strongly from the first CARPP event in February was the importance of choosing research that is significant and central to my life. I would like the research to provide a focus to draw together the different strands that I am interested in.

(Continued)

These strands are:

- complexity theory
- archetypal psychology
- organisations as religion – this could be a further image of organisations to be added to Gareth Morgan's (1997) list of metaphors, which would help locate this idea in an attractive and rigorous theoretical framework.

At the end of this first entry, I also wrote the lines:

This question of practice is extremely important, not just for the research but for my working life, as I want the research to help lead me in a direction which can reorient my work. At the moment I identify with the lines of Dante's (1949) poem:

> In the middle of the road of my life
>   I awoke in a dark wood
> where the true way was wholly lost.

I don't know if it is too much of an extravagance to hope that the research will enable the 'true way' to be rediscovered.

Personal logs and diaries

These are the records you keep of personal action, and reflection on the action, and the learning arising from it. It does not matter whether you call them logs, diaries or journals, or whether you keep a research diary and a reflective diary, or use the same journal for both purposes. It can be helpful to differentiate episodes of action from episodes of learning, for example, by using different fonts or colours. The excerpt from Paul Roberts's work above contains extracts from a learning journal.

Questionnaires

Do not rush into questionnaires. They may seem an easy way to collect data and there are many texts explaining how to construct them, as a browser search will reveal. If you do use them, use them to get a sense of trends and directions. Also if you use them, pilot them many times in advance to make sure that they are getting the kind of information you need to move your enquiry forward and not prevent learning. This advice also applies to the next item about surveys and interviews.

Surveys and interviews

You can conduct closed, semi-structured and open surveys and interviews. Closed questions that look for 'yes/no' answers are easier to analyse, but do not give much information. More open questions that allow personal responses are more difficult to analyse, but provide rich information and insights.

A closed response question

	Yes	No
Are you married?	☐	☐

An open response question

Question: What do you think of banning smoking in public places?
Answer: ....

A Likert-type scale

	Strongly agree	Agree	Don't know	Disagree	Strongly disagree
Girls do better than boys at academic subjects					

Where do I gather data? When do I look for data?

Places for gathering data

The kind of data you are looking for is to be found in the textual accounts of people's practices, both documented and living. The practices in question can be current or historical.

Documented practices

Documents are both private and public, and record current and past practices. Diaries, autobiographical narratives, and personal letters are examples of private records. You can also look at public records such as institutional archives, agendas and minutes of meetings, and policy statements. These records will contain information about what people were thinking and doing at a particular time and place. They can be invaluable for helping you address your questions, 'What is my concern?', 'Why am I concerned?' and 'How can I produce evidence to show my concern?', because they may show whether the values that guide your own work also guided the practices in earlier situations, or not. Accessing and looking at records such as these is often called 'desk research' or 'library research'.

Living practices

You would gather most of your data within your research site, where you and your participants meet together. You would gather data about the current action.

In some cases you would also be able to gather data about your learning as it happens, but this may not always be the case, because sometimes it is important to step back from the action in order to make sense of it. Schön (1983) talks about this as reflective practice that involves both 'reflection in action' and 'reflection on action'. In order to make practical decisions about the next move, we have to reflect in action, but often it is not until later in a quiet space that we reflect on action. This reflection on action involves learning, which is still a form of action and needs to be recorded. Remember that you are monitoring your learning as well as your social actions.

You can also set up situations so that people can explore their learning and find ways of articulating it. Some examples of how you can do this are as follows.

Role play and performance

You can set up role-play and performance situations where participants take the part of others and then offer feedback on the experience. It is important for them and you to keep records of their experience and learning from these episodes.

For example, Jack Whitehead (2004b) includes a performance text in his enquiry into 'How valid are multi-media communications of my embodied values in living theories and standards of educational judgement and practice?' To communicate the meanings of his embodied values of academic freedom and social justice, Whitehead reconstructs his response to a Senate Working Party on a matter of academic freedom in a performance text that includes a videotaped extract in the visual narrative.

Artworks

You can encourage participants to produce their original visual representations in the form of artwork. You would ask the participants themselves to give their own interpretations of how their artworks represented their experience and learning, and you would keep records of these interpretations.

For example, have a look at the prologue of the PhD submission of Eleanor Lohr at http://www.jackwhitehead.com/elFront%202.htm. See how she uses artwork and video as an integral aspect of her evidence.

Video

Video is becoming increasingly popular because it enables you to move beyond written accounts and show the actions as they happen. This can be especially powerful when you come to generate evidence in support of a claim to knowledge. When you say, for example, 'I am claiming that I have influenced the quality of relationships in my workplace,' you can produce videotaped material that shows people's visual expressions and bodily language to communicate how they are feeling. The development of multimedia narratives is an exciting and important innovation in the field. Significantly, these have now been accepted by prestigious universities such as the University of Bath in support of higher degree dissertations and theses. This theme is developed in Chapter 19.

When do I gather my data?

A certain amount of entrepreneurialism is called for in data collection. As well as planning to gather the data, you also have to be on the lookout for opportunities. The most obvious place to gather data is in your direct research practice, when you interview participants, say, or conduct an observation. Many opportunities arise, however, out of hours and also off-site. You may meet a colleague while walking the corridors, or in a park. These are wonderful times for quiet and relaxed conversations and reflections.

As well as these informal encounters, aim to gather data formally as part of the research process. The frequency with which you gather data depends on the overall length and intensity of your project. As noted earlier, if it is short term, say three or four weeks, you will need to gather data every few days. If it is long term, say three or four months, every week or so will do. You will soon get a sense of what is right for you.

Do not avoid data gathering or put it off, especially in the early stages. If you are wondering where to start, tape record a conversation with a trusted colleague about why you are doing your job and what keeps you doing it. This should help you (and the colleague) to clarify and articulate the values that inform your work. Keep the tape and transcript carefully, and refer back to it when you are making a claim to knowledge. Having got your tape, which should enable you at least to become aware of your core values, now you can begin to look carefully at practice.

You can record data about your reflections anywhere you have a quiet space. You can reflect on the bus, in the shower, or while watching television. Have a notebook handy for recording thoughts, and write them down immediately. Do this systematically. An idea that seems utterly obvious in the middle of the night can flit away at daybreak.

It pays to carry a workbook with you everywhere, even outside your research site. Keep your rough field notes, ideas and reflections in this workbook and sort them and write them up later. Ideas about your research may occur to you during other work activities.

2   SORTING AND STORING THE DATA

Remember that you gather data in order to generate evidence. Generating evidence involves analysing data, and analysis is greatly aided if you know what to look for and where to find it. The more systematic you are about storing your data, the easier it will be when you come to select those pieces that you want to stand as evidence.

Your accumulated data are called your data archive. You may store a lot of data on your computer, and you may store your physical artefacts in a box or in your bag. It is not a good idea to put material into a box in a haphazard way. Aim to sort it regularly into categories.

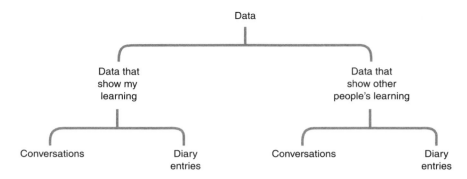

FIGURE 14.3   Organization of data into categories

When you begin gathering data, do so with a few broad categories in mind, such as

- data that show my learning
- data that show other people's learning.

Put the different data into their own files. Now, sort the data into more refined categories, such as

- File 1: data that show my learning

   conversations
   diary entries

- File 2: data that show other people's learning

   conversations
   diary entries.

You could regard the job of organizing your data archive something along the lines of Figure 14.3.

Organize your data into as many categories as you need, and put them into different files or containers (modified cereal boxes are good). Colour coding your files can be helpful. If you are storing data on your computer, work out a similar coding system. As your research progresses, the number of categories will increase, along with the increasing depth of analysis. 'Conversations' may turn into 'conversations with participants' or 'conversations with critical friends', and 'diary entries' may become 'diary entries about reflection' or 'diary entries on the research experience'. Keep on top of your data. Visit them regularly and frequently. Sort them into new categories and new files, and keep your filing system on the move. This does take time, and also space if you are saving the data in physical files, all of which has to be negotiated with colleagues in your workplace, or with family members if you keep them at home.

Finally, you have a data archive to be proud of. Now comes the task of analysing it and turning it into evidence. This is the focus of Chapter 15.

Also note the following.

Keeping references

References in the literature are not data, though they refer to where the data can be found, but the same advice about regular and systematic record keeping refers also to references. Whenever you read a book, have your 'References' workbook with you. Keep a record of what you have read. Write it like this:

> Authors' family name, initial (date of publication) title. town of publication, publisher.

This gives you:

> Jones, B. (1996) *Working with Data*. London, Sage.

If you read a particular phrase or sentence that you like, write it down accurately, word for word, and note the page number. When you use quotations in your reports, you must give a page reference. Do not ignore this advice. It can take hours to track down a missing page reference, and it is virtually impossible if the book is back in the library. Don't forget to record the page numbers of the chapter in your references if you are quoting from a book or a journal article.

SUMMARY

This chapter has offered advice about gathering, sorting and storing data. It has talked about different data gathering techniques, and which ones may be appropriate for different purposes, whether recording the action or recording learning. It has also talked about putting together a data archive in a coherent way.

The next chapter gets to the heart of the matter by discussing how you can select key pieces of data and turn them into evidence in support of your claim to knowledge.

15

Turning the Data into Evidence

You now have substantial amounts of data, and you need to turn them into evidence to support your claim to knowledge. Producing evidence is about establishing the validity, or truth value, of a claim. For example, if you say, 'This way of working is better than previous ways,' you need to support that claim with evidence, otherwise what you say could be construed as your opinion.

Evidence is not the same as data. 'Data' refers to the pieces of information you have gathered about what you and others are doing and learning. All these data are in your data archive. Your task is to turn some of these pieces of data into evidence. These will be those special pieces of data that you identify specifically in relation to your claim to knowledge. The pieces of data do not change their form, but they change their status. A comment remains a comment, and a picture a picture, but it now comes out of the larger body of data to stand as evidence. It no longer keeps company with other data; it now keeps company with a claim to knowledge.

It is important also to remember that evidence is more than illustration. Illustration is used when you organize your data to show a point in action. You could, for example, produce documentation around a new work schedule, or a videotape to show you mentoring a colleague. These uses of data remain illustrative, because you do not make a value judgement about whether they show an improvement on a previous practice, or offer an explanation for why they are better.

Generating evidence is a rigorous process which involves

1   Making a claim to knowledge
2   Establishing criteria and standards of judgement
3   Selecting data
4   Generating evidence

This chapter is organized as four sections to address these issues. Two examples are given at the end to show the processes involved.

1   MAKING A CLAIM TO KNOWLEDGE

When you make a claim to knowledge you say that you know something now that was not known before. This knowledge is being put into the public domain for the first time and is adding to the public body of knowledge. The knowledge may be about a substantive issue, such as a new clinical nursing practice, or it may be about the process of creating new ideas and explanations. If it is about substantive issues, the knowledge is usually about practice. If it is about explanations, it is usually about theory. Knowledge generated through action research is about both practice and theory. You offer descriptions of what you did, and explanations for why you did it. Your descriptions and explanations together become your theory, your theory of practice.

Your claim to know in relation to practice would be something of the kind:

- I have developed a new work schedule.
- I have improved my mentoring practice.
- We have created better communications in our office.

Your claim to know in relation to theory would be something of the kind:

- I have developed my understanding of the need for a good work schedule.
- I have created my theory of mentoring practices.
- We know how and why to communicate better in our office.

Both kinds of claims are related. One cannot stand without the other. Your theory of practice (explanation for practice) has been created from within the practice. You can describe and explain your improved mentoring practice because you have studied your mentoring practice and worked systematically to improve it. You know what you have done and how and why you have done it.

We have said throughout that the need to show how you are contributing to theory and not only practice is important in all action research, and especially in reports that are submitted for accreditation. The criteria for accreditation usually state that a candidate has to show that they are making a claim to knowledge (see page 151). If the report shows that the candidate is making a contribution only to practice, the report could well be rejected.

2   ESTABLISHING CRITERIA AND STANDARDS OF JUDGEMENT

Making a judgement about something involves using criteria and standards of judgement. Criteria and standards of judgement are different though intimately related. The criteria for safe driving, for example, would involve observing traffic flows, and driving within speed limits. A driving instructor would probably bring a checklist of criteria to a driving test, and tick them off when the learner driver did these things. Whether or not the driver passed the test, however, would depend on how the instructor judged the driver to have done them. How did the driver negotiate the traffic flows? Did they drive responsibly within designated speed limits? The instructor uses these values of safe and responsible driving as their standards of judgement. When you make judgements about your practice it is not enough simply to work to criteria in the form of achieving targets, such as 'I took the patient's temperature' or 'I completed my work on time', although these are important elements. You also have to explain the nature of what you did and why you believe it should be perceived as good.

When we make a judgement about something, we do so in relation to specific standards. Having standards is important to ensure that our work is good quality. However, questions need to be asked about which standards are appropriate, who sets the standards, and who says.

Which standards? Whose standards?

Many debates about quality say that practices should be judged in terms of practitioners' performance, in relation to specific skills and competencies, which often appear as targets. In many instances in the UK, ambulance drivers and fire crews have to reach their destination in a specific amount of time, and hospitals must achieve a designated turnaround of patients. The emphasis on quantity can, however, jeopardize quality. Stories are sometimes told of patients not receiving quality care because doctors have to achieve their quotas of patient appointments. This approach to target setting and performance is part of the current managerialist and consumerist culture.

Professionals use different kinds of standards to judge the quality of their work, related to the values that inspire the work. An educational manager may judge her leadership by how well she encourages motivation and purpose among employees. A foster-parent may judge their success in fostering by their capacity to love in times of trial. Professional values are to do with care, compassion, and respect for the other. Most action researchers try to find ways of living these values. The educational leader judges her work in relation to employees' increasing motivation and purpose. The foster-parent judges his work in relation to the foster-child's capacity to develop independence through loving relationships with the new family.

As a practitioner-researcher, your job is to set your own standards of practice and judgement, and show how you are fulfilling them. In relation to practice, do you live out your values of love, compassion and purpose? In relation to judgement, do you use these values as your standards? Furthermore, do you articulate these standards, and communicate them to others, so that others can see how you judge your practice, and negotiate your judgement with you? If you are submitting your work for higher degree accreditation, the validating institution will have its own criteria and standards of judgement. You have to show how you are fulfilling those, as well as any that you set yourself.

For example, Mary Hartog (2004) submitted her PhD thesis to the University of Bath, to be judged according to the University's criteria, which were:

- that the thesis demonstrates originality of mind and critical judgement
- that the extent and merit of the work are appropriate
- that the thesis contains matter worthy of publication.

As well as observing and fulfilling the official criteria, Mary asked her examiners to consider the standards of judgement she had chosen for herself. In her opening pages she writes as follows.

STANDARDS OF JUDGEMENT

Mary Hartog

If this Ph.D is differentiated or distinguished as a research process, it is because its methodology is underpinned by the values I as a researcher bring to my practice. It is with this in mind that I ask you to bring your eye as examiners to bear on the following questions, asking yourself as you read this thesis whether these questions are addressed sufficiently for you to say, 'Yes, these standards of judgment have been met':

- Are the values of my practice clearly articulated and is there evidence of a commitment toward living them in my practice?
- Does my inquiry account lead you to recognise how my understanding and practice has changed over time?
- Is the evidence provided of life-affirming action in my teaching and learning relationships?
- Does this thesis evidence an ethic of care in the teaching and learning relationship?
- Are you satisfied that I as a researcher have shown commitment to a continuous process of practice improvement?
- Does this thesis show originality of mind and critical thinking?

Your judgment may be supported by applying the social standards of Habermas's 'truth claims':

- Is this account comprehensible?
- Does it represent a truthful and sincere account?
- Is it appropriate – has it been crafted with due professional and ethical consideration?

Mary's examiners made their professional judgements about the quality of the work in relation both to the University's established criteria and also to Mary's personally selected standards of judgement, and she was awarded her doctoral degree (see http://www.bath.ac.uk/~edsajw/hartog.shtml).

3   SELECTING DATA

Having established your criteria and standards of judgement, you now need to search your data archive and find instances of values in action. The educational leader (see the example on page 153) may select the minutes of a meeting where she urged people to have faith in themselves, promising that she would support them. She also selects a memo sent to her by a colleague to say that they were organizing a staff get-together. The foster-parent may produce a card from a previously fostered child, now a mature person, expressing their thanks to the parent for helping them get through a difficult adolescence. These physical artefacts may be seen as containing participants' testimonies to practitioners' capacity to live their values in practice.

4   GENERATING EVIDENCE

In the same way, when you produce evidence to support your claim that you have improved your work, you search the archive and find artefacts that contain data, such as tape-recorded comments, pictures, field notes, and minutes of meetings. You take out of these data those specific instances that you feel show your values in action, such as a special comment, or a picture, or a field note. You use those data in your research report, but now you explain how they represent both your capacity to realize your values in practice, and also your capacity to articulate and communicate your specific standards of judgement.

Your explanation is key. In your report you specifically articulate the fact that you are producing evidence in relation to your clearly articulated standards of judgement. You say you know what you are doing and why you are doing it. You explain that the values and principles that underpin your work (your ontological commitments) have now emerged as living standards of practice, and you are articulating and communicating them to others as the living standards by which you judge your claim (your epistemological standards of judgement) and the validity of your contribution to new knowledge.

Here are two examples to show this transformation of ontological values into epistemological standards of judgement. The first example is fictitious. The second is an extract from a validated PhD study (Punia 2004). These examples show how people specifically articulated their standards of judgement as part of their process of making a claim to knowledge.

THE EDUCATIONAL LEADER'S STORY

I work in a college of further education. I understand that quality learning by students can be influenced by the quality of teaching of staff. In order to teach in a way that inspires enthusiasm and a sense of purpose among students, teachers themselves have to have a sense of purpose. How do I inspire them to develop that sense of purpose?

I take as one of my guiding principles the idea of commitment to learning. As I study my own practice I note how I try to communicate my own commitment to learning to staff, so that they also develop a sense of purpose about their work as teachers, which in turn they communicate to their students.

As I monitor my work I gather data around my research issue. I conduct surveys, make audiotapes and videotapes of myself in interaction with staff, and of their interactions with students and one another, to see whether a development of that commitment is evident. I store my data in colour-coded files in my office.

I take the idea of a commitment to learning as the core value that inspires this aspect of my work. As I sort through my data I note specific instances where I see demonstrations of this commitment. I see Teacher M teaching in a way that enthuses his students to learn more. I see two students asking for time to go to the library for independent study. I see myself listening carefully to teachers and suggesting ways in which they could do things differently, with the urge to try them out and see. I see these actions as instances of the demonstration of my value of commitment to learning in action.

I think of how I am going to generate evidence. I first need to establish criteria. My criteria are around commitment to learning and whether others and I demonstrate it. I observe from the data that this is the case, so I can say that my criteria are being met in my own and other people's practices. I can say that my standards of practice are being fulfilled. What about standards of judgement?

I begin to think about turning the data into evidence. Now I need to take those special pieces of data out of my archive, and place them in relation to what I say I believe is happening, that is, what I now know (because it seems to be happening) that I didn't know before (because it wasn't happening). I look at the survey results, the audiotaped and videotaped data, and I say to my critical friends: 'Look. Here are examples of how I believe my value of a commitment to learn is being demonstrated in practice. Here are data to show the realization of that value.' In articulating this, I am showing how I am using specific standards of judgement to judge practice. The main standard of judgement I use is related to my original value of a commitment to learn.

I am actually doing more now than just making explicit my standards of practice and judgement, and showing their significance for my own and other people's learning. Because I explain to my critical friends that I know what I am doing and why I am doing it, I can now claim that I am developing my own theory of practice. My theory of practice is my theory, not anyone else's, and can therefore be seen as my original contribution to knowledge.

MY CV IS MY CURRICULUM: THE MAKING OF AN INTERNATIONAL EDUCATOR WITH SPIRITUAL VALUES

Ram Punia

This autobiographical self-study presents my living educational theory of lifelong learning as an international educator with spiritual values including belief in cosmic unity, and continuous professional development for personal and social development of life in general. The landscape of knowledge includes India, UK, Singapore, Hong Kong, Fiji, Samoa and Mauritius in several roles including a lecturer, teacher trainer, change agent in curriculum, staff, school development, a training technologist in corporate learning and a student in the University of Bath.

A living educational theory approach begins by asking questions of the kind, How do I improve my work? Practitioners produce accounts of their learning. A living educational theory is living in two ways: people and their theory change as a result of learning and they are living what they learn. New knowledge emerges in the process. A useful epistemology of lifelong learning of an international educator has emerged from this inquiry. Taking responsibility for my roles and contextualising problems and solutions to problems to match the contexts were the essential dimensions of my lifelong experiential learning. These dimensions originated from my spiritual belief in cosmic unity of life and ethical aims of education.

The originality of my contribution to the knowledge base in the living educational theory approach to action research is how I integrated my spiritual and ethical values with technical knowledge to enhance the quality of my professional development and the development of technical and vocational education in the international context.

You can access Ram Punia's doctoral thesis at http://www.bath.ac.uk/~edsajw/punia.shtml You can access other masters and doctoral abstracts in the 'Living theory' section of http://www.actionresearch.net

SUMMARY

This chapter has taken you through the different stages of generating evidence. These stages are

- deciding on what you are going to claim
- establishing criteria and standards of judgement
- selecting data
- generating evidence in relation to your criteria and standards of judgement.

You have executed the procedures of generating evidence, but you now have to test its validity. This involves processes of private and public testing, which are dealt with in the next part.

Part V

How Do I Test and Critique My Knowledge?

This part deals with testing the validity and legitimacy of your claim to knowledge. Validity is to do with establishing the trustworthiness of a claim, which is largely a matter of methodological procedure. Legitimacy is to do with getting the claim accepted in the public domain. This is largely a matter of power and politics, because people have different opinions about who is entitled to speak and whose voices should be heard. At a deeper level, this means that people have different opinions about which knowledge is valuable and who should be accepted as a knower.

The part contains these chapters.

Chapter 16 Testing the validity of your claims to knowledge
Chapter 17 Establishing the legitimacy of your claims to knowledge
Chapter 18 Engaging with the politics of knowledge

In terms of your own action enquiry into the nature and uses of action research, you are now at the stage of testing your understanding, and you are asking, 'How do I validate my knowledge? How do I show that any conclusions I have come to are reasonably fair and accurate?'

16

Testing the Validity of Your Claims
To Knowledge

Having generated your evidence, you now have to show its validity. After that, you have to seek legitimacy for the account. Validity and legitimacy are different things. Validity refers to establishing the truth value of a claim, its authenticity or trust-worthiness. This is a matter of rigorous methodological procedure. Legitimacy refers to getting the account accepted in the public domain, by getting people to listen to you and take your work seriously, in the hope that they may be open to learning from it or trying out something similar for themselves. Establishing legitimacy is a matter of power and politics, because people may or may not want to listen, in spite of your having demonstrated the validity of your work.

This chapter deals with issues of validity. The next chapter deals with legitimacy. Both aspects are inseparable. We are setting these issues out as separate for purposes of analysis, but they are intertwined in the real-life contexts of getting people to listen to you and see the importance of your work.

The chapter is organized as two sections.

1   Validating your claim to knowledge
2   Examples of validation procedures

1   VALIDATING YOUR CLAIM TO KNOWLEDGE

By producing authenticated evidence, you have satisfactorily demonstrated to yourself the internal validity of your claim to knowledge. You now need to get other people to agree that your claim to validity is credible. If you want to engage in public debates, it is no use talking only to yourself. You have to talk with other people and get them to engage. This means you have to put your claim into the public arena with an explicit articulation of your procedures to demonstrate its methodological rigour, so that its validity can be tested against other people's critical assessment. Once they agree with you, you can regard your claim as valid (but see next paragraph), and proceed with greater confidence. It may be of course that in the process of public testing, they may not agree with you, so you may have to go back and think again. This can be difficult for several reasons, including the common reaction that people tend to see critique as critique of themselves and not of their ideas. Critique is, however, an essential part of scholarship (and of many other human practices), so do not avoid it. Go for it with vigour, and show that you do have something important to say, and make sure that you are listened to.

As noted earlier, bear in mind that in some situations, such as in the case of Galileo (see page 166), when people in authority judge you to be mistaken, you may in fact be correct. Although having your claim judged democratically goes a long way towards testing its validity, this does not necessarily establish the validity of your claims. You may in fact be right when others are mistaken. If you are convinced that you are right, and can justify your stance to yourself, you have good reason to stand firm. This is, however, a risky business and you need to be aware of the risks involved.

Arranging for critique

If you are on a professional development or award-bearing programme, you may be assigned a supervisor to offer you critique. Do not expect your supervisor to tell you that your work is good when it is not. Their job is to guide you and invite you to question your own assumptions, so do not get hostile when they ask problematizing questions about your work rather than give you immediate affirmation. They should give you affirmation when it is deserved, but they should also encourage you to extend your thinking. You can see some excellent examples of one-to-one critical supervision at http://www.bath.ac. uk/~edsajw//multimedia/jimenomov/JIMEW98.html in the multimedia account, 'How valid are multi-media communications of my embodied values in living theories and standards of educational judgement and practice?' (Whitehead 2004b).

You should also look for critique from groupings of critical friends. The kind of constructive, unsentimental feedback you are looking for will probably come from people who are sympathetic to what you are doing but are also aware of the need to challenge your thinking, especially in relation to your own assumptions and established ways of thinking. They will probably be drawn from your circle of colleagues, peers, students, parents, friends or interested observers. There are no rules about who to invite.

Having identified these people, you now need to invite them to act as critical friends and companions. Explain carefully in advance what this will involve. They will have to meet with you throughout your research, listen to you explain what the research is about, look at your data, and consider contextual aspects and the internal coherence of the research. Above all they have to be prepared to offer critical feedback, to enable you to see things you have perhaps missed, or to find new directions. It is their job to help you to see whether you are extending your thinking and developing new insights, or whether you are doing your research to justify and continue your existing assumptions.

Critical friends

Ideally your critical friends will agree to stay with you for the life of your research, but this is often not possible. Some may drop in and out. You do need one or two people, however, who are going to stay the course, so that they can give feedback about how original issues have developed, especially in terms of your own learning.

You may meet with your critical friends singly or in groups, depending on your needs and their availability. Treat them carefully. They are valuable people, essential to your research, and you need to maintain their goodwill. Write to them about meetings, and give them plenty of advance notice. Write a thank you note after your meetings. Never abuse their kindness. They are giving their time and energy for free and this needs to be acknowledged gracefully.

After each meeting with a critical friend, write a brief record of the event and sign and date it. Give two copies to your friend, and ask them to counter-sign and date them. One copy is for their files, and one for you. This copy can stand as a powerful piece of evidence when you come to show the integrity of the procedural aspects of your research.

Validation groups

Your validation group will consist of three to ten people, depending on the size of your project. You may invite any or all of your critical friends to join this group, and you can also recruit new people. Again, they should be drawn from your professional circle, but this time you should aim to include people who are not directly involved in your research or associated with you, such as the head of another department or an interested outside observer, or perhaps someone from the business community. As before, they should be competent to offer you educated feedback, not be unnecessarily picky, but be seen as capable of offering an informed and reasonably unbiased opinion.

The job of your validation group is different from that of your critical friends. They have to meet with you at regular intervals to listen to your account of your research. Accept that not all members of the group may be available on all occasions, but try to ensure continuity. The job of your validation group is to listen to you, scrutinize your data and evidence, consider your claims to knowledge, and offer critical feedback. Validation meetings are seldom cosy or comfortable experiences for researchers, because the aim is to raise questions and to critique, and not approve anything without solid evidence that shows its internal validity. This means that you have to articulate the standards of judgement you have used, and show that you are aware of the problematics of generating evidence. Your validation group would also expect you to be able to articulate the potential significance of your work, and indicate some of its implications.

Validation groups can convene to consider work in progress and also final submissions. Meetings to consider work in progress act as formative evaluation meetings, while those that consider final submissions act as summative evaluation meetings. For your formative evaluation meetings, you should prepare and provide a progress report that outlines the research design, work done so far, any preliminary findings, provisional conclusions on those findings, and comments on whether the research is proceeding satisfactorily or any suggestions for possible new directions. Summative evaluation reports, that is, final reports, should set out from the start what your claim to knowledge is (you may make several claims), and how you feel you are justified in making the claim. This will involve an explication of methodological issues, such as research design and processes, and also explain how evidence has been generated from the data in support of your claim. It will also contain epistemological issues of why you feel you are justified in claiming that you have developed your own theory of practice. This means that you are able to describe what you did and how you did it, and also explain why you did it and what you believe you have achieved in terms of your educational and social goals. You are able to articulate the standards of judgement you have used in making your claim to knowledge, and explain their part in the development of your theory of practice. Showing how your work can constitute a theory of practice is essential if you wish it to be seen as a potential contribution to educational theory (see Chapter 7).

As with critical friends, do not take your validation group for granted. Let them know that their help is appreciated. Give them advance notice of proposed meetings and enquire about their availability. People have busy diaries and need time. Try to negotiate travel expenses for those at a distance. If this is not possible, say so, and thank them for their effort and commitment.

In advance of the meeting, send a briefing sheet to each member of the group (see the example on page 161). After each meeting, write up a record of what was said, sign and date it, and send two copies to each member of the group. Ask them to countersign and date these, keep one copy for their files and return one to you. Keep this carefully, and produce it in your final report as evidence both of what was said in response to your claim to knowledge, and also of the meticulous care you paid to the methodological aspects of your research.

It can help to secure the services of one of the group as a minuting secretary. They do not need to keep detailed minutes, or notes of individual speakers' comments, but they do need to keep a reasonably accurate record of what points were made and what actions recommended. If no one volunteers, you will have to keep minutes yourself. This can be difficult because you will be focusing on responding to questions, so try to get someone else to keep records for you. Give them an exemplar sheet such as the below to help them.

Remember in validation meetings that you have little control over what happens and what people will think and say. This is one of the reasons why careful preparation is important. You have to prepare a case for why others should believe you and acknowledge your credibility and the legitimacy of your research.

2 EXAMPLES OF VALIDATION PROCEDURES

Here are some ideas about how to draw up a briefing sheet for a validation meeting, and also how a validation meeting might be conducted.

Validation meeting briefing sheet

If you are presenting your work, please check:

1 Have you said at the beginning what you are claiming to
   have achieved through the research?
2 Have you made clear

   • your research question
   • your reasons for doing the research
   • the conceptual frameworks you have used
   • your research aims and intentions
   • your research design
   • an awareness of ethical considerations
   • the methodology you chose, and why
   • how you monitored practice
   • how you gathered data, interpreted the data, and
     generated evidence
   • the criteria and standards of judgement you used
   • how you came to some provisional conclusions?

3 Are you explaining that you are now testing your claims
   to knowledge? Are you inviting critical evaluation of
   the claims?
4 Do you show how doing the research has led you to
   develop new forms of practice and new learning?
5 Do you show the significance of your work in terms of
   your possible contributions to new practices and new
   theory?

If you are listening to a presentation of research, please check:

1 Does the researcher make an original contribution to knowledge? In what way?
2 Does the researcher demonstrate critical engagement throughout? In what way?
3 Does the researcher demonstrate an awareness of ethical considerations?
4 Does the researcher make clear the standards of judgement used to test claims?
5 Does the research contribute to new educational practices and new educational thinking? In what way?
6 Does the researcher present the work in a way that clarifies its significance and future potentials?
7 Does the researcher show a critical engagement with the ideas of others?

Minutes of a peer validation group meeting, 20 November 2004, University of Limerick

PRESENT

Margaret Cahill (PhD candidate)
Máirín Glenn (PhD candidate, presenting)
Breda Long (PhD candidate)
Patricia Mannix McNamara (PhD candidate)
Caitríona McDonagh (PhD candidate)
Jean McNiff (supervisor)
Mary Roche (PhD candidate)
Bernie Sullivan (PhD candidate)

Máirín Glenn presented her research account to the validation group covering all aspects of the briefing sheet supplied. She was closely questioned about the validity of her claim to knowledge, and critical issues were raised about

• The justification of her standards of judgement. Some members of the group requested further evidence to be supplied at the next meeting in relation to Máirín's claim that she was encouraging the growth of new knowledge through the development of interconnected virtual communities of practice.
• Her claim to be developing an epistemology of practice. Further evidence was requested.

RECOMMENDATIONS OF THE VALIDATION GROUP

Máirín should continue her research in its present form, but attend to the issues raised by the validation group. Further evidence to be supplied at the next validation group meeting on 9 March 2005.

RESPONSES FROM CAITRÍONA TO MÁIRÍN

Validation session 20 November 2004

Máirín, I heard you explain a new epistemology of practice, which you have developed in your research. You have come to a theory of multiple ways of knowing. Within the metaphor of a web of ongoing, relational ways of coming to know you have demonstrated a new understanding of knowledge acquisition.

You have contributed to new educational thinking in that you have positioned learning and knowledge generation as verbs, which form a process in which epistemology and knowledge (nouns) are the products. You have critically engaged with theories of knowledge.

You have contributed to new educational practice through engaging with the spirituality and creativity of your work with your pupils. I have witnessed how you have extended this beyond your classroom to the larger world in the East-West project and in the local community. From your practice you have reached the understanding that knowledge cannot be reified. In your research, which you represent as a learning journey, your holistic perspectives have focused on an inclusive, relational epistemology. As you have engaged in your research your values have shifted.

A validation group meeting with non-peers

One of the best examples of a validation group meeting is in the MA dissertation of Martin Forrest (1983). As a professional educator, Martin's concern was to investigate the quality of his educational influence in the professional learning of the teachers he supported. To judge the quality of his work, he posed two questions:

1   How can we know that an improvement has taken place in the school classroom? What criteria do we use to judge whether an innovation has led to an improvement in the quality of learning?
2   In the context of my work as an in-service tutor, how effective am I in my role as a disseminator and supporter of innovation? What evidence is there to support my claim to be helping teachers to improve the quality of their children's learning?

He decided to investigate his practice especially in relation to how he supported two primary teachers, who were themselves interested in evaluating their use of historical artefacts in the classroom. One of the teachers, Sue Kilminster, took as her standards of judgement the then current Aims of School Education (DES 1981), which included:

- to help pupils to develop lively, enquiring minds, the ability to question and argue rationally and to apply themselves to tasks and physical skills
- to help pupils acquire knowledge and skills relevant to adult life and employment in a fast-changing world.

In an attempt to encourage these capacities in her pupils, Sue developed the idea of a 'feely box', which was a closed cardboard box into which artefacts were placed, and the children were invited to 'feel' the objects through a hole in the side of the box and guess their identity. The event was videoed. The children were invited to discuss their ideas as they explored, and at the end of the lesson, when the objects were revealed, their group discussion was also recorded.

At a validation group meeting, Sue said, 'I was amazed at the quality of the questions being asked by the children, because they were actually thinking about the time of the object and asking questions about that time.'

Members of the validation group were given Martin's two questions (see above) as the basis on which to make their judgements. Comments from the validation group included the following:

'The thing that impressed me most was the way, somehow, these children came to their conclusions through dialogue and discussion themselves.'

'I just wanted to say that I was very impressed by the evidence of lively enquiring minds.'

'"It couldn't be a library book because you couldn't keep a book out of the library for as long as that." Obviously they've got some concept of time, haven't they?'

During subsequent validation meetings, Martin was questioned closely about his role, and required to produce documentary evidence to support his claim that he had exercised his educational influence in the learning of the teachers he was supporting.

SUMMARY

This chapter has set out ideas about establishing the validity of a claim to knowlege, that is, showing its truthfulness or trustworthiness.

This is done primarily by arranging for critique. This may come from critical friends or validation groups.

The chapter has also given examples of documents used in validation procedures.

The next chapter deals with establishing the legitimacy of your claims to knowledge.

17

Establishing the Legitimacy of Your Claims To Knowledge

If validity is about establishing the truth value of a claim, legitimacy is about establishing its acceptance in the public sphere. Both processes involve getting the agreement of others that what you have to say should be believed and incorporated into public thinking. While you have some control over validation processes, by showing the internal logic and methodological rigour of your claim, you have less control over legitimation processes, because you are presenting your claim within the socio-political context of other people's interests, including their personal and professional ambitions. This can be tricky, because those people may or may not agree that your work is valuable depending on how its suits their purposes.

In other writings (McNiff et al. 2003; McNiff and Whitehead 2005), we have cited the examples of Galileo and Bruno, who were made to suffer for their work. In both cases the validity of their ideas was clearly demonstrated, yet they were silenced (Bruno was burned alive) when the dominant institution, which at the time was the Church, mobilized its resources of power against them. The same has happened to people throughout history. Jesus and Socrates are outstanding examples. People in power have silenced others who have something useful to say, yet which seems to threaten the authority and stability of their own power base. This has also happened to action researchers (see the case of Geoff Suderman-Gladwell (2001). How do you prevent it happening to you? How do you show both the validity and the legitimacy of your research in a way that engages the attention of all and ensures its acceptance in the public domain? You need to know that in some cases this is not possible, and you have to find new strategies for dealing with the situation (see next chapter).

This chapter gives advice on how you can show the value of your research so that it stands a good chance of getting accepted. This involves showing the value of your research to the audiences you are speaking to. One of your greatest strengths is that you are both a practitioner and a researcher. In both contexts you will be recognized as a member of that particular community of practice, and can speak to other people's experience. However, we have made the point throughout that, while you are likely to be recognized readily by the community of practitioners as capable of making valuable contributions to practice, there may be some resistance to recognizing you as a member of the community of researchers, when you maintain that you are advancing knowledge.

Here are some ideas about how you can deal with the situation. The chapter is organized as two sections.

1 Getting recognized by the community of practitioners
2 Getting recognized by the community of researchers

1 GETTING RECOGNIZED BY THE COMMUNITY OF PRACTITIONERS

The significance of your practice

Getting recognized involves methodological and political aspects. The community of practitioners will be interested in seeing how your work is relevant to them, which means demonstrating the significance of your practice. People will listen if they can see how your ideas can enrich their own lives. This is good news for you because you can immediately show what others can learn from what you have done. It can also be problematic, because often people say, 'Tell me what you did. Tell me how I can do the same.' There is often an expectation that you should give them ready-made answers, which they can apply to their own practice. Action research does not work like this. People have to do it for themselves. This is also why it is important that you do not present your work as a finished product, which you now expect others to apply to their practice. In your report you explain how you have learned from the experience, and what they could also learn by doing something similar in their own context. You are showing the significance of your learning, and inviting others to learn with and from you in significant ways.

You can do this in relation to several learning contexts.

Your own learning

By producing your account of what you have done, you show how you have learned to do things differently and better. Your new learning has fed back into new action, which has in turn generated new learning. This is an ongoing process, and has become a way of life that will continue into the future.

The learning of others in your workplace

By accessing your account, other people in your workplace and professional contexts can see how they can do something similar in their own contexts. They will not necessarily do the same as you, because you have not presented your account as a model. You have learned by doing, about what worked and what didn't, so next time you do it, you may do things differently. Your story shows how you constantly tried to live in the direction of what you believed in, and how you transformed your present context into a new one in which all were benefiting from working together.

The education of social formations

Jack Whitehead (2003; 2004a) speaks about 'the education of social formations', that is, helping others everywhere to understand how they can work together in a way that will help them to improve their social contexts. This is especially important for understanding how practitioners can act as agents. A social context is not a free-standing entity, but comprises people who make decisions about how they should think and act. Sometimes these decisions become solidified into accepted rules and structures, and sometimes the rules and structures take on a life of their own, and rise above the heads of the people who made them in the first place (Habermas 1987). People come to serve the rules, rather than have the rules serve them, and see the rules no longer as temporary answers, which were appropriate for a particular situation at a particular time, but as fixed norms. They also often do not see that it is in their power to change the rules, even when the rules are out of date. Your strength as a practitioner-researcher lies in how you can show that you have changed the rules of your context by changing your practice. You have deconstructed old ways and have established new ones that are recognized by others as an improvement. By accessing your account, other people can see that they can do this too. When they see that you have done it, they will understand what it takes for them to do the same.

Many accounts show how this can be done. Ivan O'Callaghan (1997) showed how he reconceptualized his work as a principal to develop new forms of participatory working. Jackie Delong and Heather Knill-Griesser (2002) show how they integrate issues of power and ethics in valid explanations of their educative influence as a teacher-consultant and a superintendent (see also Delong 2002 and Knill-Greisser 2002 for their higher degree accounts). Dave Abbey (2002) explains how he develops his teacher-consultant's role in developing and facilitating an interdisciplinary studies course. Melanie Rivers (2003) shows how she created an inclusive atmosphere to support an autistic student in her classroom. These stories of scholarly practice are in the public domain and accessible to all. (For workplace accounts see http://schools.gedsb.net/ar/passion/pppii/index.html and http://schools.gedsb.net/ar/passion/pppiii/index.html. For higher degree accounts see http://schools.gedsb.net/ar/theses/index.html. See also http://www.actionresearch.ca/) On page 175 in this book, Ruth Deery explains how she has reconceptualized her nursing midwifery practice in a way that ensures an improved life experience for all (see also Deery and Hughes 2004), and explains how she had to engage with the politics of institutional knowledge in order to do so.

By producing your account of practice you are not only helping other practitioners to see how they can help themselves but also contributing to the public evidence base of practice, and to the public knowledge base of theory (see Section 2 of this chapter).

Strengthening the evidence base of practice

As noted earlier, getting recognized involves both methodological and political aspects. Both are equally important.

Methodological aspects

First, it is vital to show the methodological rigour of your evidence base for your claims of the kind, 'I have improved my practice.' You show how you have collected data to support your claim to knowledge, which you have authenticated and subjected to the critical judgement of others, so that you can now claim it as evidence. The claim appears robust.

Political aspects

Your account now goes into the public domain and joins many others already there. The mass of public accounts comes to form a large body of knowledge, itself an evidence base that supports the idea of practitioner research. This body of knowledge comprises accounts of the personal theories of practitioners as they study what they are doing, and show that they know what they are doing and why they are doing it. Further, the accounts show how practitioners have learned from one another, and how this process has influenced their future lives and learning. For example, Eleanor Lohr (see Lohr 2004) writes:

> Having just submitted my PhD thesis I am thinking, 'Ah well, so that's over. Now I can get on with the rest of my life!' But that's not possible. In wanting to hold to what I have learned in writing my thesis, I find that I must continue to write, to reflect, to act, to inquire. And by returning, by reworking, by thinking through my action research journey within a community of others on similar expeditions, I hope to continue to reform myself and thus improve what I do with others on similar expeditions. (posted 1 December 2004, retrieved 2 December 2004 from the 'discuss the article' section of http://www.arexpeditions.montana.edu/articleviewer.php?AID=80)

Politically, you are showing that you are not alone. Your voice is one among many, all of whom are doing similar things to yourself. Voices in community usually have a much stronger influence than lone voices.

2   GETTING RECOGNIZED BY THE COMMUNITY OF RESEARCHERS

Getting recognized by the community of researchers can be far trickier, because practitioners have not traditionally been perceived as thinkers. Their job has been to do, rather than think, and now here you are claiming to be both a thinker and, by making your account of thinking public, a public intellectual who has something to say about what social practices should look like and what form they should take. You have suddenly become potentially dangerous.

Public intellectuals

The idea of you as a public intellectual is important and worth considering further. A common understanding of intellectuals is that they are an elitist group who have something to say about high culture. While this may be the case in some quarters, it is different in others. Gramsci (1973) talked about organic intellectuals who are 'directly connected to classes or enterprises ... to organize interests, gain more power, get more control' (Said 1994: 3–4). Said also talks about public intellectuals, whose work is constantly to pose awkward questions about current social practices so that the status quo is interrogated and its discourses interrupted. Chomksy (1988) says that the responsibility of intellectuals is to tell the truth and expose lies. This also means digging beneath the propaganda systems that many elites put in place to keep ordinary people under control and prevent them from asking too many questions that might expose the real intentions of elites. These issues are especially relevant to you, because practitioners are often the targets of such propaganda systems. Messages communicated through public discourses systematically aim to persuade practitioners that they cannot think for themselves, that they are not capable of talking intelligently about knowledge, and that they should leave these matters to those who are publicly recognized as capable, that is, intellectuals (see, for example, Hammersley 1993). More will be said about these issues in the next chapter.

This also raises questions about who qualifies as an intellectual. An intellectual is someone who works with their intellect, not only their bodies. On this view, people in shops and on street corners who have something to say about social orders should be seen as intellectuals. As an action researcher you are special, because you show how working with your intellect is an embodied practice. Your work as an intellectual and as a practitioner is integrated. You are not an intellectual on Wednesday and a practitioner on Thursday. You are a thinker and a doer all the time.

So how to communicate this to those who believe that intellectuals working in publicly recognized research institutions are the only ones who are capable of advancing knowledge? How to persuade them that you also have something enormously valuable to say, that they can learn from you, and that they should consider regarding themselves as practitioners?

One of the ways is to show how you as a practitioner are contributing to others' learning. This involves showing the validity of the work, as discussed in the previous section. Another is to persuade intellectuals working in elite institutions to regard themselves as practitioners who are learning with and from other practitioners about how to improve their own work. This involves referring to those accounts by higher education personnel who already regard themselves as practitioners, and explaining that a large body of knowledge already exists to show how and why they should do this. Large bodies of evidence go a long way to influencing public opinion and to persuading others to adopt similar practices.

Large bodies of knowledge do exist, produced by scholar-practitioners working in higher education. For example:

- Je Kan Adler-Collins works at Fukuoma University. His research question is, 'What am I learning as I research my life in higher education as a healing nurse, researcher, and Shingon Buddhist priest and as I pedagogise a curriculum for healing nurses? Weaving the webs of consciousness' (Adler-Collins 2004).
- Margaret Farren works at Dublin City University. Her research question is, 'Developing my pedagogy of the unique as a higher education educator. How can I co-create a curriculum in ICT in education with professional educators?' (Farren 2004).
- Mary Hartog works at Middlesex University. Her research question is, 'How can I improve my practice as a higher education tutor?' (Hartog 2004).
- Patricia Mannix McNamara works at the University of Limerick. Her research question is, 'How do I develop educative relationships?' (Mannix McNamara 2003).
- Mohamed Moustakim works at St Mary's University College. His research question is, 'How do I encourage the active engagement of students in the teaching/learning process whilst enabling them to gain the skills, knowledge and understanding upon which they are formally assessed' (Moustakim 2004).
- Ram Punia works as an international consultant. His research question is, 'How do I fulfil my spiritual values through my work?' (Punia 2004).

Many other stories exist, and their numbers are increasing by the day. You can access many of these in the living theory section and masters programme section at www.actionresearch.net and at www.jeanmcniff.com.

What is special about all these stories is how their authors position themselves as practitioners who are generating their theories of practice. If you are on a programme leading to accreditation, your story of how you have improved your practice by improving your learning can stand with them. As someone who is studying for a degree, you are automatically positioned in higher education. This positioning would probably be contested, however, by those who regard themselves as specialists in knowledge, which returns us to the issue of power and politics. These issues are everywhere, and serious. You need to get on the inside of what the issues are, so that you can deal with them. This brings us to the next chapter about the politics of educational knowledge.

SUMMARY

This chapter has dealt with ideas about establishing the legitimacy of your claim to knowledge, that is, getting it accepted in the public domain. Because you are claiming to have contributed both to new practices and to new theory, you have to secure the approval both of the community of practitioners and of the community of researchers. This second aspect is often more difficult than the first, and can mean engaging with the politics of knowledge. This issue is dealt with in the next chapter.

18

Engaging With the Politics of Knowledge

Sometimes action researchers work in contexts that do not support their research. The lack of interest can range from apathy to outright hostility. In many cases, the root of the difficulties is in matters of power and prestige, in relation to jobs and earnings. Those already in powerful positions make every effort to prevent others' voices from being heard. If you are in such a context, and want to continue doing your research, you need to be clear about how cultures of power operate, so that, as well as surviving, you can also transform the hierarchical power into democratic power, and go on to develop a culture of enquiry. This may take time, but it can be done.

This chapter is in two sections.

1   Understanding oppression
2   Strategies for transformation

1   UNDERSTANDING OPPRESSION

The foundations of oppression lie in one person's wish to control the other. People achieve this through strategies aimed at control and domination. They tend ontologically towards self-interest, using a form of thinking that sees the self as the centre of the universe, and all other entities, including people, as things that can be manipulated in order to serve their own interests. It was this kind of thinking that led to early experiments on animals, asserting that they were mechanical objects whose screams were caused by the movement of their limbs, and to a view of people as disposable (Bales 1999). Practices that see a person as less than human stem from the basic assumption that one person has the right to make judgements about the potential value of another, and to impose their will so that the other is made invisible if necessary. This can extend to controlling the entire environment. The planet is seen as a limitless resource to be exploited for cash.

Practices of domination and oppression are elements of unilateral power. However, according to Foucault (1980), power is not a thing, but is in the relationships of people as they interact. It moves through their relationships like quicksilver, permeating personal boundaries and infiltrating attitudes and discourses.

In many organizational contexts, the person in power is the one who can exercise most control. In contemporary post-industrial knowledge-creating societies, where knowledge is the most prized possession, the person in power is the one who knows most. Because knowledge can be exchanged for cash, the person with the most knowledge gets the position and the money. Foucault (1980) knew this when he said that power and knowledge were inseparable.

In traditional organizational contexts, people tend to be organized in hierarchical structures, which are presented usually as hierarchies of responsibility but are actually hierarchies of power. Those at the top are publicly acknowledged as the best people. In knowledge contexts, they are the ones who know. It can be pleasant at the top, so they tend to resist any claim by pretenders, such as practitioners, that they also deserve to be seen as knowers. Sometimes those at the top go to extraordinary lengths to put down any rebellion or attempt to revolutionize the system that legitimizes their own position. They do this by using a range of strategies of control. This is where the discussion becomes significant for you.

Strategies of control differ according to the political nature of the context. For example, in a dictatorship, according to Chomsky (1988), where human rights can be violated without fear of reprisal, it is commonplace to suppress insurgence by violent means. Those who protest are silenced by being made invisible, often by incarceration or death. In democratic societies, however, where laws protect citizens from violence, other means have to be sought. These, according to Chomsky, take the form of the control of the public mind, using strategies of persuasion. These strategies can range from gentle cajoling to forms of manipulation that have people colluding in their own subjugation and claiming that it was their idea in the first place.

In contexts of educational knowledge, the orthodoxy is that professional researchers are capable of doing research and generating theory, while practitioners are not. So commonplace is this view that many people, researchers and practitioners alike, come to believe it sincerely. Some researchers write books and articles that adopt a benevolent tone, as they explain how they will relieve practitioners of the responsibility of doing research (and presumably thinking for themselves). In practice contexts, the situation can become quite severe, when those in power refuse to allow practitioners to do their research because it may threaten the status quo. One such story is told by Ruth Deery.

HOW COULD I HELP MIDWIVES TO CLARIFY THEIR SUPPORT NEEDS AND PLAN FOR CHANGE?

Ruth Deery

The context of my study

I currently work as a midwifery teacher in a university in the United Kingdom (UK) and I still undertake some clinical practice on a busy delivery suite in order to maintain my clinical skills and credibility within the student body. I have been part of the National Health Service (NHS) since 1972 and a midwife for 28 of those years. During this time I have experienced a rapidly changing NHS as well as unprecedented change within the maternity services. Unfortunately the changes do not appear to have given due regard to long standing cultural and organisational barriers that prevent such change taking place. This has often led to midwives feeling stressed and unsupported. The story I relate here is mainly concerned with my relationship with the organisational culture of the NHS and midwifery. There are also many parallels with the educational institution where I work as a teacher.

I undertook an action research inquiry to find ways of helping midwives plan, implement and test a model of support that would enhance their own sense of wellbeing. I worked with a team of eight community midwives for three years, helping them to acknowledge and address their support needs at work. However, as my inquiry progressed, I was drawn into a minefield of uneasy working relationships between midwives and managers, as well as between the midwives involved in the project and myself. Some of the encounters I had with these midwives and their midwifery managers kindled previously unresolved issues and associated emotions I had experienced during my career as a midwife. For example, my nurse training was disappointingly authoritarian. We learned by rote and were not allowed to speak to senior students or senior members of staff. We were kept firmly in our places and not allowed to express ourselves. There were 120 students in my group, and I could easily lose myself, remain silent, and hide behind others. To this day I continue to experience acute anxiety in the presence of authoritarian people, even though I understand more about oppression and power relations.

Tensions and difficulties also became apparent between the way in which the needs of midwives did not match the changing culture of the NHS. In this new culture, hospitals were managed as hierarchically organised places of employment. I was therefore required to practise midwifery in a culture that had become dominated by a medicalised model rather than a social model of childbirth. This often left me feeling isolated and unsupported, which was also the experience of the midwives whom I wanted to support in my project.

(Continued)

Why did I choose this topic?

So here I was, faced with the challenge of being asked to provide high-level support for women in pregnancy and childbirth, yet I experienced a lack of support myself. The midwives in my action inquiry also recalled similar experiences.

I value women and the concerns they express about their lives, so I constantly strive to improve women's status and their ways of working. I dislike social injustice and hierarchy and prefer to work collaboratively with others. I therefore decided to find new ways of helping midwives, in order to develop mutual support. I decided that action research best suited my inquiry, because this meant I could help the midwives and myself find a way forward together. This was easier said than done, because, although I wanted to establish equal power between myself and the midwives, they insisted that I was the only person who had the power to change things. This went against my democratic and educational values.

How did I explore this further?

I interviewed the midwives individually to find out their views and experiences of support in clinical practice. The midwives reported feeling threatened by the massive changes that were taking place in the maternity services. Change was felt to have been imposed, and had brought uncertainty to their working lives. Interestingly, in order to cope with this uncertainty, the midwives sought to control and direct their own working lives, and their clients' lives, by exerting their own professional power. One way they could do this was to withhold information from their clients and from each other. This is exactly the same strategy used by obstetricians who want to direct and control women and midwives by arguing that birth must be managed by 'experts' for a normal outcome and to reduce uncertainty. A medicalised model of childbirth therefore persists in UK midwifery practices where traditional knowledge of midwifery is subjugated by the authoritarian knowledge of obstetricians. At the same time, however, the experiential knowledge of childbearing women is in turn subjugated by midwives as professionals. Midwives can therefore both experience subjugation and subjugate others (Kirkham 2000).

The midwives who took part in this action enquiry also experienced subjugation on a much more intimate level within their own work team. Excessive organisational demands and limited resources meant that the midwives did not want to undertake anything that was outside their work schedule. Despite my efforts to help them imagine a way forward, they constantly used self-denigration as a way of discounting their own needs. I sensed a culture of 'them and us', not only between hospital and community midwives, but also between midwives and their managers. This situation reinforced the hierarchical structure of the NHS

(Continued)

and the maternity services. When negotiating different ways of working with managers, or working in different settings, I found midwives were forced to internalise the values of those they perceived to be in power. Theorists such as Freire (1972) and Roberts (1982) describe this as common behaviour for those individuals with lesser standing in hierarchies. Midwives working in the hospital, and midwifery managers, were viewed as the dominant groups and thus seen by the midwives working in the community as those with the power. Sometimes when I worked as a clinical midwife in the hospital I felt intimidated by some of the midwives who were renowned for their superiority and lack of support for midwives with less experience. I often became inexpert and awkward as I felt harassed by the hospital midwives. One of the midwives in my action enquiry referred to hospital midwives as 'dinosaurs'. She also referred to 'little dinosaurs' as those midwives who were being oppressed by the 'dinosaurs' while exhibiting similar characteristics to the oppressors.

Focus groups as a forum to reflect on support needs and change

I organised focus groups to observe and explore how the midwives interacted with each other. This also helped me gain further insight into working relationships. One of the focus groups also turned out to be a forum where the midwives expressed their anger and resentment at midwifery managers. The managers were perceived as not keeping their part of the bargain in terms of support for the enquiry, even though I had negotiated extra help and support for the midwives beforehand. The collaborative and participative elements of my action enquiry were unfamiliar to the midwives, despite my efforts to encourage them to work with me and take ownership of the project. I realised that these were practices that they had not experienced previously. Their reluctance to participate and collaborate seemed to parallel their own struggle in response to the need for reciprocal relationships with clients and managers. The midwives implored me to re-negotiate support for the enquiry with midwifery managers but they refused to accompany me to do this. In order to maintain their participation I reluctantly agreed to act on their behalf. They wanted me to speak for them, whereas I wanted them to speak for themselves.

In final individual interviews the midwives said that the support mechanism they devised was beneficial. However the challenge that I presented to them, through action research, seemed to present an opportunity that they were unable to deal with. Midwifery managers had pledged their support for the enquiry, but in the absence of this support, a passive resistance to change developed. This seemed to reinforce the pressure for midwives to meet organisational demands rather than their own or their clients' needs. Although the midwives constantly perceived the managers and hospital midwives as having more power, they used their own 'power' to constrain and limit the progress of my enquiry. They chose to limit their involvement and the scope of the enquiry by establishing some constraining ground rules at the outset. This sort of imposition was disappointing, as one of the aims of the study was to plan a means of gaining support with the midwives through mutual collaboration.

(Continued)

What have I learned from the process?

Midwifery continues to be restricted and confined by rigid institutional routines and practices. These do not take account of midwives' struggles for autonomous practice. Throughout my enquiry this situation has mirrored my own struggle to overcome being silenced and being prevented from living out my own midwifery values. The complex interpersonal demands of my enquiry led to turbulence and heartache. This discomfort became even more painful as I unpeeled power structures and relationships to examine midwifery work more closely.

Incorporating different perspectives into midwifery practice has often resulted in revealing contradictions and conflicting values. This highlights the need for a different way of thinking. There is a need to address the bureaucratic, hierarchical nature of the maternity services and the prevalent medicalised paradigm of health care that is intolerant of these different ways of thinking.

I will continue to use action research as a means to influence change in midwifery although I acknowledge that it is not a magic wand. The potential of action research to incorporate direct participation in strategic planning cannot be ignored. This needs to be embraced by midwifery as a means to integrate education, research and practice development.

2   STRATEGIES FOR TRANSFORMATION

As Ruth Deery discovered, complex difficulties can be addressed and transformed, albeit sometimes with difficulty. It is in your power to change the situation. Here are some ways in which you can do so.

Your aim is to transform a situation in which your values are being denied into one in which they are realized. This usually involves developing a range of strategies to be used according to the situation. Not all strategies are appropriate to all circumstances, so it is important to develop some political sophistication in knowing how to deal with each situation as it arises, in as useful a way as possible. Here are some strategies you can consider.

Confrontation

This is seldom the best strategy, but it is sometimes the only option, especially when you are in a situation that is damaging to you or someone else, such as when you are in the company of someone who is talking or acting in destructive ways. Sometimes it is necessary to fight fire with fire. Although action research is about educational wellbeing, you may find yourself dealing with people who are committed to their own self-interest, and you have to resort to non-educational ways. Confrontation is not the best, because it involves bringing a situation to complete closure, where one side wins and the other loses, with no way out for either party. This is a strategy of containment, not of potential development, because development means that the conversation remains open so that everyone can return to the issue and find a way forward without losing face. This is important, because people seldom adopt new practices when they feel disgruntled or begrudging. Avoid confrontation where possible, but if it is a case of stopping a potentially destructive situation, such as bullying, don't hesitate. Just be aware of the potential fallout if you do.

Negotiation

This is usually a better option, because it leaves opportunities for new conversations and new practices. Negotiation can be far more difficult than confrontation, which is sharp and definite, because negotiation means compromise, which can be rather difficult for those of us who do not easily tolerate thoughtless behaviour. It can also seem like hypocrisy, when you find yourself dealing with someone who lives in the direction of life-distorting values such as cruelty. Negotiation is, however, essential if you are to create new opportunities for the exercise of your influence. You are in fact trying to persuade people to change their minds, and your attitude of openness in negotiation will in most cases be far more effective than the finality of confrontation. Negotiation means always leaving a loophole for the other to change their mind publicly, without damage to their image and self-esteem. Be sure that they, and you, know what is going on, but in situations of conflict it is essential that you both play a politically strategic game so that both emerge as winners.

Creative compliance

In 1987, Barry MacDonald spoke about the need for creative compliance, that is, a form of resistance that recognizes the constraints of a current situation, and finds ways of working within the constraints in order to achieve one's own aims. This does not mean giving in to dominant systems. It means being pliable and bending with the prevailing wind, but not breaking. It means adapting to imposed systems but working creatively within them in order to find a way through. For some, it means working within and changing systems from the inside. This can be a most creative experience. The aim is not to change the external 'system' so much as to influence people within the system, so that individual practices realize their potential for transforming wider thinking.

Build your own power base

This is a wise and powerful strategy. Building your own power base means that you can act from a position of publicly recognized strength, and you have resources behind you to back up what you say. These resources come in the form of people and profile.

Remember that the currency you are using is knowledge. You may be dealing with people who are vying for power in the form of knowledge. They wish to be acclaimed publicly as knowers, and often they are seeking to establish their own power base at the expense of others, by refusing to acknowledge them as knowers. If you are to engage, it is best to do so from a position of strength in your own knowledge. Your best strategy is to secure as much public legitimation as possible for yourself. You can do this in the following ways.

Get accreditation

The academy is still the highest body for the recognition and legitimation of knowledge. If you want to engage politically, the more accreditation you have, the better. As well as offering opportunities for your own intellectual develop-ment, programmes leading to awards are also pathways to acknowledgement. Once you have a degree, it is difficult to take it away. You are acknowledged publicly for ever. People know that it takes disciplined scholarship to get a degree, so they will regard you with respect, if not affection.

Get published

Publication is one of the most powerful resources, especially if your work proves popular. You may find, as in Jack's case, that ideas which have previously been rejected actually come to form the basis of official programmes (see http://www.actionresearch.net/bk93/0con.pdf for the story of Jack's struggle for the academic legitimation of his ideas). You may find, as in Jean's case, that her accessible style of writing, which was critiqued as non-scholarly in the early days, proves popular with scholars who use her texts rather than more inaccessible ones. In an earlier conversation with Noam Chomsky, when Jean explained that academic communities tended not to reference her work, even though her books sold in thousands, his comment was, 'You must be doing something right if they are trying to ignore you.' If people know that you have a reputation, and also have access to print, they will treat you with respect. You do not necessarily need their friendship, but you do need them to allow you untrammelled freedom to exercise your influence.

Get the ear of policy makers

If policy makers perceive that you are a person with clout, they will make room for you. It is easier to gain access to them if you have some public standing. They will also look with interest at what you are doing, to see whether opportunities exist for their own self-advancement. In the 1980s, Jack's work was rejected by his university, and Jean ran the gauntlet of the hostility of other academics who saw her as a threat to their own positioning. Those same people and institutions now write in affirming terms about the value of the work. We are all human, and we all do what we can to further our own ambitions. If your ambition is to influence individual and collective thinking in such a way that systems will change to allow others in, you need to find ways of doing this. Furthermore, your work may come directly to influence policy makers. Recent initiatives such as the Best Practice Research Scholarships, awarded to teachers in schools to study their own practice, have arisen out of the early work of pioneers in action research, many of whom have now retired or gone on to do other things. Influencing the public mind can take a long time and we often do not see the benefits in our lifetime, but that should not stop us from building for a better future for others.

Get popular

You are working with practitioners, and persuading them to find ways of improving their work, and also to improve their own capacity for publishing the work and contributing to new theory. The kind of theory they produce is practical theory grounded in practice. This new form of theory is contributing to the knowledge base that influences policy (Chapter 25). You can popularize your own ideas by making them accessible to others, and encouraging others to see that what you are advocating is well within their grasp. Once people can see that they can achieve on their own terms, they will have more confidence to stand up for themselves and mobilize. Mobilization is essential, because collective voices are stronger than lone ones. If possible, you can then show people how they can become active in their own interests, perhaps by finding ways of making their own work public, or by organizing themselves to offer resistance to the use of unilateral power and injustice, with a view to transforming those situations into new opportunities for others.

Mind yourself

Be aware of your own capacity at all times. While you can probably do more than you believe yourself capable of doing, you are also still human and can do only so much. Do not take on the worries of the world. Do what you can, from your own position. Often people find that they fight so hard that they have little energy left after the battle to begin reconstruction. It is important that you pace yourself and stay reasonably within your own capacity. You are less use to people dead, but while alive you can achieve much. Find allies, develop economical strategies, be shrewd. Your own energy is limited, so use it with care. Find ways of supporting yourself, with caring people and the affirmation of your own productive work. You need others, but at the same time, never underestimate the power of your own voice of passion, and your own capacity for influence.

SUMMARY

This chapter has set out ideas about the politics of educational knowledge and how to deal with them. Dealing with power begins by understanding its nature clearly. Power and oppression are not 'things', but aspects of the practices of real people, who aim to meet their own interests. It is important to be imaginative in finding strategies for survival, and also strategies that will help you transform negative situations into life-affirming ones.

One of the ways you can develop your own strategies for transformation is by making your work widely available and showing its significance for developing learning in order to improve practice. This is the focus of the next part.

Part VI

How Do I Represent and Disseminate My Knowledge?

This part is about sharing and disseminating your work. Communicating the value of your work to different audiences can sometimes mean learning their languages and organizing your ideas in ways that will speak to their experience. The chapters give practical advice on how to do this.

This part contains the following chapters.

At this point in your own enquiry into action research you are asking, 'How do I communicate the significance of my research? How do I show the value of studying my learning in order to improve my practice?' Your own interest is now developing into how you can best show the importance of your research for learning, both your own and others'.

19

Telling Your Research Story

Now you need to tell others about your research. However, producing a text can be complex, because speaking about experience is different from experiencing the experience itself. Furthermore, the process of communication is itself an experience, both for you and your reader. You are trying to communicate what is 'in here' to someone 'out there'.

You have to produce a text that is high quality. Like it or not, your work is going to be judged in terms of the quality of your text. People are more likely to listen to you if they can see immediately what you are doing, and what the significance of your work is. If they have to struggle to understand you, they may put your text down, or worse, read someone else's. This carries big responsibilities for you. You have to use a language that your reader can easily comprehend, and make sure your message captivates their imagination even though some of the ideas may be complex and will need disciplined study to understand fully. Moreover, 'texts' can be visual and oral as well as written. Whichever form of expression you choose has to communicate the reality of your experience, both what you did and what you learned, and the potential significance of your work for the learning of others.

You can of course do this, but to do so you have to tell your story in such a way that people will want to listen, and will see immediately what you are getting at.

This chapter therefore asks two questions.

1 How do you get people to listen to you?
2 How do you show what you are getting at?

1   HOW DO YOU GET PEOPLE TO LISTEN TO YOU?

Habermas (1987) tells us that ideally we should

- speak comprehensibly
- speak truthfully

- speak authentically
- speak appropriately.

This has implications for you. How do you tell your story in a way that is comprehensible, truthful, authentic and appropriate?

Speaking comprehensibly

When you speak, you speak to a listener. When you write, you write for a reader. You may speak and write for yourself when you are preparing your text, but when you present it publicly you do so for someone else. This means that you have to grip their imagination through language.

Here are some ideas to help you do this.

Get passionate

Getting people to engage with you and maintaining their interest means that you have to show your own enthusiasm for your work. Encourage them to believe that if you can do it, so can they.

Show that you believe in your work, yourself, and others. Believing in your work means that you know how important it is. You need to say this. Believing in yourself means that you had the courage of your convictions to do the research. Explain how you had to draw on your own inner strength, and on the support of allies, and how you won through eventually. Audiences love to hear victory stories, but the most authentic ones are those that tell of the struggles involved. Don't present yourself as a victim. You are a responsible practitioner who has been fighting for justice for yourself and others. Believing in others means that you were guided by your own commitment to other people's capacity to think for themselves and make their own decisions. Be up front in saying to people, 'You can do this too. Believe in yourself.'

Get personal

Speak in a way that your audience can understand. Don't use unfamiliar words. If you have to use professional jargon, explain what it means in ordinary language.

Do not tell people what to do. Adopt throughout an invitational stance. This means relating well to your audience. If you are speaking, establish eye contact. If you are writing, establish mind contact. Draw your reader into your text, and invite them to consider ideas, rather than impose them. Keep a light touch throughout. If you have some serious critique to make, do it in a constructive way, and move on. Never alienate your audience by talking down (or up) to them, and make the case that you also can be mistaken.

Use the language of the community you are addressing. If you are writing a scholarly document, use a scholarly language. If you are talking to a group of parents, use a language that relates to their experience. You have to become fluent in your audience's language, not the other way round (see below, 'Speaking appropriately').

Get clarity

Say what you mean to say, clearly and directly. Never use two words when one will do. In your case, less is more. Producing a text that is simple and straight-forward without jeopardizing the quality of ideas is difficult, and takes time and concentration. In a written text, you will spend ten times as long editing as producing a first draft. For every book that is published, many more go in the bin. Do not expect to get a text right in one go. The most experienced authors often spend days working on a few pages. This is what it takes to produce a quality text.

Get working

Get on with it. Don't spend time and energy finding other jobs to do. It is easy to put things off indefinitely. What can you do tomorrow that you cannot do today? If you are finding it hard to get started, write anything. You don't have to begin at the beginning. Begin half way through, or at the end. You are going to edit the text anyhow, and achieving a few sentences, even of lesser quality, is an achievement which will inspire greater achievement. Don't think you are the only one who is struggling. Everyone struggles. If you want to do it, just do it.

Speaking truthfully

You show that people can believe what you say by demonstrating your credi-bility. Whatever you claim to have happened, you show it to be true by pro-ducing evidence, and also by saying that you are doing so. People will believe you because you are prepared to subject your claims to critique and not hide behind anything. You explain that this is your original work, and you demon-strate consistently your capacity for critical engagement.

Speaking authentically

Throughout you use your practitioner-researcher voice, not the voice you may normally use as a primary teacher or psychiatrist or nursing practitioner. Your practitioner voice is incorporated into your research voice (see also next section).

As a researcher you explain how you have aimed to live true to the beliefs you hold as a practitioner through doing your research. You explain how the conduct of your research programme itself is consistent with your beliefs. Your participative and inclusive methodology demonstrates participation and inclusion in practice, and your willingness to subject your provisional findings to critique demonstrates your commitment to holding your findings lightly and resisting the idea of a final truth.

Speaking appropriately

Sometimes researchers find it difficult to speak in a researcher's voice, especially when they are with, say, primary children for most of the working day. Bear in mind which community of practice you are now with. When you are in your primary classroom you are with your community of primary practice. When you write your report you write it for your community of scholarly practice. For your report, you leave your primary teacher's voice in your primary classroom, although you are telling the story of your practice in your primary classroom. Each community has its own language. Speaking appropriately means using the right language, that is, using language in a way that shows you are aware of the normative assumptions that you are making. Many practitioner-researchers have to learn the language of scholarship, and this can take some time. Again, do not think you are the only one. As with everything, practice makes perfect. If you are unfamiliar with scholarly language, read other works such as dissertations and journals to see the kind of language used, and note it carefully. Do not copy or model your work directly on exemplars, but do aim to develop a language that is appropriate for the job of producing a research report. Always produce your own original text, but make sure that it will be received well by the audience you are writing for. When you go on to write your textbooks, you will use a different voice again, this time the voice of practitioner-researchers. We authors are writing this book using a different voice than the one we use in our scholarly articles, which are written for a different audience. We are deliberately positioning ourselves as practitioner-researchers, and using the language of practitioner-researchers. This does not mean that we are avoiding scholarly issues – indeed, this book has dealt throughout with scholarly issues – but we are using a form of expression that is more appropriate for the community of practitioner-scholars than for the community of scholar-practitioners.

2   HOW DO YOU SHOW WHAT YOU ARE GETTING AT?

We said above that texts may be presented in different forms. In the next two chapters advice is given about the content and form of written reports, because writing is still the most common form of expression, and is expected by accrediting institutions. However, many higher education institutions now accept multimedia forms as part of degree submissions. While they would probably not accept extreme forms such as graphic accounts, as in graphic novels, or video narratives as entire theses, they would certainly accept those forms as supplementary to the main text. Also a text may be incorporated into a visual narrative to guide the reader through the interconnections of meanings.

Excellent examples of these approaches are now available to show the potentials of multimedia forms of representation for global networks of communication. Seminal texts are Jack Whitehead's (2004c) 'Action research expeditions: do action researchers' expeditions carry hope for the future of humanity? How do we know? An enquiry into reconstructing educational theory and educating social formations'. Part II of this account takes you into Jack's (2004b) multimedia account: 'How valid are multi-media communications of my embodied values in living theories and standards of educational judgement and practice?' The form of these papers is extraordinary, because they really do constitute the message they are communicating. They are saying that communities of practice come into being, and sustain and develop themselves, by showing how they are consistent with their underpinning values and commitments to inclusional and relational forms of living. These commitments enable people to work together in ways that honour the capacity of the other to think for themselves and to engage critically with the ideas and work of others. The communities develop themselves as good social orders by their commitments to create their own new futures, and also to test their claims that what they are doing now has the potential to develop into a new future that is grounded in values that give promise for the future of humanity. Furthermore, each community has the potential to influence other communities, by sharing and critiquing what they are doing and thinking. The way they share is by forming networks. The networks are interconnecting branching networks, forming a global network that connects networks to one another in multiple innovative ways.

These networks have special features. At a surface, physical level they are groupings of people connected to other groupings, and each grouping can connect with any other anywhere in the world. At a deep level of commitment they are held together by bonds of common purpose. Their underlying ontological commitments are the 'ties that bind' (Bateson 1972). These ontological commitments emerge as epistemological standards (see page 152), when members of communities tell one another what they know and how they have come to know by generating their claims to knowledge and testing them against the critical insights and practices of themselves and others. These 'ties that bind' form an unseen web of interconnection, what O'Donohue (2003) calls a 'web of betweenness', similar to Capra's (2003) idea that the invisible threads between the networks are what power the creation and sustaining of the networks themselves.

As noted earlier, Foucault (1980) wrote about power and power relationships. He said that power was not a 'thing', which one person had and often used to dominate the other, but was in relationships. He spoke about 'capillary action', as power moved back and forth along the invisible strands that connect parties in relationship. This idea sits well with the idea of interconnected branching networks of global communication through education (Whitehead and McNiff 2003). The form of these networks is not centre-to-periphery, but multidimensional, each network forming a node, which itself is a dynamic network of shifting relationships. There is no central point anywhere. The power of influence is in the people and their relationships, in their own contexts. No one manages these networks. They manage themselves, and are self-sustaining and self-regenerating. Power is everywhere. It is in the relationships that hold the networks together and enable them to develop at both a practical and a theoretical level (see page 63). Each person within each network has the power of influence. Each has the capacity to influence their own learning and the learning of others. Each has to learn to exercise their influence in such a way that the other will also learn to exercise their power for influence for educational sustainability.

It is easy to become part of the networks. Wherever you are, whatever your context, you can link with other practitioner-researchers who are asking, like you, 'How do I improve what I am doing?', and make your story public so that they can respond critically and so influence your learning, as you are hoping to influence theirs. You are already a participant in physical space, in your own workplace, where you can share your reports, and you can connect virtually, through sharing your ideas electronically. There is simply nothing to stop you. This brave new world of educational influence has come into being through the commitments of people like you. You need to tell your story of what you are doing to sustain it and develop it even further.

SUMMARY

This chapter has offered ideas about how you can get people to listen to you, and how to explain clearly what you are getting at. It has used Habermas's ideas of speaking comprehensibly, truthfully, authentically, and appropriately as the basis for your own communicative action. The chapter has gone on to suggest how you can get involved in networks of communication, and has offered ideas about the nature and formation of these networks.

The next chapter moves on to the practical business of writing a report.

20

Writing a Workplace Report

This chapter gives advice on possible frameworks and contents for an action research report about workplace learning. The next chapter is about reports submitted for higher degree accreditation. Please note that this division of chapters is for emphasis of content only. Many workplace reports come to stand as reports submitted for degree accreditation. Therefore, what is said in this chapter is also relevant to submitting a report for accreditation.

It is important also to bear in mind that the ideas presented here are suggestions only. You should decide what is right for you, and then adapt the ideas here to your own purposes and in your own way. Many people, including those whose work is cited in this book, used ideas like these to get them started, and then modified them as they created their own narratives. Others organized their ideas into their own frameworks and representations. It does not matter how you organize your ideas, provided you meet all the criteria for writing a quality research report that shows how you have met the criteria for doing a quality action research project. The chapter is presented to show, first, how you can organize your ideas using a formal structure such as the one presented here, and, second, how you can organize your ideas in your own innovative way. The chapter is in two sections to set out these different approaches.

1 Organizing your ideas as a formal framework
2 Organizing your ideas in your own innovative way

It should also be noted that the examples cited here are both from teaching and from other professions. While action research is most strongly developed in the teaching profession, other professions use action research approaches, and high-quality reports are beginning to form a new body of professional development literature that will have significant influence.

1 ORGANIZING YOUR IDEAS AS A FORMAL FRAMEWORK

All reports, regardless of audience, should contain the following:

- Descriptions of practice – what you did.
- Explanations for practice – why you did what you did and what you hoped to achieve.
- An articulation of your theory of practice – saying that you understand how your descriptions and explanations constitute your personal theory of practice, and why it is important.

Your report will therefore be a narrative of your own learning from practice, and an ongoing analysis in the form of a reflective commentary on its potential value and significance.

Your action plan as a framework

You can use the action plan you drew up at the beginning of your project as the main framework for your report (see page 79). When you drew up your action plan you were looking forward to what you might do, so you told it in the future tense. You are now looking back on what you have done, so you tell it in the past tense. Possible section headings would therefore be as follows.

- What was my concern?
- Why was I concerned?
- What experiences could I describe to show the reasons for my concern?
- What did I think I could do about it?
- What did I do about it?
- What kind of evidence did I produce to show the situation as it unfolded?
- How did I ensure that any conclusions I came to were reasonably fair and accurate?
- How did I evaluate the validity of the account of my learning?
- How did I modify my practice in the light of my evaluation?

What was my concern?

Say what your research was about. Did you want to find better ways of working with people? Did you want to replace a hierarchical management system with flatter structures? Explain how this concern led you to decide to research the issue. Articulate your question as 'How do I …?', for example, 'How do I improve relationships?' or 'How do I introduce flatter structures into my organization?'

Why was I concerned?

Explain how the situation could be seen as a realization of, or a denial of, your values. Doing this means articulating the values that inspire your work, such as justice, freedom, and care for the other. Explain that you undertook the research in order to stay consistent with your values. You may have experienced the situation as a problem which needed a solution, or you may have been just trying to understand the situation and finding ways of living with it.

What experiences could I describe to show the reasons for my concern?

Explain that you undertook your research by first undertaking some reconnaissance (Elliott 1991) to establish what the situation was like. You did this by gathering data using different techniques. You interviewed people and used excerpts from your transcripts, or you had a conversation with a trusted colleague about how you both felt about the situation. You kept a record of the conversation. Paint a word picture for your reader so that they can see clearly what you and others were thinking and doing, and why you felt dissatisfied with the current situation. If you are using multimedia you could paint a real picture, or represent the situation using a range of still or moving images.

What did I think I could do about it?

What were your options? How did you arrive at them? Perhaps you had conversations with critical friends? Did you invite ideas about what you could do? Explain here how you thought about the situation, and how you thought you could address it. Did you see yourself doing it alone or in company with others? Did you understand this as a process of testing out possible strategies? How did you feel about this kind of open-ended enquiry? Were you looking for certain solutions, or testing out possible ways forward?

At this point also say that you were aware of the ethical considerations of involving others and also of working in a social context where your proposed action may have implications for others. How could you safeguard your own and their wellbeing?

What did I do about it?

Say what course of action you decided to follow. Explain that this was only one possible way forward, and it was provisional. You were ready to change if necessary according to the changing situation. Say whether it was problematic to go forward like this.

Set out here some of the practicalities of what this involved. Who would be your research participants? How did you select them? How long did you think the research would last? What resources did you need?

Also set out how you intended to ensure good ethical conduct. Say that you produced ethics statements and letters requesting permission to do the research, and put these letters, together with letters granting permission, in your appendices.

What kind of evidence did I produce to show the situation as it unfolded?

Bring back to mind the word or visual picture you painted to show the situation as it was, and now paint a new picture to show the situation as it developed, again drawing on the data you gathered. Explain that you used the same, or possibly different, data gathering techniques. Aim to show, at a descriptive level, what happened, and also aim to show, at an explanatory level, why you think it happened and what was achieved. What was your part in the change? How did you influence people's learning, so that they changed their own ways of being together? Remember that the focus of the research is you and your learning, and you are monitoring and recording other people's learning only in relation to your own. Your research question, 'How do I improve …?' means that you are producing evidence in relation to how other people are responding to your educative influence, and changing things for themselves.

How did I ensure that any conclusions I came to were reasonably fair and accurate?

Say that you were aware of the need to test and critique your provisional conclusions at all steps of the research. This means explaining how you put procedures in place to deal with this. You arranged for key people to be your critical friends, and you negotiated with them and others to form a validation group, who would convene at regular intervals to listen to your account of your research, and critique your provisional findings. Say whether they agreed, or requested further and more quality-controlled evidence, or asked you to go back and think again. Explain why you chose those people and not others, and also how you ensured that you made clear that you were testing your ideas throughout and not presenting them as fact. Set out the main recommendations of your validation group and include their reports as an appendix to your report. Say also whether you took or rejected their advice, or adapted it to suit your own needs.

How did I evaluate the validity of the account of my learning?

Say that you took care in the methodological procedures involved in making your claim to knowledge. Say what your criteria and standards of judgement were, and that you were aware of their significance for evaluating the validity of your account of learning. Say that you specifically drew these matters to the attention of your critical friends and validation groups, and that you emphasized how you were producing explanatory accounts of learning and not only descriptive accounts of activities.

How did I modify my practice in the light of my evaluation?

Set out how doing your research has led to the development of new practices and new thinking (theorizing). Whose practice has changed, yours or other people's or both? How can you show that this new practice is an improvement on previous practices? Are your values now being realized? On reflection, could you or should you have done things differently?

Explain that although this may appear to be the end point of one research cycle, it is not the end of your enquiry. You now need to test the new practice, which means undertaking a new project that will help you to evaluate what you are doing and how to improve it where necessary. You will generate new practices and new thinking, and you will evaluate them so that you can say that these are an improvement on the previous situation. Think about the idea that it is impossible to arrive at an end point because wherever you are on the journey is always half way to the end. Doing action research legitimates the idea of half way there. You are not aiming for an end point or a final answer. You are looking for provisional answers that describe and explain the journey so far. Your story is about making the journey, not about arriving, because we never actually arrive. However, half way to somewhere is a new beginning, and new beginnings carry with them their own intent. Set out what your new beginnings involve, and how you intend to live for the time being.

Examples of the framework in use

Many examples exist to show how people have used this framework. Two of the best examples are in the collections of work supported by Jackie Delong in Ontario, Canada, and Moira Laidlaw in Guyuan, China.

Collection 1

Jackie and her colleagues have produced four volumes of *Passion in Professional Practice*, containing narratives of colleagues' improved practice through action research. These are available in hard copy (Delong 2001; Delong and Black 2002; Delong et al. 2003; Delong et al. 2005) or electronic form. You can access Volume II at http://schools.gedsb.net/ar/passion/pppii/index.html and Volume III at http://schools.gedsb.net/ar/passion/pppiii/index.html. The books contain dozens of case studies from teachers across a range of levels. Here are some.

Sandy Fulford asks: How can I use electronic portfolios to create a reflective record of the highlights of my students' school year?
Her abstract says: I worked with George Neeb to develop student electronic portfolios that combine computer technology with traditional portfolios. Students collected examples of their work, digital photos and reflective evaluations to create a record of the highlights of their school year. Working with colleague and mentor George Neeb, various techniques and approaches were developed to have students complete personal portfolios using Corel presentations for the school year.

Dan Mattka and Heather Knill-Griesser ask: How can we support primary teachers to implement a Balanced Literacy Program to improve student learning based on the Provincial Ministry initiative, 'Schools in Need of Extra Help', as an administrator and teacher-consultant?

Their abstract says: Princess Elizabeth School is a Junior Kindergarten to Grade 6 school with a student population of 260. It exists in a mixed residential area in Brantford where Ontario Housing provides residence to a significant number of students, where one in four families are single parent households. Grade 3 and 6 Education Quality and Accountability Office (EQAO) provincial testing results have placed many of the students below the provincial standards. The authors examine their educative influence as administrator and teacher-consultant as they answer the question, 'How can we support primary teachers to implement a Balanced Literacy Program to improve student learning?'

Lindsey Huyge asks: How can I improve my effectiveness as a learning resource teacher (LRT) through the development of partnerships with my colleagues so that the specific needs of my students can be met or accommodated?

Her abstract says: The student population at Walsh Public School, from junior kindergarten to grade eight, is 434. It is situated in a rural area where farming is an important source of income for many families either directly or indirectly. At this school students are very diverse and require a community where they can actively participate in their education and can gain the necessary skills for success in a challenging world. Teachers at Walsh P. S. take every opportunity to create a uniform atmosphere and appreciate open communication.

Collection 2

The collection of case stories compiled by Moira Laidlaw and colleagues can be downloaded from http://www.bath.ac.uk/~edsajw/moira.shtml. This collection includes the following accounts.

Liu Binyou asks: How can I cultivate my non–English students' interests in English?

Her abstract says: In my case study I reveal how I changed my methods to enable students to take a more active part in lessons. I found new ways to attract their interest and helped to motivate them. These methods consisted of introducing issues of personal interest to the students, and paying attention to the learning needs of individuals. I also describe in detail the responses of one student to a new method of teaching, in which his own talents as a poet are harnessed to motivate him to study English. I show how changing my methodology has helped my students to become better learners.

Li Peidong asks: How can I improve my students' self-confidence in their class work?

His abstract says: This paper is an account of what I have done in the very first cycle of my educational action research, which lasted about one year. I have struggled and explored myself within this long duration with the question: How can I help my students to improve their self-confidence in their classwork? I reasoned this as the extrinsic cause influencing learners' conversational performance and communicative motivation. The article records the process of how I came to my present action research questions with see-sawing inquiry and evaluation of my imagined solutions, all of this with respect to humanistic approaches and educational values based on my insights and learning about the New English Curriculum. I used questionnaires, interviews and my own observations to triangulate and draw conclusions.

Cao Yong asks: How can I improve the pronunciation and intonation of the first-year English Majors to meet the demand of the New English Curriculum?

His abstract says: In my report, I present my [action research] work on how I used action research in teaching pronunciation and intonation for the first-English majors. My concern reveals itself to be closely associated with the bases of the four language skills of speaking, listening, reading and writing. I put forward a case that the effort to master the sound system and to pronounce correctly are key aspects of learning a second language. As clarification I give some technical details on aspects of sounds of speech, including articulation, vowel formation, accent, inflection, and intonation, with reference to the correctness or acceptability of the speech sounds. I also provide some descriptions of new classroom teaching methods for pronunciation and intonation. I include comments from students, reveal statistics of their scores, quote from expert sources in linguistics, and show the results of a questionnaire. I conclude that by researching my practice in terms of targets for the New Curriculum for the teaching of English in China, there is the potential for my work and similar enquiries to be of educational benefit for schools and other colleges in China.

2   ORGANIZING YOUR IDEAS IN YOUR OWN INNOVATIVE WAY

We said at the beginning of this chapter that you should feel free to organize your ideas in a way that is right for you. We encourage you to experiment and find your own way, while bearing in mind the need for methodological rigour. Here are three examples of how people have done that.

From Ruth Deery and Deborah Hughes

Ruth Deery is a Senior Lecturer in Midwifery (see her story on page 175). Her article, together with Deborah Hughes, a Sure Start Midwife and Deputy

Programme Manager, 'Supporting midwife-led care through action research: a tale of mess, muddle and birth balls', is in *Evidence Based Midwifery* (Deery and Hughes 2004). The article tells of an action enquiry to 'identify changes in care given by midwives, to offer developmental opportunities to midwives to support the continuation of a midwife-led ethos and to examine the process of cultural shift created by relocation to shared facilities' (2004: 52). Using an action research approach, the findings of the study were that: 'Key weaknesses were identified within a midwife-led unit (MLU) and actions agreed and taken to address these, with a resulting strengthening of midwife-led care. The reflective process, an integral part of action research, fostered a shared concept of midwife-led care and an expanded skill-base for the facilitation of physiological childbirth' (2004: 52).

The framework used to conduct the research was adapted from McNiff et al. (2003):

- We review our current practice,
- identify an aspect we want to improve,
- imagine a way forward,
- try it out, and
- take stock of what happens.
- We modify our plan in the light of what we have found, and continue with the action,
- evaluate the modified action, and
- reconsider the position in the light of the evaluation.

The headings used for the article follow the same plan.

From Colin Smith

Colin Smith is a seconded teacher, now working as a university-based researcher. Smith's (2002) article 'Supporting teacher and school development: learning and teaching policies, shared living theories and teacher–research partnerships' appears in *Teacher Development*. In the article he draws on Jack Whitehead's idea of living educational theories, and develops it into the idea of shared living theories, that is, the articulation of a group's shared commitments to improved learning and practice. To organize his research, he used this outline.

- I experience a concern when my values are negated in practice.
- I imagine a way forward.
- I act.
- I evaluate.
- I modify my concerns, ideas and actions in the light of my evaluations. (Whitehead 2000: 93)

Commenting on the process of the research, Smith says:

> This research cycle follows Whitehead's framework. If a school asks how something can be improved, it is experiencing a concern that a value is being negated in practice. How it deals with this will depend upon where the value derives from … and the power relations involved. It then imagines a way forward, acts, evaluates and, if necessary, modifies what it believes and does in light of those evaluations. By making public the theory behind its practice and its evaluations, the school can contribute to educational knowledge. The links between research and practice are strengthened and support for both teacher and school development from the research world is given new direction and relevance.

While he did not directly use this framework to write up his work, it is worth noting that he used a framework that he found in the literature, and adapted it for his own use.

From Kathryn Yeaman

Perhaps the most striking example of a researcher deciding to go her own way is from Kathryn Yeaman's (1995) report 'Creating educative dialogue in an infant classroom' for her masters module in research methods. Here is the introductory section of her report, which can be downloaded from http://www.bath.ac.uk/~edsajw/module/kathy.htm.

A LIVING EDUCATIONAL THEORY!

Kathryn Yeaman

I am not used to the idea of theory being something which can be alive. So often it is something once studied, perhaps partly assimilated into one's teaching, then long forgotten. The view that educational theory can be something less abstract and more meaningful is an exciting one.

I have found action research to be an empowering process. It has led me to what is right or educational and in doing so it has empowered me to follow this path. It is empowering in that it shows your actions to be the right ones and in doing this you [demonstrate] to yourself that your ideas work. They then become more than ideas; they change into truths.

The following action research was undertaken as a single module towards an M.A. at the University of Bath. I chose action research as I wanted my study to have direct relevance to my work in the classroom as a teacher. It is possible to have what might be termed a 'good

(Continued)

knowledge' of educational theory without actually using it in one's own situation. It could then be argued that this superficial learning is not in fact knowledge at all. In doing my action research I have discovered for myself the relevance to me of some traditional, propositional theories and also discovered gaps and contradictions in the field of educational theory.

The 'living educational theory' for me is not an alternative one or indeed a subversive one as some might suggest (see Newby 1994), but one which combines traditional theories with practice to form a new understanding and in doing so provides new theories which may have some generalisability to the profession as a whole.

> Critical research is praxis. Praxis involves the inseparability of theory and practice – i.e. informed practice. We must understand theoretical notions in terms of their relationship to the lived world, not simply as objects of abstract contemplation. (Kincheloe 1991)

Schön stresses the need for such research to be 'I'-based. Such research can construct a new theory of a unique case. My action research report is written in the first person, as this is how it was. The research was done by me. 'I' was at the centre of my research question. If others as they read wish to propose what might happen to others in a similar situation, that is for them to imagine. I am concerned with the specifics of my research, not, in the report itself, with generalities or indeed with relevance to other situations. I will however consider these points after the report. I have also chosen not to write an introduction for readers, as I would like them to read the report and find significant points themselves.

My reasons for presenting this report are many. I am making public my action learning. I am presenting it as evidence of my own professional development. I would like fellow professionals to learn from it. In presenting my findings my intention is not to be prescriptive but to demonstrate some insights into the subject of educational dialogue. I hope too, that by revealing the self-educative nature of action research I will inspire others to become involved. I would like others to question and research for themselves my findings and those of others; I would like others to become involved in creating their own educational theory. As teacher-researchers, by focusing our enquiry on our children's learning and integrating the insights of existing theories into our enquiry we can make a significant contribution to educational knowledge.

By adopting this stance, Kathryn seems to be inviting her readers to draw from her research report those aspects that speak to their own experience. She uses her capacity for originality and critical engagement in order to encourage others to do the same.

It is important to bear in mind that you are at liberty to create the report that most clearly communicates your experience. Provided you produce a report that shows the rigorous process of conducting the research and articulates the development of your own living educational theory, you can have confidence that you have done what it takes to achieve recognition.

SUMMARY

This chapter has offered ideas about writing a workplace report. It has offered a basic framework, and given examples to show how this can work in practice. It has, however, emphasized that you should develop your own framework to suit your own purposes as you tell your story. Further examples have been presented to show how this can be achieved.

The next chapter considers how to write a report for formal accreditation.

21

Writing a Report for Higher Degree Accreditation

If you are on an award-bearing course, you may prefer the framework outlined in this chapter. It is tried and tested, and if you use it you won't go far wrong. It deals with the same issues as in Chapter 20, but also covers different ground. For a degree, especially a higher degree, you would be expected to engage with the literature, and be clear about conceptual frameworks and more theoretical issues. This framework has proved useful to many practitioners as a starting point for their writing. Most have then adapted it for their own purposes and contexts.

The chapter is in two sections.

1 Outlining the framework
2 Examples of the framework in action

1 OUTLINING THE FRAMEWORK

The framework uses the following chapter/section headings.

- Abstract
- Introduction
- Background to the research
- Contexts for the research
- Methodology
- Gathering and interpreting data and generating evidence
- Main findings and significance
- Implications

Here is an outline of how you can use this framework and what should go into each chapter.

Abstract

This is a summary of what the research was about and its main findings. The abstract is about 200–300 words in length. It is not the place to put in quotations or descriptions of practice. It sets out what the claim to knowledge is, and shows how the claim can be seen as valid through the production of authenticated evidence. It is important to say that you are presenting your work as work in progress, which you are now presenting for public testing and critique.

Introduction

Introduce yourself and your research. Say who you are and where you work, and anything special that will help your reader to see the significance of your work and why they should read this document. You should immediately tell your reader what you believe you have achieved. Do this in terms of stating your claim to knowledge, probably in terms of having generated your own theory of practice. Explain why you wanted to do the research and why this may have been problematic, possibly in terms of your experience of yourself as a living contradiction and how you wanted to find ways of living more fully in the direction of your values. Say why it was important to adopt an action research approach, but don't go into detail here because you will develop these ideas in your methodology chapter. Feel free to cross-reference to your different chapters and sections within your report. If this is a scholarly document, set out what your conceptual frameworks are, that is, the main fields of enquiry or key ideas that informed your research, such as issues of justice, gender, or ecological sustainability. These issues will be related to your values. You should say that your research enables you to participate in and contribute to these debates in terms of how you are contributing to new practices and new theory.

Give a brief summary of your chapters and explain whether the reader should read the whole as a beginning-to-end story, or whether they can move around the work without losing the thread. Always tell your reader what you want them to know and help them to see how they are coming to know it.

Background to the research

This is where you set out the background to the research in terms of what inspired you to do it. Some researchers like to combine their background chapter and introduction. Most find that it can be helpful to treat the background as a separate issue, especially as it relates to the values that underpinned the work. For example, you may have experienced bullying or marginalization in the home or the workplace, of yourself or someone else, and this has led you to find ways of overcoming the pain and creating new life-affirming ways of working. Or perhaps you wanted to evaluate your practice and see whether you were living in accordance with your own rhetoric.

Contexts for the research

This is your opportunity to set out in detail the contexts for your research. You may want to analyse them in terms of specific categories such as the following.

Personal contexts

What was going on in your personal/professional life that inspired you to do the research? Were you dissatisfied with the situation you were in? Why? How can your reader see your situation clearly?

Theoretical contexts

How could you relate your research issue to what you were reading in the literature? Could you see issues of injustice that you could relate to the work of Paulo Freire (1972), or issues of freedom that you could relate to the work of Isaiah Berlin (1998), or issues of ecological sustainability that you could relate to the work of Zimmerman et al. (2001)? Were gender issues important, or issues of 'difference', or political action? Aim to establish a link between your own ideas and the ideas in the literature, and show how you drew on the literature to help you develop and test your own thinking. The concepts you are dealing with come to form your conceptual frameworks.

Policy contexts

What was happening in the contexts of policy formation and implementation? Did this affect you and your research? Did policy enable you to work in a way that was consistent with your values? Or not? Did policy allocate funding to privileged groupings rather than the underprivileged groupings you were supporting? Was there a policy on assessment that used benchmarking and standardized testing, which were inappropriate for the kind of work you were doing? Did policy require you to practise in a way that was not consistent with your own preferred way of working? Could you do anything about it? Did you feel that you could contribute to policy by doing your research?

Any other relevant contexts

Mention here any other contexts that may be relevant. Perhaps you are a member of a wildlife trust, which may be significant if you are finding ways of protecting the environment; or you may be in the police service, which will be relevant to exploring how you can improve working practices in rehabilitation centres. Whatever is particularly relevant should be mentioned here. If you work with sexual offenders, or are partially sighted, or a member of a political action group, say so. Let your reader see why your contexts are important to your research.

Methodology

In this section you outline how you planned and carried out your research. Give details of

The research design (plan)

- What was the time scale?
- Where was the research conducted?
- Who were your research participants? Why did you invite these people and not others?
- What resources did you need?
- Whose permission did you need to get? Did you get permission? If so, where can your reader see letters asking and granting permission? If not, why not?

The methodology

- Why action research? Why self-study?
- How did you monitor your actions and your learning, in relation to other people's action and learning?
- How did you plan to gather data and interpret them?

Ensuring ethical conduct

- Say that you were aware of the need for ethical considerations, and sought and obtained permission at all stages of your research as necessary.
- Say where your reader can find your ethics statements and letters of permission.

Gathering and interpreting data and generating evidence

Set out here how you gathered the data, which data gathering techniques you used, and why you used those and not others. Say that you were looking for data in relation to your research issue. Make it clear that you gathered data about your action and your learning.

Explain clearly how you gathered data systematically, so that you could track changes in the ongoing action and possibly see an improvement in terms of the realization of your values. Explain how you sorted your data into categories of analysis, such as conversations and transcripts, and that you began to focus progressively as the data began to form patterns about how you were beginning to influence other people's learning. Also explain how you decided to interpret the data in terms of your values, and the extent to which these values were being realized, and that the values began to emerge as the standards by which you made judgements about your work. Show that you understand the difference between data and evidence, by explaining how you pulled out of the data those pieces that you wished to stand as evidence in support of your claim to knowledge.

Remember that data and evidence can show that a belief may be mistaken as much as justifiable. You may find that the data show that something is not going as you wish, and that you have to rethink the situation. In this case, the data could generate powerful evidence for your claim that you have learned from experience.

Let your reader know that you were aware of the need to submit your data and evidence to the critical scrutiny of others. Say how you negotiated with colleagues to become your critical friends and validation group, how often you met, and what kind of feedback they offered on your work. Say whether you acted on the feedback, or not, and why.

Main findings and significance

At this point, set out what you believe you have found out. This should be both about substantive issues, such as how to manage your budget more efficiently, and about your learning, such as the insights you developed about the need for budgeting. Link your findings with your claim to knowledge. You are saying that you know something that was not known before. You have created your own theory of practice. You can show how you have incorporated ideas from others in the literature, and how you have reconfigured that knowledge in terms of your own context. Do not present your findings as final answers so much as tentative theories, which you are now subjecting to testing and critique. This is the spirit of research: you always regard a solution as provisional and open to refutation and modification.

One of the most important claims you can make is that you have influenced learning for improving practice. This can be in terms of

- Your own learning: you have learned through the process of being aware of your own capacity for learning.
- Your colleagues in your workplace: perhaps they have learned from you and are trying things out for themselves.
- The learning of wider social formations: people have learned from you how to work together so that they too can influence learning.

Explain the significance of your work. Say that you have contributed to new practices in terms of showing how it is possible for people to change their own situations. Say that you have contributed to new theory by explaining how your own thinking and ideas have improved, and how you have deepened your insights around the issue you have been investigating. By focusing on your learning you have come to know differently, and you are making your theory of practice public in order to test and validate your theory and have it accepted as a valuable contribution to the existing body of knowledge. Be confident about saying that people should listen to you and learn from what you have done, both in terms of practice and also in terms of knowledge generation. At this point also be clear about how you have drawn attention to your awareness of the need for methodological rigour in presenting your account of learning. Be clear that whenever you have made a claim to knowledge, you have also articulated the criteria and standards of judgement you have identified. It is as important to say that you have done these things as to have done them.

Implications

What might be the implications of your research for other people? Perhaps they will learn to see things differently, because you have made them think about things in new ways. Perhaps they will begin to think differently, because they will see the world through new eyes. Perhaps they will act differently, because their new thinking will inspire them to develop new practices.

One of the most valuable (and difficult) things to do is persuade people to begin to question their own prejudices. If you can do this, your research will have been most worthwhile. Just as important is to lead people to be aware of their own capacity for learning, where they come to see themselves always as in process, on the edge, never at a point of closure. Perhaps one of the most valuable things action researchers can do is to allow their work to promote new perspectives that celebrate open-endedness, lack of certainty, and a tentative view towards the planet and the life it supports.

2   EXAMPLES OF THE FRAMEWORK IN ACTION

Here are some examples to show these ideas in action. Our own collections of work can be accessed through our published papers and books, and also via our websites: see www.actionresearch.net and www.jeanmcniff.com.

Jean has supported masters-level work in Ireland, and now supports doctoral studies at the University of Limerick. None of these has as yet been submitted for accreditation. Examples of the masters work are available on her website, and show how the above framework has enabled practitioners to organize their ideas in relation to their own contexts.

In the first example, the contents of the chapters are given in expanded form. In the following examples, chapter headings only are given.

HOW CAN I RAISE THE LEVEL OF SELF-ESTEEM OF SECOND YEAR JUNIOR CERTIFICATE SCHOOL PROGRAMME STUDENTS AND CREATE A BETTER LEARNING ENVIRONMENT?

Marian Nugent

Here is the abstract from Marian's dissertation and a summary of her chapters (Nugent 2000). You can access the entire dissertation from http://www.jeanmcniff.com

Abstract

This study shows, I believe, an improvement in my teaching of the Junior Certificate School Programme (JCSP) students. The philosophy of the JCSP is that every student is capable of success. It describes the shift in my thinking and practice from a view of reality as objectified to a view of reality as holistic and integrated. Carr and Kemmis (1986: 24) state: 'A humanistic perspective emphasises that education is a human encounter whose aim is the development of the unique potential of each individual.'

I believe my practice demonstrates this quality. The question which informed my research is: How can I raise the level of self-esteem of second year JCSP students and create a better learning environment? I set out to explore this question in a number of ways: in terms of my own professional development as a reflective practitioner and in terms of the students' development.

In my work with the students I have attempted to develop their respect for one another, within managing behaviour and classroom discipline. I have fostered a climate of mutual respect between the students and myself as year head. The research was in the overall context of classroom management and I followed an action research methodology to locate my research.

A problem which I encountered was that as an authority figure it is easy to maintain the status quo but it is difficult to imagine how things could be different. I have implemented practices, which can be used in order to show a move to a different style of discipline, to teaching and care for the students.

(Continued)

Action research aims to improve our practice and our understanding of that practice. For me, my educational journey has evolved as a result of participation on the MA in Education programme, and I am now further towards my goals of being more understanding of the students and their needs and of encouraging students to believe in their own powers of learning.

Contents

Introduction

To the research project.

Chapter 1   Reasons for doing the research

Here I reflect upon the values I hold that inform my practice as an educator. This chapter also deals with why I want to research this topic and my values underpinning my research. It explains the aims and objectives of the research.

Chapter 2   Contextualisation

This chapter deals with my present context as class teacher, year head and the JCSP coordinator in an inner city school designated disadvantaged. It allows the reader to connect with the relevant background of the school. The descriptions here will act as the background for the research and indicate the reasons I give for the course of action taken during the research project.

Chapter 3   Methodology

This chapter deals with issues of methodology and epistemology. I describe the three main educational research paradigms and compare and contrast the advantages and limitations of each paradigm. I show my responsibility as a researcher by providing an analysis of the main research paradigms, which will include a short history of their origins, and I explain my methodology stating why I have chosen action research and the problematics of action research. I describe in this chapter how important ethical values are to my work and how I maintained them throughout the research. I aim to support my claim that an action research methodology was the best form of research for me to use while I researched this question.

Chapter 4   The project

Here I tell the story of the project. My research question is: How can I raise the level of self-esteem of second year JCSP students and create a better learning environment? This chapter

(Continued)

describes how I set about researching this question and how I discovered through critical reflection and moved on and explored alternative ways of improving my practice, such as encouraging more student participation. I have also described the data gathering methods I used and their value to me, and I supported my descriptions with evidence and validation to show that the claim to improvement in my practice can be reasonably justified. This chapter is built on an action research plan:

- I experienced a problem.
- I sought a solution.
- I implemented the solution.
- I evaluated the outcomes of my actions.
- I reformulated the problem in the light of my evaluation.

I present my findings as a result of this analysis, and show the evidence of my findings.

Chapter 5   Significance of the research

This chapter deals with the significance of my research for the JCSP class and myself. I hope to show the relevance and significance of the study, show my own professional learning and what it has done for my workplace and me. I hope to do this by reflecting on, observing and evaluating the feedback from the students.

Conclusion

I hope to show progress of how I changed my practice and moved from using an authoritarian teaching style to a more caring teaching style. By implementing a class code of good behaviour I have learned the importance that a positive approach can have on the students and how they can benefit from this approach. I will return to my aims and objectives and see how far I have fulfilled them. I will critically review the limitations of the study, and indicate avenues for further possible research.

HOW CAN I HELP THE PRIMARY SCHOOL CHILDREN I TEACH TO DEVELOP THEIR SELF-ESTEEM?

Sally McGinley

Here is the abstract from Sally's dissertation and a summary of her chapters (McGinley 2000). The entire dissertation can be downloaded from http://www.jeanmcniff.com/sally.html.

(Continued)

Abstract

This dissertation tells the story of a study I carried out in my primary classroom in answer to the research question, how do I help the primary school children I teach to develop their self-esteem? Through the process of doing this research, I learned that focusing on care in relationships and care in the learning process can impact positively on the children's self-esteem.

In undertaking this study I had two aims:

- To understand the ways that self-esteem develops and the impact of the classroom experience on that self-esteem, and
- To reflect on and improve my own practice with a view to creating an atmosphere where the children could be enabled to view themselves in a more positive light.

I used an action research methodology, because my intention was to improve my own practice and to involve and learn from the participants in order to enhance the learning experience for all. Through the process of doing the research I learned to reflect on my values, attitudes and relationships with the children as they impacted on my practice and on the children's view of themselves.

In doing the research I developed an enhanced awareness of the emotional needs of the children in my class and a greater understanding of their individuality. I came to understand the impact of self-esteem on learning and I developed a respect for the children's capacity to make decisions about their own learning and for the level of trust they place in me as their class teacher.

In the course of the research I developed an awareness of the need to create a caring practice centred on values of gentleness, respect, kindness and awareness of individual needs. This has implications for the ways I organise learning, attend to individual needs and help the children to manage their relationships with each other and, most importantly, for the way I as teacher show respect for each child.

Contents

Chapter 1   Introduction

(Continued)

Chapter 2   The contexts of the study

2.1   Autobiographical context
2.2   Locational context
2.3   Policy/historical context
2.4   Theoretical context

Chapter 3   Methodology

3.1   Views of knowledge
3.2   Views of knowledge and educational research
3.3   Views of knowledge and of the purpose of researchers
3.4   Methodological and epistemological considerations
3.5   Action research
3.6   The design of the study

Chapter 4   Analysis, interpretation and validation of data

4.1   My aim in engaging in this study
4.2   Overview of this study
4.3   The process of analysis of data
4.4   The story of my research study
4.5   Validation

Chapter 5   Discussion of findings

5.1   The teacher as significant other
5.2   Defining self-esteem and the role of the teacher
5.3   Levels of self-esteem and behaviour
5.4   Autonomy and the enhancement of self-esteem
5.5   The role of programmes in self-esteem enhancement
5.6   The learning context and self-esteem enhancement
5.7   A lived caring vision

Chapter 6   Conclusion

6.1   Research question and aims
6.2   My broad areas of learning
6.3   How my learning relates to the aims I set out
6.4   The limitations of this study
6.5   Future research possibilities

Bibliography and references

Appendices

Jack supports doctoral studies at the University of Bath. Here are some examples of completed studies.

HOW DO I, AS A TEACHER AND EDUCATIONAL ACTION-RESEARCHER, DESCRIBE AND EXPLAIN THE NATURE OF MY PROFESSIONAL KNOWLEDGE?

Kevin Eames

Here is the abstract and summary of chapters from Kevin's PhD thesis (Eames 1995). You can download the entire thesis from http://www.bath.ac.uk/~edsajw/kevin.shtml.

Abstract

This thesis is an attempt to make an original contribution to educational knowledge through a study of my own professional and educational development in action research enquiries of the kind, 'How do I improve what I am doing?' The study includes analyses of my educative relationships in a classroom, educative conversations and correspondences with other teachers and academics. It also integrates the ideas of others from the wider field of knowledge and from dialectical communities of professional educators based at Bath University, Wootton Bassett School and elsewhere. The analyses I make of the resulting challenges to my thinking and practice show how educators in schools can work together, embodying a form of professional knowledge which draws on Thomism and other manifestations of dialectical rationality.

Contributions to educational knowledge are made in relation to educational action research and professional knowledge. The first is concerned with the nature of professional knowledge in education, and how action research can constitute the form of professional knowledge, which I see lacking at present. The second contribution is concerned with how we represent an individual's claim to know their own educational development. These contributions contain an analysis in terms of a dialectical epistemology of professional knowledge, which includes contradiction, negation, transformation and moral responsibility within a dialogical community.

Contents

Chapter 1 An outline of my thesis
Chapter 2 Personal growth through students' reviewing of their own writing
Chapter 3 Dialogues and dialectics: action research and a dialectical form of classroom-based educational knowledge
Chapter 4 How action research can be used in an educational community
Chapter 5 Rethinking teachers' dialogues as educational knowledge

(Continued)

HOW DO I AS A TEACHER-RESEARCHER CONTRIBUTE TO THE DEVELOPMENT OF A LIVING EDUCATIONAL THEORY THROUGH AN EXPLORATION OF MY VALUES IN MY PROFESSIONAL PRACTICE?

Erica Holley

Here is the abstract and summary of chapters from Erica Holley's (1997) MPhil thesis. You can download the entire thesis from http://www.bath.ac.uk/~edsajw/erica.shtml.

Abstract

My thesis is a description and explanation for my life as a teacher and a researcher in an 11 to 16 comprehensive school in Swindon from 1990 to 1996. I claim that it is a contribution to educational knowledge and educational research methodology through the understanding it shows of the form, meaning and values in my living educational theory as an individual practitioner as I researched my question, How do I improve what I am doing in my professional practice?

   With its focus on the development of the meanings of my educational values and educational knowledge in my professional practice I intend this thesis to show the integration of the educational processes of transforming myself by my own knowledge and the knowledge of others and of transforming my educational knowledge through action and reflection. I also intend the thesis to be a contribution to debates about the use of values as being living standards of judgement in educational research.

(Continued)

Contents

Introduction

SUMMARY

This chapter has outlined a basic framework for writing a report for accreditation. Examples from a range of settings are offered. The chapter has also emphasized that, while the ideas here can act as a guide, individual people have adapted them to their own needs, producing reports of outstanding quality for higher degree accreditation. Examples are given to show the range and variety.

The next chapter deals with issues of further dissemination.

22

Publishing and Disseminating Your Research

You have completed your research and produced your report. Now what? Your report is not much use locked away. You have to put it to use and let it serve your purposes. This chapter gives ideas about how you can do this, and why. It contains these sections.

1   Publishing and disseminating your research
2   Contributing to the knowledge base
3   An example of a significant contribution

1   PUBLISHING AND DISSEMINATING YOUR RESEARCH

You can disseminate your work to an increasingly wide audience – workplace, professional, global – and in a variety of forms – written, oral, multimedia.

Potential audiences

Colleagues in your workplace

Throughout your project you have kept colleagues informed. Now you need to tell them your findings, and why these may be important for them (see Chapter 23 for the significance of your work). You will need to get permission from your manager to disseminate your work, certainly in the workplace, if not for wider audiences. Always check beforehand. Try to get their active support by asking them to mention your work at a staff meeting or write a cover note for the report as an endorsement. Aim to communicate to colleagues how much you have learned, and suggest diplomatically that they could learn too.

Your professional field

Take and create opportunities to connect with wider professional circles, explaining the significance of your learning and its potential for their own. Emphasize that you are contributing to new professional practices and knowledge. They can do the same and can form new communities of practice that can link with wider global communities. Most of the people whose work is cited in this book have published for their professional communities in a range of different ways. Publishing your work may sound daunting, but it is achievable. Don't leave it to someone else to publish the ideas you have already thought about. Get on and do it yourself.

The wider public

Be bold in publishing your work for global dissemination. Write articles and books. Even the most widely published authors had to start somewhere. Learn how to write for the market (see next section). Study journals and see the kind of articles that are accepted, and the language they use. Learn how to write a book proposal. Many publishing houses have websites that give guidelines on submitting proposals. Editors are constantly on the lookout for promising proposals, and most are prepared to work with you to refine your proposal and get your book published. It is a competitive market, so basic advice is to take your work seriously and professionally, learn how to write for the market, and be prepared to work hard. You must be in love with your subject matter, because you are going to live alone with it for a very long time.

Form of publication

You can publish your work in a range of forms.

Written reports

Aim to write reports, articles and books. Your initial publication will possibly be your research report, but you can adapt that for new outlets. Being serious about disseminating your work means studying the market. Where do other people like you publish? Which journals and magazines? Which publishing houses? Search engines can be valuable. Type in an author's name and you can gather a lot of information by following the links. Library databases are great if you have access. The most important resource, as always, is yourself and your own passionate commitment that you have something to say that other people should hear. The golden rule for publishing is to study and learn to write for a particular market. Writing is a job, the same as any other job that takes preparation and practice. Learn to accept critique, and don't be dismayed if your work is rejected initially. Learn from the experience. What did you do right? What could you have done better? It can take years for work to get published, but if you have faith that you have something to say that other people should hear, you will succeed.

Oral presentations

Getting people to listen to you means engaging and sustaining their interest so that they will want to hear more. You can do this by developing specific presentation skills, including these.

Believe in yourself and others
Let your passion show through. Say that you had a dream and you now want to share it. Let your audience know that they too can do similar things and can also contribute to other people's improved learning and practice.

Get maximum participation and involvement
Don't tell other people what to do. Suggest that they can do what you have done. Be inviting. Relate well and maintain eye contact. Keep a light but serious touch throughout. Get involvement. Set up instant pair work, or conversations in threes. You can do this with an audience of hundreds, but negotiate before-hand that they will stop when you give the signal. Once people begin talking about something that interests them, they often don't want to stop.

Watch your language
Always talk in the language of the community you are addressing. If you use a new professional word, say so and explain it, but don't talk down to anyone. Engage them as educated participants who are interested in what you have to say. Keep it simple and accessible.

Organize your material
Plan in advance what you are going to say, and then say it. Don't get side-tracked, and stick to the point. If someone raises a question, make sure you address it at some point. If you can't, say so. People will respect your lack of knowledge but they will not respect you if you dodge the issue. If you are speaking from notes, do not read them but glance at them occasionally to keep you on track. Speak from the heart, not from notes.

Electronic communication

Electronic communication can put you in touch with virtually anyone any-where. You can disseminate your work through your own or your organization's website, or by sending it to an e-mail list which you or others may compile.

This is a wonderfully attractive and valuable form of dissemination because you can use multimedia, and also connect people to others by using live links, which relate your work to others in the field. You can immediately show the significance of your research by disseminating its relevance to the field, and explaining how people can renegotiate their meanings so that practice and knowledge can advance. As with other forms of dissemination, you have to learn how to do this, which takes time and practice. One of the rewards of electronic communication is that you tend to get rapid feedback, so the sense of isolation that many writers experience in conventional print publication tends to be reduced.

2   CONTRIBUTING TO THE KNOWLEDGE BASE

A knowledge base refers to everything that is known in a particular field. The knowledge base is usually found in the publications of that field.

The idea of creating a new kind of knowledge base is well developed in the teaching profession. In 2001, Catherine Snow, then President of the American Educational Research Association, called for the development of a knowledge base that was created by teachers for teachers. This, she said, would enable teachers to access developments in the field and see what they had to do to advance it further. The work reported in this book is already making that contribution. We now want to extend the idea from the teaching profession to embrace all professions. We want to strengthen the idea that all practitioners should regard themselves as involved in education, though not necessarily in the teaching profession, with important things to say about learning, and how to develop learning through the systematic testing of knowledge claims.

Bear in mind that one kind of knowledge base already exists, but not in the form that all practitioners can access, or that has direct relevance to everyday practice. This knowledge base resides in the publications of the professional elites that Schön (1983) mentioned. These publications usually take the form of the exposition and linguistic analysis of ideas, which are often unrelated to practice. The accumulation of articles and books tends to be written for peers in the professional elites, not for practitioners, and this reinforces the idea that one grouping is designated an elite who can understand these things, while another grouping is designated a learner group, some of whom are incapable of understanding, let alone contributing. We are saying in this book that all are capable of both understanding and contributing, and should contribute, and ways need to be found to communicate this message and show its truth.

One of the ways to communicate the message is to develop a knowledge base by practitioners for practitioners. This knowledge base should incorporate the ideas of professional elites and develop them through systematic critique, for example, by showing their relevance (or not) to practice. Similarly, the work of practitioners should be incorporated into the thinking of the elites, and tested for validity in relation to whether practitioners support their claims through stringent methodologies. This will take time, given the current situation, but it is already happening in many places. One of the outcomes that is already happening, as demonstrated in this book, is that previously artificial categorizations of elites and practitioners disappear from the culture and the language. People may work in different settings and have different responsibilities, but all are equal in status and in the recognition that they are valuable people who have the right to be listened to when they stake their claims about how they wish to conduct their lives.

Doing this can be risky for anyone who positions themselves in what is still seen as one camp or the other. It can be risky for those who regard themselves as belonging to an elite, because it means relinquishing the power that this positioning gives them, and recognizing themselves as practitioners. It can be risky for practitioners, too, because it means leaving the security of subjugation. It is easy to grumble about a situation, but rather difficult to find the energy to do something about it. It is risky for all who run the gauntlet of the comments of peers, many of whom also wish to keep them in their place. Breaking down barriers and coming out from hiding takes energy and commitment, a willingness to move forward while accepting the hazards involved. This is well demonstrated in the work of Joan Whitehead (2003), who speaks of 'making the probable possible'. Joan Whitehead and Bernie Fitzgerald (2004), who are practitioners in higher education, have renegotiated roles and responsibilities with others whom they support on schools-based mentoring programmes, a practice that has involved the development of new relationships and ways of working between university staff and school-based mentors, and confronting the hierarchy which had previously existed. Such renegotiation is often not easy, because it means all have to unlearn what they have previously learned from the culture, and change their language accordingly. It means developing new cultures that have to be tried out, and developing new languages that often take time to learn. Joan and Bernie show how this can be done.

Contributing to the knowledge base takes time, energy and commitment. It takes the efforts of all to build up the publications and disseminate the work. This is essential if ideas are to be disseminated and take hold in the public mind. The position in contemporary work is that there are two knowledge bases, the traditional propositional one of those who still position themselves as professional elites, and the newer person-centred one of those who position themselves as practitioner-researchers. Whereas these knowledge bases used to be in an asymmetrical relationship of power, they are both now concurrent. It is well to bear this in mind, and also the constant struggle involved, because a knowledge base is developed through regular maintenance and constant regeneration. This means regular contributions from the community of practitioners whose ideas make up the knowledge base. If the energy flags, it is salutary to remember that practitioners in the other knowledge base are working hard to build their own platforms, from which they can speak with authority. This may be a game, but it is a seriously important game, in which there are winners and losers, some of whom are the people you work with now and future genera-tions of practitioners. The future, it is hoped, will be that the two knowledge bases will merge, and all will learn how to learn from the other, so that all work is regarded as potentially valuable and as contributing to a wider understand-ing of creating a better world. For the meantime, for the current practitioner-researcher knowledge base to remain intact, and grow, you have to become an active participant.

3   AN EXAMPLE OF A SIGNIFICANT CONTRIBUTION

Here is an example of one such contribution. It is the entire proposal for a symposium at the 2004 American Educational Research Association (AERA), one of the most prestigious educational research associations. It is significant in several senses. First, it shows how practitioners from all education sectors and from different countries came together with shared intent to make their research findings public and to test them against the critical perspectives of others. Second, the symposium was significant in the sense that it constituted a shared living theory that Colin Smith has spoken about (page 198). What is particularly striking is, third, how the symposium itself represents generative transformational capacity, both in terms of how the settings develop from individual classrooms to worldwide systems, and in terms of the transforma-tion of ontological commitments into epistemological standards of judge-ment, which in turn transform into social practices which have potential for global influence.

We are using this also as an example of how to submit a proposal. Further examples are given in the following chapters. Getting a proposal accepted for a paper or a symposium is competitive, so you have to observe all protocols carefully and write to a high standard. The AERA and other research organi-zations require proposals to be presented anonymously. Even citations from the literature should not give away the proposer's identity. In the example, we have added the names and affiliations of the presenters in square brackets, to honour them and their contributions. You can see other proposals also on our websites. They are there to help you organize your own proposal for successful submis-sion, and contribute to the growing knowledge base yourself.

The transformative potentials of individuals' collaborative self-studies for sustainable global networks of communication

16 April 2004 from 12.25 p.m. to 1.55 p.m. in the San Diego Marriott – Columbia 2, North Tower, Lobby Level

[SYMPOSIUM PARTICIPANTS AND THEIR AFFILIATIONS

- Caitríona McDonagh, Bernie Sullivan and Jean McNiff from the University of Limerick
- Joan Whitehead and Bernie Fitzgerald from the University of the West of England
- Cheryl Black and Jackie Delong from the Grand Erie District School Board
- Jack Whitehead of the University of Bath and Margaret Farren of Dublin City University]

AIMS OF THE SESSION

This session aims to demonstrate the transformative potential of individuals' collaborative self-studies for the development of sustainable global educational networks of communication. For this potential to be realised we see certain practices as necessary. Here we explain some of these practices and how we believe we are achieving and justifying them by making our evidence base and the outcomes visible through multimedia representations of our learning.

We are a group of teachers, professional educators, and education administrators, working across the levels of education systems. Each of us asks, 'How do I improve what I am doing for personal and social good?' Each of us aims to generate our personal educational theories (23) to show how we are doing so through our contributions to the education of social formations in our own settings. This symposium is an opportunity to test the validity of these claims against the critical judgement of peers, in the spirit of the AERA organisers' themes, to make public a consideration of 'what counts as evidence in high-quality educational research, how educational research informs and is informed by practice, and the nature of the social, political, and historical contexts in which educational research is conducted and used' (see http://www.aera.net) (25). We are claiming that we are not only fulfilling those high principles, but also transforming them into the kinds of practices that contribute to sustainable forms of living worldwide (5).

Given the fragility of the world we are in, we believe that educational endeavours should increasingly focus on developing international understanding in the interests of nurturing forms of life that respect the integrity and right to self-determination of all (3, 20). Our symposium explains how we try to do this. We believe that the validity of our efforts lies in the generation of educational theories of professional practice. A criterion for the legitimation of such validity claims is the capacity of educators to show how they are holding themselves accountable for their work as they seek to exercise their educative influence at local and global levels. In our symposium, we explain how we are fulfilling our understanding that acceptance of individual responsibility for ourselves and to each other through collaborative self-study is at the heart of global influence (2), and we are testing our claims in the public domain.

We aim to produce evidence to support our claims that we are contributing to more sustainable forms of global understanding through education, by offering descriptions and explanations of our practices in different education settings, as we try to exercise our educative influence for social good. We show how our public accounts of theory generation contribute to a systematic knowledge base (22). From the ground of clarifying the meanings of our embodied values and using them as educational standards of judgement we show how contributing to this knowledge base constitutes a form of theory generation that has profound implications for educational practices worldwide.

Our presentation is substantively and methodologically transformational, and takes the form of four papers presented collaboratively. Each of the papers explains the learning processes of the authors, as they research the realisation of their educational values within their social situations. The series of papers shows the transformation of influence, from a consideration of the moral commitments of self-study, through the realisation of those commitments across a range of professional practices and through expanding spheres of systemic influence.

EDUCATIONAL SIGNIFICANCE

The educational significance of our presentation lies in showing how, in response to Snow's call to systematize our professional knowledge base (22), the collaborative production of evidence-based accounts can contribute to this knowledge base, and how this knowledge base, in response to Coulter and Wiens (4), Feldman (9) and Noffke (18), can influence the trajectories of social change. We show how what begins as the personal accountability of self-study has the potential to impact on processes of organisational and social change at local levels, and how this can transform into the education of social formations at global levels. We explain how the knowledge base, which contains multimedia presentations (8) of personal enquiries undertaken collaboratively, can be disseminated through global networks, in live and electronic forms; how these networks contain the potentials for sustainable forms of education that have implications for future educational practices (13); and how these practices have reciprocal influence at local and global level. Drawing on Bateson's (1) idea that the patterns that connect need to manifest generative transformational potential, we explain how our educational practices are realisations of metaphors of transformation through reciprocal mutuality. We explain how the social processes of local and global education interactions are sustained through their capacity to inform one another. We also explain how these social processes constitute a form of living theory generation that feeds back into practice, so that new practices become the grounds for new forms of theory. The significance of our individual and collaborative work lies, we believe, in its capacity for reciprocal epistemological and social transformation. Our presentation offers theoretical justification for our work, and shows its practical consequences in the lives of real people.

SUMMARY OF PRESENTATIONS

PAPER 1   ONTOLOGICAL COMMITMENTS IN SELF–STUDY

Presenter 1   [Jack Whitehead, University of Bath]
Presenter 2   [Jean McNiff, University of Limerick]
Presenter 3   [Margaret Farren, Dublin City University] (for Margaret Farren's website
               see http://webpages.dcu.ie/~farrenm)

An elementary moral principle is that no one should expect another to do some-thing they are not prepared to do themselves. In our paper we explain how this commitment acts as a core principle for our work as professional educators and educational theorists, and we set out the ideas and values to which we hold ourselves accountable.

We are each undertaking our separate enquiries as we support educators in higher degree study in different countries. Our enquiries focus on explaining what we do as professional educators that will influence the quality of learning of others.

We encourage educators across the professions to ask questions of the kind, 'How do I improve what I am doing for personal and social benefit?' as we do. We make explicit the kind of educative influence we hope to exercise by producing authenticated accounts of our work, which contain evidence that shows how we hold inviolable the endowment of all to exercise their originality of mind and critical judgement.

Theorising processes of self–study, we believe, should go beyond conceptual analyses of the potential worth of self–study, and explain how the worth is embodied within the practice. Accepting that self–study is a form of educational research that has significant potentials for the education of social formations, we therefore aim to transform discourses of regulatory principles into discourses of political practices (17) which show the passionate investment involved in a commitment to living in the direction of one's educational values. These are ontological commitments that embed issues of epistemology and methodology.

In our efforts to create a systematic knowledge base, in response to Snow (22) and Hiebert, Gallimore and Stigler (12), we make available the work of ourselves and those we support as learning resources for use worldwide. Our work in education knows no frontiers. We explain how we are transforming the social, political, and historical contexts within which our research is located into new forms of global influence (see 11). Our methodologies are first to exercise self–critique in relation to the professional judgements we make; second to invite critique through our networked communications with peers; third to present that critical process to an expanded critical forum in the shape of this presentation. We hope in this way to strengthen our interconnecting networks of communicative action in which individuals, groups, communities and networks can share accounts of learning in order to live more fully their educational values in their varied contexts.

The papers that follow demonstrate the reciprocal influence between ourselves and others with whom we work in a variety of education settings.

PAPER 2   LEARNING FROM AND WITH OUR PUPILS

Presenter 4   [Caitríona McDonagh, University of Limerick]
Presenter 5   [Bernie Sullivan, University of Limerick]

Our work as primary teachers in Dublin focuses on helping our pupils to maximise their own potentials for learning. Our professional commitments are informed by our values of social justice that hold as sacred the right of all to learn, regardless of social or academic positioning, as well as our educational values to do with the right of all to exercise their originality of mind and critical judgement in order to learn in ways that are appropriate for them.

We work in separate schools, both with young children with so-called 'special educational needs'. Some of these children come from the Traveller community, a community that is educationally marginalised in Ireland (14). Through studying our practices, we have been able to crystallise our initially tacit concerns into explicit concerns about how our children were not learning because they were systemati-cally disadvantaged by the traditional socio-political contexts of education that banish children who are 'different' to the educational margins (10, 19). In trying to teach our children so that they could learn, we concluded that our traditional pedagogies were contributing to the marginalisation, and we needed to develop new pedagogies that were grounded in the pupils' ways of learning. Our research, as adults involved in professional learning and mindful of the new challenges of educational theory and practice (21), involved generating evidence to show how we could support our claims that our new ways of working had implications for organ-isational and social change (16). Our evidence demonstrates the validity of theoris-ing our practices as a new (for us) integrated model of professionals' and pupils' learning, rather than perceive teaching and learning as separate realms of discourse. At our presentation we will produce some of this evidence, using multimedia forms of representation. We also hope to explain how our research is impacting on our institutions, and on what counts as good professional practice in Ireland.

PAPER 3   EXPERIENCING AND EVIDENCING LEARNING: NEW WAYS OF WORKING WITH MENTORS AND TRAINEES IN A TRAINING SCHOOL PARTNERSHIP

Presenter 6   [Joan Whitehead, University of the West of England]
Presenter 7   [Bernie Fitzgerald, University of the West of England]

As the organisers of AERA have identified there is a questioning of the role of higher education institutions in the initial training and continuing professional develop-ment of teachers. This questioning has also been evidenced in England and has led to government requirements for greater involvement by schools in initial teacher training and a central determination of training outcomes. This has tended to minimise innovation and produce a culture of compliance.

More recently the social and political context has begun to recognise the limitations of centralised control and the government has encouraged schools, in collaboration with higher education institutions, to explore and try out new approaches to training teachers, to carry out and use teaching research.

As university-based teacher educators involved in a Training School working with PGCE (Postgraduate Certificate of Education) trainees and school-based mentors, we have been involved in developing a model of mentoring which has given trainees and mentors a critical voice and vocabulary of reflection whilst building a more democratic community of professional practice. In this process we have reflected on our own learning and on our commitments and values. This has caused us to reappraise the interconnectedness of our training partnership and the implications for our own practice and that of others.

We see as key to this new model, which involved using multimedia to record collaborative reflection and critique by mentors and trainees, a particular quality of relationship between them and between university- and school-based staff. This we believe is best characterised by a climate of professional learning involving mutuality, trust, and respect as well as the kind of open-mindedness espoused by (24). Such qualities have enabled dialogue to take place, and the situated learning of mentors, tutors and trainees to be recorded and, as (12) have advocated, to be made public via a multimedia website thereby contributing to a professional knowledge base for teaching. This process has enhanced the learning of participants as well as contributed to a network of communication about the nature of professional knowledge and learning within and beyond this particular community of practice (15). We see this presentation as another way of communicating our work to ascertain its credibility and usefulness to other teacher-researchers and to those involved in formulating and enacting policy about teacher training and development.

Our intent is, and continues to be, to rethink the respective contributions of higher education and schools to the professional development of new and more established members of the teaching profession, to open up our current thinking to critique by others and to explore its transformative potential for ourselves and for others locally as well as globally.

PAPER 4   HOW CAN WE IMPROVE OUR PRACTICE OF SUPPORTING TEACHERS IN OUR SCHOOL SYSTEM, AS THEY RESEARCH THEIR PROFESSIONAL PRACTICE TO IMPROVE STUDENT LEARNING?

Presenter 8   [Jackie Delong, Grand Erie District School Board]
Presenter 9   [Cheryl Black, Grand Erie District School Board]

This paper describes our work in a school district as we research our support for other educators who are researching their practice. In our respective roles as a school superintendent and an elementary school principal, we have worked as co-researchers with teachers, consultants and administrators, in our school system, in the successful completion of our masters and doctoral self-study degrees. In both roles, we model our commitment to research our own professional practice. These practices include our engagement with the political processes related to the provision of resources for learning. In our presentation we will produce authenticated evidence to explain our influence as we investigate our ability to support teachers in their quest to improve student learning, as we research together. Some of the evidence will be drawn from a successfully completed, six-year doctoral programme into the support provided by a superintendent for the development of an action research approach to professional development (6). Other evidence will be drawn from our work together as co-researchers and critical friends within our school board as we supported a successful cohort of some 14 teacher-researchers in their own masters enquiries (7).

Responding to Snow (22), the paper will show the ongoing contribution of teacher-researchers in a school board to the professional knowledge base of teaching, both in published books and in the electronic journal, *Ontario Action Researcher*. This contribution will include an analysis of the significance of social context in influencing our practice and learning.

Evidence of our influence will come from our personal journals, interviews with those we are supporting, together with validated narratives from ourselves and teachers. It will include an analysis of our educational influence in the Ontario Educational Research Council and the communication of our ideas in international forums of educational researchers. The processes of validation will focus on the responses of validation groups to our claims to know our own learning, the teachers' learning and improvements in student learning. They will also focus on our claims to know our influence in the education of a school culture and in the social formation of a school board.

STRUCTURE OF THE SESSION

The presentations will be linked by participants' critical commentary, as they explain what may be the significance of these individual and collective enquiries to sustainable educational networks of communication. They will invite critique from the audience on their claims to be contributing to the development of sustainable global networks of self-study researchers through the extension of their relationships in Ontario, Ireland and the UK to self-study researchers in Japan, China, Israel, India and Australia. Members of the audience will be invited to comment on how they themselves might contribute to strengthening these networks of communicative action, by showing how they hold themselves accountable for their work as they share their narratives of learning.

REFERENCES

1   Bateson, G. (1979/2002) *Mind and Nature: A Necessary Unity.* Cresskill, NJ, Hampton Press and the Institute for Intercultural Studies.

2   Chomsky, N. (1996) *Powers and Prospects: Reflections on Human Nature and the Social Order.* London, Pluto Press.

3   Chomsky, N. (2000) *Chomsky on MisEducation.* New York, Rowman and Littlefield.

4   Coulter, D. and Wiens, J. (2002) Educational Judgement: Linking the Actor and the Spectator, *Educational Researcher* 31 (4): 15–25.

5   Dallmayr, F. R. (2001) *Achieving Our World: Toward a Global and Plural Democracy.* New York, Rowman and Littlefield.

6   Delong, J. (2002) *How Can I Improve My Practice as a Superintendent of Schools and Create My Own Living Educational Theory?* PhD thesis, University of Bath. Retrieved 27 July 2003 from http://www.actionresearch.net/delong.shtm.

7   Delong, J. and Black, C. (eds) (2002) *Passion in Professional Practice*, Vol. 2. Retrieved 27 July 2003 from http://www.actionresearch.ca/

8   Eisner, E. (1997) The Promise and Perils of Alternative Forms of Data Representation, *Educational Researcher* 26 (6): 4–10.

9   Feldman, A. (2003) Validity and Quality in Self–Study, *Educational Researcher* 32 (3): 26–28.

10   Gillborn, D. (1995) *Racism and Antiracism in Real Schools.* Buckingham, Open University Press.

11   Herman, E. S. and McChesney, R. W. (1997) Alternatives to the Status Quo?, Chapter 7 in *The Global Media: The New Missionaries of Corporate Capitalism.* London, Continuum.

12   Hiebert, J., Gallimore, R. and Stigler, J. W. (2002) A Knowledge Base for the Teaching Profession: What Would It Look Like and How Can We Get One?, *Educational Researcher* 31 (5): 3–15.

13   Hochschild, A. R. (2001) Global Care Chains and Emotional Surplus Value, in W. Hutton and A. Giddens (eds) *On the Edge: Living with Global Capitalism.* London, Vintage.

14   Kenny, M. (1997) *The Routes of Resistance: Travellers and Second–Level Schooling.* Aldershot, Ashgate.

15   Lave, J. and Wenger, E. (1991) *Situated Learning.* Cambridge: Cambridge University Press.

16   McNiff, J. with J. Whitehead (2000) *Action Research in Organisations.* London, Routledge.

17   Mouffe, C. (2000) For an Agonistic Model of Democracy, in N. O. Sullivan (ed.) *Political Theory in Transition.* London, Routledge.

18   Noffke, S. (1997) Professional, Personal, and Political Dimensions of Action Research, in M. Apple (ed.) *Review of Research in Education*, Vol. 22. Washington: AERA.

19   O'Boyle, M. and MacAonghusa, M. (1990) *The Alienation of Travellers from the Education System: A Study in Values Orientation.* MEd thesis, University College Dublin.

20   Russell, B. (1932) *Education and the Social Order*. London, Unwin.

21   Schoenfeld, A. H. (1999) Looking Toward the 21st Century: Challenges of Educational Theory and Practice, *Educational Researcher* 28 (7): 4–14.

22   Snow, C. E. (2001) Knowing What We Know: Children, Teachers, Researchers. Presidential Address to AERA, 2001, in Seattle, *Educational Researcher* 30 (7): 3–9.

23   Whitehead, J. (1989) Creating a Living Educational Theory from Questions of the Kind, 'How Do I Improve My Practice?', *Cambridge Journal of Education* 19 (1): 137–153. Retrieved 27 July 2003 from http://www.bath.ac.uk/~edsajw/writings/livtheory.html.

24   Zeichner, K. M. and Liston, D. P. (1996) *Reflective Teaching: An Introduction*. Mahwah, NJ: Lawrence Erlbaum.

25   AERA (2003) 2004 Annual Meeting Theme: Enhancing the Visibility and Credibility of Educational Research. Retrieved 29 July 2003 from http://www.aera.net/meeting/am2004/call04/theme/.

SUMMARY

This chapter has talked about how you can publish and disseminate your research for a range of different audiences. The chapter has also made the point that your report now contributes to the knowledge base, so others may access your work and learn from it. In this sense, your report represents a contribution that has profound significance. An example is given of such a significant contribution.

The next part goes on to explain the nature of that significance, and how it can contribute to the education of social formations for the development of good social orders.

Part VII

How Do I Show the Significance of My Knowledge?

Part VII explains how you can communicate the significance of what you have done and learned through engaging in your action enquiry. It contains the following chapters.

These chapters show how a personal action enquiry has the generative transformational potential to influence thinking and practices in a wide range of contexts, especially in terms of the development of new organizational cultures of enquiry, and potentially with global influence.

In terms of your own action enquiry, you are now asking, 'How do I use what I have learned for my own and others' benefit? How do I explain the significance of my learning and my practice for encouraging the kind of learning that will transform my own and wider organizational and social practices?'

23

Explaining the Significance of Your Research

The significance of action research as a form of enquiry is in relation to its capacity to generate and test theory to improve learning in order to improve practice. In other words, it is possible through action research to offer explanations for processes of improving learning. The significance of your action enquiry is that you are able to generate and test your living theory of improving learning, in relation to your own learning, the learning of others in workplaces and social situations, and the education of social formations. This chapter discusses these issues. It is in three sections.

1 The significance of your research in relation to your own learning
2 The significance of your research in relation to the learning of others in workplaces and social situations
3 The significance of your research in relation to the education of social formations

1 THE SIGNIFICANCE OF YOUR RESEARCH IN RELATION TO YOUR OWN LEARNING

You are claiming that your practice has improved in an identifiable way. This did not happen by accident. It happened because you studied what you were doing, and made specific decisions in relation to possible choices. You became aware that your learning was the grounds for your practice. As you began to critique and modify your existing practice, you became aware of how you could do things differently. You tried out new ways, and you tested your provisional thinking about their effectiveness in informing other people's learning by listening to what those people said about you and how they were responding to you. You are able to stand back and comment on those processes that involved your own and other people's learning.

Here are some examples of how people have done this, taken from work submitted for higher degrees. Once again most of these examples are taken from people working in education. There is urgent need for practitioners in other professions to make their stories of learning public, so that others may learn from them.

Ivan O'Callaghan (1997) writes the following abstract for his masters dissertation:

> My concern in undertaking this research was to study my role as principal of a second level school, with a view to understanding how I might improve my practice. This concern arose out of my belief that the role of principalship, in the mid-nineties, calls for improved awareness of the human factors which influence the school environment. People are, in my view, the *raison d'être* of the educational system. Yet it is my experience that administrative efficiency due to the demands of a commercialised market approach has replaced the enhancement of holistic human development as a central tenet …
>
> I have as a result of this research committed my own values and beliefs to paper, which has had the benefit of clarifying the thought processes I apply in conduct-ing my practice. I am more convinced than ever as a result of my findings and published research, that the delivery of education should focus its attention on holistic human development rather than on commercial technical excellence for the benefit of the school community.

As part of his understanding of the significance of his work, he writes:

> I am acutely aware of my influence in the role of principal on the effectiveness of the school community in achieving its educational goals. I can see it in the faces of those who interact with me on a daily basis. It is a humbling experience to know that I can influence so many lives through my practice. This is why it is so important for me to establish as often as possible by means such as used in this research study positive direction from and for that community … If [teachers] are dissatisfied with my practice then it can result in a reduction of effort on their part in maintaining the momentum necessary to derive maximum potential for all concerned.

Thérèse Burke (1997) writes the following abstract for her masters dissertation:

> My research recounts the steps I took to address my professional concerns that my belief in the values of education as emancipatory and the uniqueness of the indi-vidual were denied. It shows how I attempted to develop a theory of learning difference through action and reflection, as I researched the question, 'How can I improve my practice as a learning support teacher?' …
>
> In my dissertation I intend to show how I moved from a deficit model of learn-ing remediation to a theory of learning difference. I investigated new methods of learning support, which I believe resulted in the development of a more collabo-rative consultative model of practice.
>
> Finally, I hope my dissertation demonstrates that I have taken my first tentative steps towards the development of an emancipatory theory of learning difference.

Reflecting on the significance of her work, she says:

> Most importantly the critical self-reflective aspect of my work required me to look at who I was and where I was situated, both personally and professionally, as I approached my twenty-fifth year of teaching … This recognition of my own professional development complements my own theory of learning difference. I no longer view the child as the sum of all her parts, but as an individual with her own ontological and epistemological needs, a person who can engage with others and use her potential to learn at this moment … I am now conscious of what I would like to name as an 'epistemological equality' between myself and my students. I do not have a monopoly on knowledge: mine is not the only way of knowing … This was a significant learning experience for me as a practising teacher. There can be a smugness about those in education, myself included, who suggest that the values of the school system are the only values that matter, and that what it offers is the only way to be. I challenge this assumption. I believe the theory of individuality which is at the basis of an understanding of learning difference makes a nonsense of this. When I reflect on who and how I was in the past, I realise that I would always have paid lip service to this theory, but now I know its truth and I claim it as an educational value of my own.

2   THE SIGNIFICANCE OF YOUR RESEARCH IN RELATION TO THE LEARNING OF OTHERS IN WORKPLACES AND SOCIAL SITUATIONS

You can explain how your work has influenced the learning of others so that they have been inspired to investigate how their learning can improve practice. Your theory of practice is yours alone, yet it has the transformative potential to influence new theories, that is, the ones that your colleagues and others in wider fields will create to account for their own practices. Those new theories will contain descriptions of what people did, that is, what aspects of practice they changed, and also explanations for why they did what they did and for what purpose. Your theory of practice therefore has the potential for transformative influence in relation to practice (what is done to improve learning), and also in relation to theory (how explanations can be offered for the learning processes involved).

Here is an example to show how this can be done.

Karen O'Shea (2000) writes the following abstract for her masters dissertation that sets out the aims of her research:

> This research is rooted in the act of reflective enquiry and focuses on my practice. [I am] a human rights educator who is concerned that students of all ages and abilities have access to an education that includes a strong commitment to human rights and citizenship education, [and] it illustrates how I set about influencing a national curriculum. It aims to contribute to the field of human rights and citizenship education by illuminating the curriculum development process and highlighting how it can benefit from personal reflection and collaboration.

It also documents how I, by seeking to become an agent of change in my own context, was drawn into a deeper exploration of my values, which in turn challenged me to explore my understanding of my practice. I reached a stage in my research where I describe my educational practice as a reflective, value-based community activity that seeks to encourage the development of a more just society within which all can reach their fullest potential. Thus the research highlights how understanding can be generated through the process of action and reflection ...

From my research I suggest that educational practice is generative in nature in that it is in a continual state of growth and development. In conclusion, I explore the implications of my learning for educational theory and practice, in particular for the development of communities of learning and on-going teacher education. I suggest that teacher education is a life-long process and that developing an understanding of one's practice provides an ideal starting point for on-going professional development.

Commenting on the significance of her work, Karen says:

As a result of my research I would now suggest that my practice is a reflective, value-based community activity, which seeks to encourage the development of a more just society within which all can reach their fullest potential. As both a human rights educator and curriculum developer my practice is concerned with the betterment not only of the educational experience of young people in the classroom, but also with the development of educational experiences for teachers and others. My practice is therefore a hopeful activity.

In relation to my emerging understanding of my own practice I would suggest that reflectivity is concerned with remaining attentive to what is going on within myself as a practitioner, how I am responding to people and events within my everyday practice. My practice does not exist outside of the relationships I live every day. It exists in relationship to my co-workers, my colleagues, teachers with whom I work on a number of curriculum development projects. The idea of being a reflective practitioner is core to how I develop these relationships in ways which are just and respectful. The idea of reflectivity is also important as it challenges me to go to the heart of what I do. To be willing to ask questions about myself, my motives, and to regularly confront such questions as 'what is really going on here?' ... From the evidence I have provided this understanding is more than simply a theory of practice but is a living theory (Whitehead 1989). It resides in me and emerges through my reflection and action.

3   THE SIGNIFICANCE OF YOUR RESEARCH IN RELATION TO THE EDUCATION OF SOCIAL FORMATIONS

By 'the education of social formations' we mean changes in the rules that regulate social organizations and that move the social formation in the direction of values that carry hope for the future of humanity. This involves the learning processes that people engage in when they decide to improve their collective capacity for generating theory for improving learning. This is a crucial aspect of social renewal, and has deep implications for policy formation and implementation (see Chapter 25). Most theories of social renewal are grounded in bodies of propositional work that tell how social renewal can come about: the development literatures are frequently grounded in analyses of the flow of economic capital; the literatures of peace education tend to be grounded in analyses of the distribution of justice and entitlement; and the literatures of social renewal are often grounded in analyses of social interactions and activities. While these literatures are enormously valuable, they tend to stay at the level of grand narrative, offering solutions to problems, on the assumption that theory can be applied to practice. What is needed is a complementary body of small local narratives, which show how people thought about what they were doing in relation with one another, in order to improve their own personal and social lives as they lived and worked together. We need not only advice about the development of communities of practice (Wenger 1998), but also stories that show the living processes of people negotiating their meanings so that the freedom of all is safeguarded to make their contribution and be listened to when they say they wish to live their lives in ways of their own choosing.

Here is an example of how this can be done. It is also another example of what aspects of a proposal for a prestigious conference can look like.

As a group of practitioner-researchers, we came together to make our individual and collective stories public. We wanted especially to show how, by working collaboratively and with a common purpose, we could claim that we were influencing the education of social formations. We put our claim together in the form of a proposal for the 2004 British Educational Research Association Annual Meeting. Here is the summary of the successful proposal.

Have we created a new epistemology for the new scholarship of educational enquiry through practitioner research? Developing sustainable global educational networks of communication

PARTICIPANTS

Jack Whitehead, University of Bath
Jean McNiff, Máirín Glenn, Caitríona McDonagh, Bernie Sullivan, University of Limerick
Joan Whitehead, Bernie Fitzgerald, University of the West of England
Marian Naidoo, National Institute for Mental Health, England

We are a group of practitioner-researchers working across the levels of education systems. Each of us asks, 'How do I improve what I am doing for personal and social good?' Each of us aims to generate our personal educational theories to show how we are doing so through our contributions to the education of social formations in our own settings. We believe that the validity of our efforts lies in the generation of educational theories of professional practice. A criterion for the legitimation of such validity claims is the capacity of educators to show how they are holding themselves accountable for their work as they seek to exercise their educative influence at local and global levels. We explain how we are fulfilling our understanding that acceptance of individual responsibility for ourselves and to each other through collaborative self-study is at the heart of global influence.

We will produce evidence to support our claims that we are contributing to sustainable forms of global understanding through education. We will do this by offering descriptions and explanations of our educational practices in different settings, as we extend our educative influence for social good. We aim to show how our public accounts of theory generation contribute to a systematic knowledge base. From the ground of clarifying the meanings of our embodied values and using them as educational standards of judgement we show how contributing to this knowledge base constitutes a form of theory generation that has profound implications for educational practices world-wide.

Each of the presenters will explain their learning processes as they research the realisation of their educational values within their social situations.

The significance of our presentation for educational research lies in showing how, in response to Snow's (2001) call to systematize our professional knowledge base, the collaborative production of evidence-based accounts can contribute to this knowledge base. We show how this knowledge base, in response to Coulter and Wiens (2002), Feldman (2003) and Noffke (1997), can influence the trajectories of social change. We show how what begins as the personal accountability of self-study has the potential to impact on processes of organisational and social change at local levels, and how this can transform into the education of social formations at global levels. We explain how the knowledge base, which contains multimedia presentations of personal enquiries undertaken collaboratively, can be disseminated through global networks, in live and electronic forms.

SUMMARY

This chapter addresses ideas about the significance of your claim to have improved learning. You are placing your account of learning in the public domain to test the validity of your claims that you have influenced the learning of yourself, of others in your workplace, and wider groupings who wish to learn how to act in ways that recognize others as able to think for themselves. You are showing how new learning can inform new practices that can influence sustainable forms of social growth.

One of the significant features of this new learning is the development of new epistemologies, and this is the focus of the next chapter.

24

Developing New Epistemologies for Organizational Cultures of Enquiry

One of the most significant aspects of your research is that you are showing how the development of new epistemologies can influence the creation of new social orders. By epistemology we mean a theory of what we know and how we come to know it. By a social order we mean the way that particular groupings live and work together, and what kinds of discourses they use to negotiate how they should do this.

The idea of a new epistemology for the new scholarship has been in the literature since the 1990s. In recent times, Jack Whitehead has extended the idea as creating a new epistemology for a new scholarship of educational enquiry, an idea that is especially relevant to you as a practitioner, regardless of your personal or professional setting. We want to develop this idea here, and show how you are contributing to a new epistemology for a new scholarship by encouraging new ways of learning in your organization, and some of the implications.

This chapter is organized as two sections that address these questions:

1 How are you contributing to a new epistemology for a new scholarship of educational enquiry?
2 What are some of the implications?

1 HOW ARE YOU CONTRIBUTING TO A NEW EPISTEMOLOGY FOR A NEW SCHOLARSHIP OF EDUCATIONAL ENQUIRY?

In 1995, Donald Schön spoke about the epistemological battle currently going on in many institutional settings, especially in higher education (see page 16). On the one hand, he said, traditional views regarded theory as a reified body of abstract knowledge. This knowledge could be applied to practice. If the task was to find ways of improving learning, the first place to go for an answer was a book that contained ideas about how it could be done. Schön made the point that, although this body of literature contained useful information from which practitioners could take ideas, the ideas were presented in a propositional form, that is, they appeared as words about abstract ideas (propositions). So, if you wanted to understand how organizations work, you would consult books such as Morgan's (1997) *Images of Organization*. If you wanted to find out about evidence-based practice, you would read Thomas and Pring's (2004) *Evidence-Based Practice in Education*. Furthermore, there was an expectation that the literatures would contain an answer, which could be applied to practice in all appropriate situations. Titles such as *The Discovery of Grounded Theory* (Glaser and Strauss 1967) implied that the answer was already there, waiting to be discovered.

Schön spoke about the need for a new epistemology in 1995. Since 1976, Whitehead has consistently spoken about the need for a new epistemology, which would involve practitioners studying their practice as the grounds for the generation of their own theories of practice. They would offer their ideas about what they know and how they have learned it, and they would put their ideas to the test both of other people's opinions, and of how well their provisional theories stood up to the exigencies of new practices. Implications of this view are that theory is not necessarily static, but is embodied in the real lives of real people: hence the idea of living theory. Schön's idea was that the development of a new epistemology would be part of the development of a new scholarship, that is, a culture of enquiry about specific practices. The new scholarship would use practices that were different from traditional scholarship; so, instead of focusing on the measurement of outcomes, as in traditional scholarship, the new scholarship would focus on the negotiation of personal and social meanings. Whitehead's idea of an epistemology of educational enquiry is that practitioners would offer their explanations of how they have learned to improve practice with educational intent.

So what are the implications for you? How are you contributing to the new scholarship, and what is special about your work that enables you to do so?

Your contribution to the new scholarship

Perhaps your most important contribution is your public acknowledgement that your practice and theory are integrated and non-divisible, in the sense of being distinct but not discrete. You are showing how your theory is grounded in your practice, and in turn feeds back into new practice. As a manager, for example, you explain how you have learned to negotiate decisions rather than make them yourself, and how you have developed new practices that prioritize negotiation. Further, you have brought this learning to your board, and begun to negotiate there also. You have explained to your colleagues on the board that you learned this new practice by studying past practice, and it seems to be influencing attitudes among the workforce. Perhaps the board should adopt it as a practice too? If you were to write an account you could show how your explanations for what you were doing could stand as a new theory, that is, a theory of management that was grounded in respect for the other (see also Reason 2002). This theory may have implications for other practices such as collective bargaining, international relations, and peace keeping.

The form of your theory is especially significant. It is not a static entity, but a living dynamic process. Your theory is in the way you are.

Schön said that the introduction of new epistemologies could reshape the way we think about how organizations develop. He spoke about the need for new institutional epistemologies. He also said that the introduction of these new epistemologies would probably involve a battle with those who still subscribed to the old epistemologies. This, he said, would be a battle of snails, as the old order waned and the new order ascended. The slowness that Schön spoke of has not, however, been the experience of many action researchers working in a living theory tradition, who have influenced the development of new organizational cultures and new ways of thinking. Nor has it always been a battle, though in some cases it has been. Some practitioners' stories show how new cultures absorbed old cultures, and transformed them into the new (Steenekamp 2004). This is important, because we have to remember that cultures are not free-standing entities, but people living and working together and negotiating how they are going to continue doing so. It is therefore a question not of developing new cultures but of influencing people to think and act in ways that will accept that seeing the other person's point of view is a core condition of successful and sustainable social growth. Some examples are given below of what this can look like and how it can be achieved through action research.

2   WHAT ARE SOME OF THE IMPLICATIONS?

There are major implications, both for practice and for theory.

Implications for organizational practices

Working in organizational settings means that you are inevitably working with other people. Organizations are not free-standing things. They are groupings of people. The word 'organization' can refer to how the groupings are organized, as well as their practices. Much of the literature focuses on this organization of people and practices, but not on the people themselves. The literature tends to focus on how groupings of people can be organized into structures such as hierarchies or networks, and offers advice about which structures seem to be the best for generating particular outcomes in practice. It focuses on how practices can be organized so that people act for greatest effect. The effect that is sought tends to be understood as efficiency in the production of goods, because that is what dominant consumerist philosophies value. Dominant literatures tend to have a thing-focus, and emphasize the organization of things (people and practices) for the most effective production of things (consumer goods), on the assumption that they can be exchanged for money (a thing), which will buy other things (freedom, power and a sense of wellbeing).

However, real people are not 'things', except in the sense that they are living bodies moving in and out of living spaces. They are persons, with feelings, values and emotions. Some people recognize others as the same as themselves, and some see others as things. 'Organization' refers to how living people organize themselves into groupings, and decide their own practices. How they decide this, and what they decide, is influenced by what they believe about how they should be together, and for whose benefit. If they place greatest value on the welfare of each person, and see each person as a valuable member of the community, they will decide collectively that all must work together for the benefit of all. Perhaps a minimum standard of judgement is in relation to the extent to which every member of the community feels valued and is able to make their active contribution. A fully realized set of standards of judgement would be in relation to the extent to which all feel valued and able to make their active contribution. This is what Sen (1999) seems to be getting at when he speaks about a theory of human capability (see page 19). All are recognized as capable. All have potentials for universal influence.

This again raises the core point of this book, about how practitioners need to be seen as theorists. This view may be realized in the reality of countless workplaces, but producing accounts of how it is realized is not yet common-place. Because those accounts are not yet available in quantity, the realities of people working to realize their capabilities do not make up a majority litera-ture, so the other view of capital accumulation remains dominant. A massive and urgent implication is that people working in person-centred communities of practice need to publish their accounts to create a new body of knowledge, so that others can see that (1) they are not alone and that the work they also are doing is valuable, and (2) precedents exist for publishing, with (3) implications for further influence.

Further, the accounts need to offer not only descriptions of what is happening, but also explanations for why it is happening, and what people them-selves want to achieve. This is action research. People need to produce high-quality accounts that comprise their theories of learning for personal and social improvement.

We have noted before that some collections of stories are now available, notably the work of Jackie Delong in Canada and Moira Laidlaw in China. Jackie, a superintendent of schools in the Grand Erie District, has been highly successful in establishing systemic structures to support professional learning across the district. She has ensured that all practitioners have the opportunity to develop their own learning pathways, and to have their learning accredited if they wish. Those practitioners have produced their accounts of practice, which are actively influencing others in workplaces and beyond. Jackie's own story of how she holds herself accountable for what she is doing is in her PhD thesis (Delong 2002), accessible at http://www.bath.ac.uk/~edsajw/delong.shtml. Moira Laidlaw has been notably successful in influencing change at national level in China. Working in a rural teachers college in an impoverished region in northern China, she has established new organizational practices that are grounded in her own and teachers' capacity to understand their work and make professional judgements about it, and to produce their own living educational theories to explain what they have done and its potential significance. In 2004, Moira was awarded the State Friendship Award for her work in China, a television documentary was made about her work for national screening, and the achievements of those she has supported have been promoted by the national government as potential exemplars of good practice (see http://www.bath.ac.uk/~edsajw/moira.shtml).

Work like this needs to be complemented by the work of others, to create new literatures and new bodies of knowledge that will, ultimately, begin to influence policy makers. This theme continues in Chapter 25. Here we summarize by saying that Schön's (1995) idea of a new epistemology for the new scholarship in institutions, that is, an account of what people know and how they learn as they organize themselves in their workplaces, is a living reality. Many more accounts are needed, such as yours, to show how this can be achieved and developed, and to raise the profile of this important new literature.

Implications for theory

As noted, the dominant form of theorizing organizational and social development is to speak about organizations as things, and groupings and their practices as structures. The aim is to produce linguistic analyses of organizations and practices such as management and leadership. The assumption is that people access the theory and apply it to their own practice. This view may be fine in theory but it often does not work in practice. Abstract theories do little to enable you to account for why you do what you do, although they may help you to make sense of what you do, and theorize it in conceptual terms, as when for example you talk about the aim of your work as your desire to achieve social justice or secure opportunities for productive work. Abstract theories do not enable you to make sense of and articulate what you personally do to achieve social justice and secure opportunities for productive work. You need to do that for yourself. Because your descriptions and explanations of what you do constitute your theory of practice, you are in fact producing theory that is different in kind from, and incorporates, abstract theories. Yours is a theory of how you live. It is your living theory.

The idea of living theory has moved into organizational studies in a range of ways. Accounts of practice show how people organize themselves and their practices from the perspective of recognizing and realizing their personal and collective capabilities. Madeline Church (2004; Church et al. 2003) tells how she works with international agencies to help them understand the nature and processes of networking for sustainable development. Madeline is a participant, not a bystander. She sees herself as a researcher in community with other researchers. Ram Punia (2004) explains how he supports the development of communities of practitioners in international settings, by understanding himself as in company with others who also see themselves in company with others. Terri Austin (2001) manages a process of communitarian growth through educational action research. Marian Naidoo (2004) encourages collectives to develop their practice through the performing arts. Many other accounts are available at www.actionresearch.net (see McNiff and Whitehead 2000 for an overview of action research in organizations).

What is special about these accounts is that they explain the form of theory they are developing, and also explain that generating the theory itself is a core practice that influences other practices in relation to living contexts. The theory is embedded in what people do. It is not a separate or conceptual entity. It is a living practice among other living practices.

This has enormous implications for new developments in theory. We have spoken throughout of the need to establish the validity of claims to knowledge. The validity of living theory approaches can be established by the living evidence of communities of practitioners who are studying their collective practices, which themselves constitute solid evidence for the power of the approach (see Black 2005).

Geras (1995) talks about the need for solidarity in the conversation of humankind, and offers ideas about how this can be achieved. The community of action researchers, however, shows how it can be done, and explains the potential implications for new organizational cultures of enquiry that are grounded in each person's capacity to ask, 'How do I improve what I am doing?' There is little doubt that people working together can influence organizational and social change. In fact, says Hazel Henderson (1996), there is no other way.

Communities of action researchers come together because all are willing to participate and hold themselves accountable. Communities do not form only because people talk about the possibilities, but because they decide to become involved in their own learning in order to take control of their own lives. It is up to each person to decide what they want to do, whether to stay on the sidelines and watch, or become actively involved as a participant. We can all do it, and life is limited. What can be done tomorrow that cannot be done today?

Here is an example of how one group of practitioners is changing their organizational culture from a culture of practical action to a culture of enquiry. It is a proposal submitted to the Educational Studies Association of Ireland for their annual conference 'Celebrating Educational Research in Ireland: Retrospect and Prospect', March 2005. The text acts as another example of what a proposal can look like. Note that the emphasis is on the production of educational theory more than the telling of workplace practices.

The transformative potentials of our self-studies for a new epistemology of educational enquiry in our university

In this interactive symposium, we aim to demonstrate the transformative potentials of our self-studies for a new epistemology of educational enquiry in our university. We explain how we have improved our learning by working as a study group, how we transfer our learning to our school-based pedagogical practices, and how we are contributing to current debates in the literature on the significance of teacher research for educational enquiry (Snow 2001).

We are five PhD candidates and their supervisor, undertaking our self-studies through action research. Each of us aims to generate our personal theories of education about how we are contributing to the education of one another, and others in our own settings. Each asks, 'How do I improve my learning to help you to learn?' Each holds herself accountable for her influence in the other's learning. This focus on personal accountability places our work within an emerging tradition of a new scholarship of educational enquiry (Whitehead 1999), which has considerable potentials for new pedagogies and for the education of social formations in our university. We claim that accepting responsibility for our influence in the other's learning has enabled us to develop a form of individual and collective practice that demonstrates the highest quality of scholarly activity, while grounded in each person's capacity to care for the other. By making our accounts public we believe we are setting precedents for forms of professional learning and institutional pedagogies (Schön 1995) from which others can learn how to improve their own practice and learning.

This symposium is an opportunity to test our claims against the critical judgement of peers. Through our oral and multimedia accounts, we hope to show how we are improving learning, in all the contexts of our professional lives.

PARTICIPANTS

Jean McNiff (chair)
Máirín Glenn
Patricia Mannix McNamara
Caitríona McDonagh
Mary Roche
Bernie Sullivan

SUMMARY

This chapter has set out ideas about developing new epistemologies for new organizational cultures of enquiry, that is, new ways of thinking that will support the development of new ways of working. The chapter explains how you can contribute to these debates by showing how your work is located within the new scholarship, which emphasizes the need to integrate theory and practice. Some of the implications of your work are that practice can come to be understood as grounded in people and their social interactions, and theory as grounded in people's capacity to theorize their individual and collective work as a form of social renewal. Both these elements are interrelated and mutually influential.

The next chapter sets out some of the even wider implications of your work, especially in relation to how you can exercise your global educational influences in learning.

25

The Amazing Potential Global Influence of Your Action Research

The amazing thing about you and your action research is that you really do have the potential to exercise your transformative influence in significant ways at global level. This may sound grandiose but it is feasible.

Achieving this potential calls for (1) vision, and (2) the political sophistication involved in finding ways of exercising that vision.

Your vision is in the idea that you can influence the education of social formations. This means aiming to exercise your educative influence to persuade different groupings that they can learn something from you, primarily that they can learn how to do things for themselves, and can change their established practices for the better.

Your political sophistication lies in appreciating that the ways that social formations work are often aspects of the formation and implementation of policy. This is important, because if you are aiming to influence the way that social formations work, you also have to find ways of influencing policy formation. Your task is therefore twofold: first, to influence general thinking and the discourses through which that thinking is communicated; second, to influence policy formation and implementation that put in place the kinds of structures and processes that support general thinking and discourses. Both these aspects are interlinked and inseparable, and they influence each other. You need to be aware of the dual nature of the task ahead, and aim to influence both contexts at the same time. This chapter addresses these issues. It is organized as two sections.

1   Influencing thinking and discourses
2   Influencing policy formation and implementation

1   INFLUENCING THINKING AND DISCOURSES

Influencing people's thinking means that you encourage them to see another way. Perhaps the greatest gift you can give to others is not only the encouragement to develop a new vision but also the idea that a new vision is possible. You are saying to people, 'It doesn't have to be like this. You are capable of rethinking the way things are and changing them.' You are showing your faith in others that they can exercise their imagination to create their own new futures. By providing your account of practice you are giving them guidance about how they can do this. If you are in any doubt that encouraging a sense of vision and providing the means to realize it is the overall purpose of your work, stop and think about the relationship between your action research and the Holocaust of World War II.

This Holocaust and other catastrophic events of pain and suffering were the direct outcome of lack of acceptance of the other, a monumental hubris that allowed some people to think they were more deserving of life than others. Holocausts are historical events. The people who are part of them are real people. Some of the people from the Holocaust of World War II are still alive. Other people in other contexts of horror are very much alive. Read any newspaper, or the literature of Amnesty International, for copious evidence. See how relationships of power and their outcomes of pain spread themselves across the pages. Listen to the rhetoric of politicians and read between the lines. 'We want people to be free,' you hear. Free for what? Free to continue serving power? Go into your workplace. See how relationships of power permeate discourses. In which direction does the power lie? Who tells others what to do? How do they do this? Do they blatantly coerce, or do they manage to get people to perform appropriately, and even come to believe that performing appropriately was their own idea?

Things do not need to be the way they are. The most amazing thing about you is that, by even considering the possibility of doing your action research, you hung onto your sense of vision that there is another way. By doing your action research you have exercised your imagination to find it. By making your account public you are saying to people, 'You can do this too.'

However, you live in the real world, and are also part of those relationships of power. You are not a fly on the wall. You are part of it. Therefore, if you want to influence trajectories of change, you have to understand what keeps this real world ticking over nicely, and find ways of disrupting the hidden assumptions in the thinking that keeps it all in order. Even when your piece of the world appears to be entirely satisfactory, you still need to dig beneath the surface to reveal those hidden assumptions and ensure that they are life-affirming rather than life-destroying. You want to disrupt the current social order and put a new one in its place, not only the social order of how people are, but also the social order of the way people think, and how the way they think influences what they do. Most importantly, you also need to encourage other people to become aware of these things, and develop their own political sophistication in finding ways to rethink what they are doing and ensure that the means are in place to help them to do it.

2   INFLUENCING POLICY FORMATION AND IMPLEMENTATION

How to do this? You need to do two things.

- First, you need to influence people that they can exercise their sense of vision and create new futures. What you have read so far has offered advice about how to influence others by showing how you are contributing to new practices and new theory and persuading them that they can do this too.
- Second, you need to influence policy makers to see the benefit of these new ways of working, so that they will put in place the basic means to enable people to continue creating their new futures.

These two aspects are interlinked. If policy makers can see that there is popular demand for new ways of working, and the demand is credible, they are more likely to put the basic means in place and ensure their continuation.

Therefore you and your colleagues need to develop your own understanding of how policy formation and implementation work, in order to ensure that your own political action will be effective.

Understanding policy formation and implementation

Policy does not come into existence by itself. It is the creation of policy makers, real people, some of whom become policy makers as a job, not necessarily because they have expertise in a particular discipline. In governments, people can go from one department to another overnight. Some politicians are deeply committed, and have extensive knowledge of the field, but not all. It is important to remember that policy formation and implementation are not a given fact, but a human practice, which, like all human practices, is grounded in different interests.

Different people analyse human interests in different ways. Habermas (1972; 1987) sets out three main forms of human interest.

- *Technical interests* focus on the production of technical rational knowledge, with the aim of controlling the environment. Knowledge becomes instrumental activity.
- *Practical interests* focus on meaning-making and interpretation, with the intention of understanding the social life world and with an awareness of its historical and political emergence.
- *Emancipatory interests* enable people to understand the influences that lead them to think and act as they do, and to liberate their own thinking in order to resist closure of any kind.

- From an action research perspective, these three interests are supplemented by a fourth *educational interest*, which focuses on establishing inclusional practices that are grounded in people's capacity and desire for relation, and self-government in communitarian work.

Which interests drive your individual and collective work? What do you hope to achieve and why? Which interests drive the work of policy makers, and why? Give this some thought, because understanding what drives policy formation will help you to find ways of appealing to the interests of policy makers.

Here are some ideas about how you can do this.

Show the value of your work for organizational renewal

In workplaces, show how your research has implications for improving practice. Explain that improved practice will raise the organization's standing in the eyes of the peer community. Raising profile meets the organizational interests of self-promotion. It also meets your own interests of promoting personal and social wellbeing through relationship. In wider contexts, explain how improving practice needs to be high on policy agendas, and how this will benefit the community as a whole.

Work all levels of the system

It is not enough to appeal only to the interests of other practitioners. It may be enough when the focus is on improving practice only, but not if you are aiming to influence policy for improving practice. Managers and organizational elites need to know what you are doing, and you need to let them see that it is in their interests to support your work. You can get their commitment by sending them copies of your reports and inviting their critical feedback. Invite them to be members of your validation groups. Ask them to attend seminars and workshops. Point out the implications of your work for organizational benefit.

Find allies

You cannot do it alone. While you may have the original vision of how things can be improved, you must find others who share your commitment. You need allies both to support you, and also to form a critical mass that will have political clout. Your single voice may be heard, but a collective voice is stronger.

Contribute to the knowledge base

Scholarly accounts of practice are still seen as the most powerful way to contribute to the knowledge base. Publishing your account will provide you with a prestigious platform from which you can speak with authority, and which will also bring kudos to any organization with which you are associated. Find outlets for publishing. Research the market to see what journals are appropriate for you and spend some time and energy in getting published. Set up your own website and make your work available on it. Set up discussion forums so that you can get instant feedback and promote your own and others' learning. Link with other websites and set up global conversations, which is easy with e-mail. If you work in higher education, use the various Research Assessment Exercises to promote your work. Although much of what is published is controlled by journal editors with a traditional bent, many new places for scholarly papers about self-study action research have become available. The journals *Educational Action Research* and *Reflective Practice* are available. New e-journals such as *Action Research Expeditions* and *Action Research International* as well as the well-established *Journal of Interactive Media in Education* are now regarded as legitimate sources for citation. Aim to create a demand, and then supply whatever will keep the demand going.

Get accreditation

It is in your political interest to achieve status for yourself. One way of doing this is to get accreditation for your work. It is possible to get the whole range of accreditation for workplace learning, from certificates to doctorates. Your accreditation will in turn reinforce a new conceptualization of what counts as knowledge. Practitioners' accounts enter the knowledge base, and stand along-side traditional propositional accounts. Doctoral theses with titles such as 'An investigation into the relationship between leadership and organizational effec-tiveness' stand alongside those with titles such as 'How do I improve my prac-tice as an educational leader?' These theses are there and will not go away. The knowledge base is changed for ever, in the same way that organizational prac-tices and systems change for ever when new practices are established.

Become a participant in the debates

Above all, if you really want to influence policy, you need to gain access to the debates, and then demonstrate that you are competent to take part. This means having the right credentials, which involves showing that you know what you are talking about, in relation both to practice and to theory. Advisers to policy makers are people who have the credentials. They have built up considerable expertise as practitioners who are able to discuss practice in theoretical terms. You have an advantage. You are competent not only to discuss practice, but also to show how you theorize practice itself. This is no small achievement, and you need to refine it to a high level of sophistication.

We are back to the Introduction. Practitioners need to position themselves as researchers and theorists if they are to have a say in what counts as good practice and which directions their professions should go and for what purposes. There are no short cuts. It is hard work, but achievable. And achievement is essential, if practitioners are to have a voice in what kind of society they wish to create for the future. The stakes could not be higher.

The positioning of managers and educational leaders

The positioning of managers and educational leaders is of special importance. In traditional forms of scholarship, managers and leaders were positioned as responsible for the creation and implementation of policy at local level, and for overseeing the implementation of higher-order, including national, policy. Many managers and leaders still feel comfortable with this positioning, and lend themselves readily to the reproduction of the status quo, which ensures their ontological and professional security. On this view, the job of managers and leaders is to move people and practices around, like pieces on a chessboard, and ensure the smooth running of the game.

Given the new scholarship focus on emancipatory learning and democratic participation, many managers and leaders prefer to reposition themselves as practitioners who are learning how to support their own and others' professional learning. 'Management' and 'leadership' turn from abstract concepts into real human practices. Management and leadership are what people do when they decide to encourage others to manage their own affairs and lead one another.

For example, Chris Glavey, working in Northern Ireland, has encouraged young people to regard themselves as educational leaders in education institutions. He has achieved remarkable developments, especially in relation to bringing communities together in strife-torn contexts. Although in a position of leadership himself, he regards his work as 'leading others to places where they have not yet been' (Donovan 1978), and enabling them to understand their own capacity as policy makers (Glavey 2004). Similarly, Séamus Lillis brings communities from the North and South together, to find ways of developing strategies for peaceful living. This shift in his professional perception came about because he undertook his action enquiry into his own learning. Séamus now sees himself as a practitioner who is supporting the development of his own and other people's understanding of management and leadership practice. In the abstract to his PhD thesis (Lillis 2001), a slightly edited version of which appears here, he writes:

> In this study I research my practice in rural community development with a view to improving it.
>
> The study reconceptualises the nature of rural community development by shifting perceptions of development as an externalised focus of study, which may be theorised about by detached 'outside' experts, to focusing on the insights from

participants' experiences. These experiential insights facilitate a process where practitioners, other stakeholders and I can generate our own theories of how rural community development is enhanced.

Long-established empirical approaches are effective in probing traditional technical, economic, practical, social and political characteristics of rural community development. But I wish to investigate the full range of the factors affecting rural communities, particularly ethical, aesthetic, spiritual, cultural and ecological influences. Here empirically based methodologies are less effective … I therefore chose action research as my methodology [as] sensitive to the emergent nature of community development, to its contextual, practice-based and relational characteristics.

The study's findings question the appropriateness of traditional approaches to training in community development, and highlight the 'knowledge in community' or wisdom shared by established communities' participants. As a teacher and adviser in horticulture [which is my professional positioning], I [previously] mediated prescriptive technical expertise to farming clients. This approach did not help advance rural community development. This was a key discovery. I recount how, as a consequence, I changed and became a learning practitioner-researcher and how that stance advances my practice. In modelling the experience through examining my own practice, I provide an imitable pattern for other practitioners.

Taking this position can be especially difficult, because personal identity is often related to professional identity, so what a person does professionally can become who a person is personally. It takes a special kind of courage and commitment to position oneself as a learner, albeit with a particular set of responsibilities, rather than as a role. Many people hide behind their roles. Those in senior positions in organizations who get rid of the role and position themselves as in a community of educational practice are special people who need to publish their accounts of work, in order to influence others in relation to practice, and also influence thinking about how management and leadership should be theorized.

What do you need to avoid doing?

It is important not only to decide what you have to do, but also to be clear about what you need to avoid doing. Primarily, you need to avoid closure of any kind. By closure we mean a situation in which you believe you have found the final answers. This means developing an awareness of what is going on in your context that may persuade you to aim for closure, in relation to ideas about epistemology, professional development and social renewal.

Avoid epistemological closure

Resist the temptation to believe that your knowledge is complete, and you have no more to learn. Some academic practitioners in established traditions deliberately work to this end, presenting their research as a definitive answer to a specified problem. Their books and papers contain messages that learning is complete, this is the way things should be, and theory may now be applied to other people's practice. This is contrary to the spirit of action research, which focuses on enquiry, on the assumption that all answers are held as provisional and open to critique and change, as contexts and understanding develop together.

Sometimes institutions actually encourage epistemological closure in order to maintain the status quo. They use a range of ways to encourage practitioners to close down their thinking and not question norms. This can take the form of straightforward bullying and threat, to more insidious forms including persuasion and flattery. You need always to be aware of what is happening to you, and avoid giving in to inappropriate persuasion through persisting in the face of pressure. This can be difficult, because human tendencies are to conserve energy by not taking action (Taylor 2004), and it takes real energy to question and resist complacency. Many of the case studies in this book are from people who are fortunate to work in institutions that do encourage change, or to find groups of allies within their institutions with whom they can work. Those are the institutions that Senge (1990; see page 72 of this book) said were the organizations of the future. The question for you then becomes, how to influence peers and managers so that they will keep their options open and see the importance of enquiry.

Avoid professional closure

It is easy to slip into professional complacency, by moving into a role or internalizing messages that tell you to go to sleep. Most people prefer to let someone else question practices or blow a whistle, knowing also what penalties may be incurred (Alford 2001). The need to belong, and to be seen as belonging, is strong, and raising questions means that individuals inevitably place themselves outside the normal frame. Said (1994) says that practitioners who position themselves as public intellectuals are always outsiders, strangers to their own, because they insist on questioning their own and other people's assumptions. 'Never solidarity before criticism is the short answer,' says Said (1994: 24). Loneliness is preferable to selling one's soul. Some organizations, however, want your soul as well as your productive work, so you have to make choices about what you are going to keep as your own and the costs involved.

Avoid social closure

Fundamentalist practices develop because some people think that they are right and everyone else is wrong. Fundamentalist practices usually lead to what Popper (1966) calls a closed society, in which people devote their energies to maintaining the status quo through the perpetuation of established regimes and apparatuses. This can be dangerous for people who step outside the norm, such as action researchers, who always look for ways of improving existing situations by encouraging new thinking. Fundamentalists do not believe their practices need improving, so they try to silence those who do. Fundamentalism in any form is anathema to the creation of open societies and the idea of social renewal. This is of course what action research is about.

Achieving your vision

So, what is the relationship between your action research and the creation of good social orders? The relationship is that future social orders begin here and now, where you are. Because of the inherent generative transformational nature of human processes, new practices, influenced by new thinking, will develop out of old ones. You can influence your own contexts, and your contexts can influence increasingly wider contexts. You really do have the capacity for global influence.

Just to show how this is possible, look at this extract from a conversation between primary teacher Mary Roche and her five-year-old children (Roche 2004).

Eoin: I am going home with so, so, so many questions in my head today!
Mary: Good, that's what school is for, asking questions and thinking about possible answers.
Aoife: Anyway, if you go home with a question and you get an answer, you can always question the answer.

Sustainable futures lie in the capacity of all practitioners to question the answer and encourage others to do the same. Practitioners do not take 'no' for an answer, but they do not take 'yes' either. The possibilities of this life end only with death, and there is a lot of living to do before that. How do people learn to live in a way that ensures not just survival, but intense and complete joy in the experience of life itself? Perhaps you have some ideas about this. If you do, tell others.

SUMMARY

This chapter has set out the potentials of your action research for influencing ideas and practices at global level. Realizing this potential involves (1) developing an understanding of the interrelated nature of public discourses and policy formation, and (2) developing the political sophistication to appeal to the interests of policy makers, primarily by showing the value of your work and its potential for new policy. The chapter sets out some strategies for how this can be done, and also makes the point that some practices are to be avoided. The overall point is, however, that you can succeed in realizing your vision, and need to exercise your tenacity and imagination to find ways of doing so.

Glossary

Action learning   A form of practice-based learning about practice, undertaken individually and collectively. It is not necessarily a form of research because it does not always aim to put in place rigorous methods for validating evidence in support of a claim to knowledge.

Action plan   A plan drawn up by individuals and collectives to guide action. Practitioners should be aware that the action does not always go according to the plan, so action plans should be regarded as notional guides and not strict sequential steps.

Action research   A form of research that enables practitioners to learn how they can improve practice, individually and collectively. The focus is on the 'I' in company with other 'I's'.

Collaborative working   People working to achieve democratically negotiated goals. Collaborative practices assume that all participants are on an equal footing and that discourses take the form of dialogues between equals.

Critical friend   A term coined by Kemmis and McTaggart (1988) to denote a person who will listen to a researcher's account of practice and critique the thinking behind the account. The term is used in a multitude of ways in contemporary literature. The job of a critical friend is to critique, not to collude or reinforce prejudices.

Critique   Critique is a part of all research and essential in action research. It refers to a process of challenging normative assumptions, that is, the thinking underpinning the research that assumes automatic justification of processes without showing why.

Data   Information about actions and phenomena that is gathered and stored in artefacts, such as diaries, computer files and videotapes. Data are the grounds for the generation of evidence.

Data gathering methods (techniques)   Ways in which data can be gathered. The number of methods available is vast, and range from questionnaires to live methods with video. Practitioners should aim to develop their own methods for their own purposes.

Epistemology   A theory of knowledge (what is known), incorporating a theory of knowledge acquisition (how it comes to be known). Action research values subjective knowledge as much as objective knowledge. Practitioner-researchers' epistemologies are rooted in their capacity to know their own practice. Action research involves studying the practice and generating practical knowledge that is rooted in the practice in relation to the ideas of others.

Evaluation   A process of establishing the value or worth of something. Action research is a form of self-evaluation, when practitioners ask, 'Am I practising in a way that is worthwhile? How do I check my assumptions?' Evaluation in action research is done by practitioners, in company with participants and others who offer critical feedback on conclusions.

Evidence   The basis for claims to knowledge. Evidence is drawn from the data, in relation to specified criteria and standards of judgement. The evidence itself has to be subjected to public scrutiny for the claim to be pronounced as valid (although sometimes validation processes are distorted within legitimation processes, as happened in the famous case of Galileo).

Human interests   It is generally acknowledged, following Habermas (1972), that there are three human interests: technical, practical, emancipatory. Action research has introduced a fourth interest of relation and inclusion in educational enquiry.

Knowledge   That which is known. Knowledge always has to be seen in relation to knowledge generation processes, which also involve logics and values. How a person comes to know influences what they know. Different kinds of knowledge exist in relation to the logics and values that are used in the knowledge creation process.

Legitimacy   A process of scrutinizing a knowledge claim and pronouncing it acceptable for the public domain. Legitimation processes are frequently power-constituted, which means that the validity of the knowledge claim is often subordinated by the power status of those who are scrutinizing the validity of the claim. Thus legitimation processes can often distort validation processes.

Living contradiction   The idea that a practitioner may hold values which are contradicted in practice. The contradiction can arise from personal or external situational constraints. The aim of action research is not always to resolve the contradiction, but to recognize it and learn to live with 'I' as a living contradiction in the narratives of lifelong learning.

Living educational theories   Practitioners can produce their own theories of living practice, which, like the practice, are transformational and developmental. Living theories are different from propositional theories, in that propositional theories are constituted in statements (propositions) and show the relationship between statements as the grounds for their validity, whereas living theories are constituted in the descriptions and explanations in practitioners' accounts of their learning through practice that show the relationship between their own and others' developing knowledge as the grounds for their validity.

Living 'I'   Practitioner-researchers are real people, whose real 'I's' are the focus of their research. Action research is a process of the 'I' investigating the 'I', who asks, 'How do I improve my learning and practice?' The living 'I' is the epistemic centre, that is, the research is about the 'I' generating knowledge. Frequently the 'I' forms a collective so that the 'I' exists in 'we–I' relationships, and the question becomes, 'How do we improve our learning and practice?'

Methodology   A theory of how to do things. Methodologies, which in research terms refer to the entire process of doing research, are different from methods, which refer to the techniques used in processes such as data gathering.

New epistemology   The new epistemology is part of the new scholarship. It refers to the development of ways of knowing that are grounded in the researcher's capacity to know their own practice. These ways of knowing often use multiple intelligences and draw on personal, propositional, dialectical and inclusional forms of logic.

New scholarship   A form of scholarship that celebrates the individual practitioner's ways of knowing about learning and practice. Whereas traditional scholarship focuses on studying subject matters that inform practice, the new scholarship focuses on studying the practice from within the practice itself in relation to a contextualized understanding of self-identity. Accounts of practice therefore come to stand as legitimate candidates for the knowledge base.

Normative   Normative assumptions are those that are usually assumed to be right without question, 'That's the way things are because that's the way things are.' Normative assumptions can also become part of normative public discourses through conscious choice. They can be carried by a culture as an unquestioned given and created through choice. Action research involves questioning normative discourses in the process of establishing the validity of knowledge claims.

Ontology   A theory of being, which influences how people perceive themselves in relation to others and the rest of their environment. A person's ontological perspective can transform into their epistemological stance and influence further practice, that is, what a person believes about themselves and others influences what they come to know about themselves and others and how they then practise in relation to others.

Participants   All the people directly involved in the action research are potentially participants. This means that they have equal rights in terms of their capacity to know and make choices and judgements. Action research processes are therefore egalitarian, and relationships need to be democratically negotiated.

Practitioner   The issue of who is a practitioner is contested. Some people assume that only those in workplaces should be seen as practitioners, whereas those in offices should be seen as something else, for example, managers. As cultural norms change, together with the research processes that investigate culturally constituted practices, the idea of practitioner has become more generic, and offices are now regarded as workplaces, and their occupants as practitioners. Consequently, many academics and managers now regard themselves as practitioners.

Practitioner-based research (enquiry)   The literature uses many terms, and often conflates and confuses them. Practitioner enquiry, in one sense, is any form of enquiry done by practitioners, so, say, ethnographic research can be practitioner enquiry as much as action research. Action research, in the views expressed in this text, must be done by practitioner-researchers, but not all practitioner-researchers do action research.

Professional learning   Learning that is done as part of the job, which is now part of many organizational practices. Many organizations put in place professional learning pathways that ensure that all practitioners have opportunities for lifelong professional learning.

Social purpose   This refers to the intent of the research in terms of encouraging social evolution. The social intent of action research is always improvement, and the main vehicle for this is practitioners' critical investigation of their own practice. The social intent underlying the research informs the entire research process, and the methodology is always oriented towards social evolution through participative critical reflection.

Validation   The process of establishing the validity, or trustworthiness, of a claim to knowledge. The validity of a claim is generally held to reside in its evidence base, although some claims, such as 'I have toothache', defy the production of objectively verifiable evidence. The claim then has to be taken on trust, so validity can come to refer to the trustworthiness of the researcher as much as the claim they are making.

Validation group   A group convened specifically to scrutinize the researcher's knowledge claims and say whether a claim is reasonable or needs further work. Knowledge claims are usually contained in formative and summative accounts of practice. The job of a validation group is to look carefully at the knowledge claim and its evidence base and agree that the claim appears reasonable, or request the researcher to rethink aspects of the research, especially any normative assumptions that have entered into the research.

References

Abbey, D. (2002) *Teacher Consultant's Role in Developing and Facilitating an Interdisciplinary Studies Course*. MEd dissertation, Brock University. Retrieved 21 January 2005 from http://schools.gedsb.net/ar/theses/index.html

Adler-Collins, J.-K. (2004) 'What am I learning as I research my life in higher education as a healing nurse, researcher, and Shingon Buddhist priest and as I pedagogise a curriculum for healing nurses?' Paper presented at the British Educational Research Association Symposium 'How Are We Contributing to a New Scholarship of Educational Enquiry through Our Pedagogisation of Postcolonial Living Educational Theories in the Academy?', UMIST, Manchester, September. Retrieved 18 January 2005 from http://www.bath.ac.uk/~edsajw//bera04/jacbera04.htm

Alford, C. F. (2001) *Whistleblowers: Broken Lives and Organizational Power*. Ithaca, Cornell University Press.

Aronowitz, S. and Gadotti, H. (1991) *Postmodern Education: Politics, Culture and Social Criticism*. Oxford, University of Minnesota Press.

Austin, T. (2001) *Treasures in the Snow: What Do I Know and How Do I Know It through My Educational Inquiry into My Practice of Community?* PhD thesis, University of Bath. Retrieved 6 January 2004 from http://www.bath.ac.uk/~edsajw/austin.shtml

Bales, K. (1999) *Disposable People: New Slavery in the Global Economy*. Berkeley, University of California Press.

Bateson, G. (1972) *Steps to an Ecology of Mind*. New York, Ballantine.

Berlin, I. (1998) *The Proper Study of Mankind: an Anthology of Essays*. London, Pimlico.

Bernstein, R. (2000) *Pedagogy, Symbolic Control and Identity: Theory, Research, Critique*. Lanham, Rowman & Littlefield.

Black, C. (2005) 'Issues regarding the facilitation of teacher research', *Reflective Practice* 5 (3): 107–122.

Boyer, E. (1990) *Scholarship Reconsidered: Priorities of the Professoriate*. New Jersey, Carnegie Foundation for the Advancement of Teaching.

Bruce Ferguson, P. (1999) *Developing a Research Culture in a Polytechnic: an Action Research Case Study*. PhD thesis, University of Waikato. Retrieved 26 November 2004 from http://www.twp.ac.nz/research.

Burke, T. (1997) *How Can I Improve My Practice as a Learning Support Teacher?* MA dissertation, Dublin, University of the West of England. Retrieved 27 November 2004 from http://www.jeanmcniff.com/

Burke, T. (2001) Doctoral research proposal. Limerick, University of Limerick.

Cahill, M. (2004) Progress report. Thurles, University of Limerick.

Callahan, R. (1962) *Education and the Cult of Efficiency*. Chicago, University of Chicago Press.

Capra, F. (2003) *The Hidden Connections*. London, Flamingo.

Carr, W. and Kemmis, S. (1986) *Becoming Critical: Education, Knowledge and Action Research*. London, Falmer.

Chomsky, N. (1965) *Aspects of the Theory of Syntax*. Cambridge, MA, Massachusetts Institute of Technology.

Chomsky, N. (1986) *Knowledge of Language: Its Nature, Origin and Use*. New York, Praeger.

Chomsky, N. (1988) *The Chomksy Reader* (ed. J. Peck). London, Serpent's Tail.

Chomsky, N. (1991) *Media Control: the Spectacular Achievements of Propaganda*. New York, Seven Stories.

Church, M. (2004) *Creating an Uncompromised Place to Belong: Why Do I Find Myself in Networks?* PhD submission, University of Bath. Retrieved 24 January 2005 from http://www.bath.ac.uk/~edsajw/church.shtml

Church, M., Bitel, M., Armstrong, K., Pryanthi, F., Gould, H., Joss, S., Marwaha-Diedrich, de la Torre, A. L. and Vouhe, C. (2003) *Participation, Relationships and Dynamic Change: New Thinking on Evaluating the Work of International Networks*. Development Planning Unit Project, University College London, supported by the USCOR Committee Department of International Development. Retrieved 16 January 2005 from http://www.bath.ac.uk/~edsajw/arsup/mcWP1210.pdf

Corey, S. (1953) *Action Research to Improve School Practices*. New York, Teachers College Press.

Costigan, A. and Crocco, M. (2004) *Learning to Teach in an Age of Accountability*. Mahwah, Erlbaum.

Coulter, D. and Wiens, J. (2002) 'Educational judgement: linking the actor and the spectator', *Educational Researcher* 31 (4): 15–25.

Cousins, J. B. and Earl, L. (eds) (1995) *Participatory Evaluation in Education*. London, Falmer.

Dadds, M. and Hart, S. (2001) *Doing Practitioner Research Differently*. London, Routledge.

Deery, R. and Hughes, D. (2004) 'Supporting midwife-led care through action research: a tale of mess, muddle and birth balls', *Evidence Based Midwifery* 2 (2): 52–58.

Delong, J. (ed.) (2001) *Passion in Professional Practice*, Vol. 1. Ontario, Grand Erie Board of Education. Retrieved 21 January 2005 from http://schools.gedsb.net/ar/passion/pppii/index.html

Delong, J. (2002) *How Can I Improve My Practice as a Superintendent of Schools and Create My Own Living Educational Theory?* PhD thesis, University of Bath. Retrieved 26 November 2004 from http://www.actionresearch.net/delong.shtml

Delong, J. and Black, C. (eds) (2002) *Passion in Professional Practice*, Vol. 2. Ontario, Grand Erie Board of Education. Retrieved 21 January 2005 from http://schools.gedsb.net/ar/passion/pppii/index.html

Delong, J. and Knill-Griesser, H. (2002) 'How do we integrate issues of power and ethics in valid explanations of our educative influence as a teacher-consultant and superintendent?', in J. Delong and C. Black (eds) *Passion in Professional Practice*, Vol. 2. Ontario, Grand Erie Board of Education. Retrieved 21 January 2005 from http://schools.gedsb.net/ar/passion/pppii/index.html

Delong, J., Black, C. and Knill-Griesser, H. (eds) (2003) *Passion in Professional Practice*, Vol. 3. Ontario, Grand Erie Board of Education. Retrieved 21 January 2005 from http://schools.gedsb.net/ar/passion/pppiii/index.html

Delong, J., Black, C. and Knill-Griesser, H. (eds) (2005) *Passion in Professional Practice*, Vol. 4. Ontario, Grand Erie Board of Education. Retrieved 12 June 2005 from http://schools.gedsb.net/or/passion/piv/index.html

DES (1981) *The School Curriculum*. Circular 6/81. Department of Education and Science. London, HMSO.

Donovan, V. (1978) *Christianity Rediscovered*. London, SCM Press.

Eames, K. (1995) *How Do I, as a Teacher and Educational Action-Researcher, Describe and Explain the Nature of My Professional Knowledge?* PhD thesis. Retrieved 12 January 2005 from http://www.bath.ac.uk/~edsajw/kevin.shtml

Elliott, J. (1991) *Action Research for Educational Change*. Buckingham, Open University Press.

Ernest, P. (1994) *An Introduction to Research Methodology and Paradigms*. Exeter, University of Exeter Research Support Unit.

Farren, M. (2004) *Developing My Pedagogy of the Unique as a Higher Education Educator. How Can I Co-create a Curriculum in ICT in Education with Professional Educators?* Draft PhD thesis to be submitted to the University of Bath.

Feldman, A. (2003) 'Validity and quality in self-study', *Educational Researcher* 32 (3): 26–28.

Forrest, M. (1983) *The Teacher as Researcher: the Use of Historical Artefacts in Primary Schools*. MA dissertation, University of Bath.

Foucault, M. (1980) 'Truth and power', in C. Gordon (ed.) *Power/Knowledge: Selected Interviews and Other Writings, 1972–1977*. Brighton, Harvester.

Frankl, V. (1963) *Man's Search for Meaning*. New York, Pocket.

Freire, P. (1972) *Pedagogy of the Oppressed*. New York, Seabury.

Fromm, E. (1956) *The Art of Loving*. New York, Harper & Row.

Furlong, J. (2000) *Higher Education and the New Professionalism for Teachers: Realising the Potential of Partnership*. London, CVCP/SCOP. Retrieved 26 November 2004 from http://www.edstud.ox.ac.uk/people/furlong.html

Furlong, J. (2004) 'BERA at 30. Have we come of age?', *British Educational Research Journal* 30 (3): 343–358. Presidential Address to the British Educational Research Association, 2003. Retrieved 26 November 2004 from http://www.bera.ac.uk/publications

Furlong, J., Barton, L., Miles, S., Whiting, C. and Whitty, G. (2000) *Teacher Education in Transition: Re-forming Professionalism?* Buckingham, Open University Press.

Gardner, H. (1983) *Frames of Mind: the Theory of Multiple Intelligences*. New York, Basic.

Geoghegan, M. (2000) *Improving the Quality of Staff Meetings*. MA dissertation, Dublin, University of the West of England, Bristol.

Geras, N. (1995) *Solidarity in the Conversation of Humankind*. London, Verso.

Glaser, B. and Strauss, A. (1967) *The Discovery of Grounded Theory*. Chicago, Aldine.

Glavey, C. (2004) Working paper. Dublin.

Glavin, T. (1998) *How Can I Improve My Evaluative and Advisory Role in a Primary School in Cork City?* MA dissertation, Cork, University of the West of England, Bristol.

Glenn, M. (2003) 'Multimedia, the celebration of creativity and multiple forms of learning'. Paper presented at the Conference 'Critical Debates in Action Research', University of Limerick, June. Retrieved 26 November 2004 from http://www.jeanmcniff.com

Glenn, M. (2004) 'How am I enhancing inter-connections with ICT?' Paper presented at the British Educational Research Association Symposium 'Have We Created a New Epistemology for the New Scholarship of Educational Enquiry through Practitioner Research? Developing Sustainable Global Educational Networks of Communication', UMIST, Manchester, September. Retrieved 26 November 2004 from http://www. actionresearch.net/bera04/bera5.htm

Goethe, W. (1988) *Die Metamorphose der Pflanzen* (1790). Reproduced as 'The metamorphosis of plants', in D. Miller (ed.) *Goethe: Scientific Studies*. New York, Suhrkamp.

Gorard, S. (2002) 'The future of educational research post RAE 2001'. Paper presented at the British Educational Research Association Conference, Exeter, September.

Gramsci, A. (1973) *The Prison Notebooks: Selections* (trans. Q. Hoare and G. Nowell-Smith). London, Lawrence and Wishart.

Grandi, B. E. de (2004) *An Action Research Expedition: How Can I Influence My Students in Developing Their Creativity and Critical Thinking? A Self Study.* MA dissertation, University of Bath. Retrieved 16 January 2005 from http://www.bath.ac.uk/~edsajw/grandi.shtml

Habermas, J. (1972) *Knowledge and Human Interests* (trans. J. J. Shapiro). London, Heinemann.

Habermas, J. (1975) *Legitimation Crisis* (trans. T. McCarthy). Boston, Beacon.

Habermas, J. (1987) *The Theory of Communicative Action. Volume Two: The Critique of Functionalist Reason.* Oxford, Polity.

Habermas, J. (1998) *The Inclusion of the Other* (ed. C. Cronin and P. De Greiff). Cambridge, MA, MIT Press.

Hammersley, M. (1993) 'On the teacher as researcher', in M. Hammersley (ed.) *Educational Research: Current Issues*, Vol. 1. London, Chapman.

Hartog, M. (2004) *A Self-Study of a Higher Education Tutor: How Can I Improve My Practice?* PhD thesis, University of Bath. Retrieved 26 November 2004 from http://www.bath.ac.uk/~edsajw/hartog.shtml

Henderson, H. (1996) *Building a Win–Win World: Life beyond Global Economic Warfare.* San Francisco, Berrett-Koelher.

Heron, J. (1998) *Sacred Science: Person-Centred Inquiry into the Spiritual and the Subtle.* Ross-on-Wye, PCCS.

Heron, J. and Reason, P. (2001) 'The practice of co-operative inquiry: research "with" rather than "on" people', in P. Reason and H. Bradbury (eds) *Handbook of Action Research.* London, Sage.

Hignell, W. (2004) *Final Report.* Birmingham, Disability West Midlands.

Hillesum, E. (1983) *An Interrupted Life: the Diaries of Etty Hillesum* (trans. A. Pomerans). New York, Pantheon.

Hitchcock, G. and Hughes, D. (1995) *Research and the Teacher: a Qualitative Introduction to School-Based Research* (2nd edn). London, Routledge.

Holley, E. (1997) *How Do I as a Teacher-Researcher Contribute to the Development of a Living Educational Theory through an Exploration of My Values in My Professional Practice?* MPhil thesis, University of Bath. Retrieved 14 January 2005 from http://www.bath.ac.uk/~edsajw/erica.shtml

Jenkins, R. (1992) *Pierre Bourdieu.* London, Routledge.

Kemmis, R. and McTaggart, S. (1988) *The Action Research Planner* (3rd edn). Geelong, Deakin University Press.

Kincheloe, J. L. (1991) *Teachers as Researchers: Qualitative Inquiry as a Path to Empowerment.* London, Falmer.

Kirkham, M. (2000) 'How can we relate?', in M. Kirkham (ed.) *The Midwife–Mother Relationship.* London, Macmillan, pp. 227–254.

Knill-Griesser, H. (2002) *A Vision Quest of Support to Improve Student Learning: Validating My Living Standards of Practice.* MEd dissertation, Brock University. Retrieved 21 January 2005 from http://www.actionresearch.ca/

Kuhn, T. (1970) *The Structure of Scientific Revolutions* (2nd edn). Chicago, University of Chicago Press.

Kushner, S. (2000) *Personalizing Evaluation.* London, Sage.

Laidlaw, M. (2002) 'How can I promote sustainable development at Guyuan Teachers' College?' Retrieved 14 January 2005 from http://www.actionresearch.net/moira.shtml

Laidlaw, M. (2004) Public lecture. Guyuan Teachers College, Guyuan. November.

Lakatos, I. (1970) 'Falsification and the methodology of scientific research programmes', in I. Lakatos and A. Musgrave (eds) *Criticism and the Growth of Knowledge*. Cambridge, Cambridge University Press.

Lather, P. (1994) 'Textuality as praxis'. Paper presented at the American Educational Research Association Annual Meeting, New Orleans, April.

Lave, J. and Wenger, E. (1991) *Situated Learning: Legitimate Peripheral Participation*. Cambridge, Cambridge University Press.

Law, J. (2004) *After Method: Mess in Social Science Research*. London, Routledge.

Lawlor, S. (1990) *Teachers Mistaught: Training Theories or Education in Subjects?* London, Centre for Policy Studies.

Lewin, K. (1946) 'Action research and minority problems', *Journal of Social Issues* 2 (4): 34–46.

Lillis, S. (2001) *An Inquiry into the Effectiveness of My Practice as a Learning Practitioner-Researcher in Rural Community Development*. PhD thesis, Dublin, University College Dublin.

Lohr, E. (2004) Prologue to PhD submission to the University of Bath. Retrieved 16 January 2005 from http://www.jackwhitehead.com/elFront%202.htm

Long, B. (2003) 'Action research in organisational change'. Paper presented at the Conference 'Critical Debates in Action Research', University of Limerick, June. Retrieved 27 November 2004 from http://www.jeanmcniff.com

Losee, J. (2004) *Theories of Scientific Progress*. New York, Routledge.

MacBeath, J. (1999) *Schools Must Speak for Themselves: the Case for School Self-Evaluation*. London, Routledge.

MacClure, M. (1996) 'Narratives of becoming an action researcher', *British Journal of Educational Research* 22 (3): 273–286.

MacDonald, B. (1987) *The State of Education Today*. Record of the First CARE Conference. Norwich, University of East Anglia.

Mannix McNamara, P. (2003) 'Exploring the nature of pedagogical relationships at third level: from reflection to action'. Paper presented at the Conference 'Critical Debates in Action Research', University of Limerick, June. Retrieved 27 November 2004 from http://www.jeanmcniff.com

Marshall, J. (1999) 'Living life as inquiry', *Systemic Practice and Action Research* 12 (2): 155–171. Retrieved 12 June 2005 from http://www.bath.ac.uk/carpp/judimarshall/LivingLifeasInquiry.pdf

Marshall, J. (2004) 'Living systemic thinking: exploring quality in first-person action research', *Action Research*, 2 (3): 309–329. Retrieved 12 June 2005 from http://www.bath.ac.uk/carpp/judimarshall/LivingSystemicThinking.pdf

McDonagh, C. (2000) *Towards a Theory of Professional Teacher Voice: How Can I Improve My Teaching of Pupils with Specific Learning Difficulties in the Area of Language?* MA dissertation, Dublin, University of the West of England. Retrieved 26 November 2004 from http://www.jeanmcniff.com

McDonagh, C. (2003) 'Presenting voice in research practice'. Paper presented at the Conference 'Critical Debates in Action Research', University of Limerick, June. Retrieved 26 November 2004 from http://www.jeanmcniff.com

McDonagh, C. (2004) 'Aware teaching, learning and research'. Paper presented at the British Educational Research Association Symposium 'Have We Created a New Epistemology for the New Scholarship of Educational Enquiry through Practitioner Research? Developing Sustainable Global Educational Networks of Communication',

UMIST, Manchester, September. Retrieved 16 January 2005 from http://www.bath.ac. uk/~edsajw//bera04/caitrionabera.htm

McGinley, S. (2000) *How Can I Help the Primary School Children I Teach to Develop Their Self-Esteem?* MA dissertation, Dublin, University of the West of England, Bristol. Retrieved 27 November 2004 from http://www.jeanmcniff.com

McIntyre, D. (1997) 'The profession of educational research', *British Educational Research Journal* 23 (2): 127–140.

McNiff, J. (2005) 'Living with foxes: learning about home, self and the other'. Paper presented at the Peace Education SIG, American Educational Research Association Annual Meeting, Montreal, April. Retrieved 25 January 2005 from http://www. jeanmcniff.com

McNiff, J. with Whitehead, J. (2000) *Action Research in Organisations*. London, Routledge.

McNiff, J. and Whitehead, J. (2002) *Action Research: Principles and Practice* (2nd edn). London, Routledge Falmer.

McNiff, J. and Whitehead, J. (2005) *Action Research for Teachers*. London, Fulton.

McNiff, J., Whitehead, J. and Laidlaw, M. (1992) *Creating a Good Social Order through Action Research*. Bournemouth, Hyde.

McNiff, J., Lomax, P. and Whitehead, J. (2003) *You and Your Action Research Project* (2nd edn). London, Routledge Falmer.

Mead, G. (2001) *Unlatching the Gate: Realising my Scholarship of Living Inquiry*. PhD thesis, University of Bath. Retrieved 16 January 2005 from http://www.bath.ac.uk/~edsajw/ mead.shtml

Mellor, N. (1998) 'Notes from a method', *Educational Action Research* 6 (3): 453–470.

Mill, J. S. (1985) *On Liberty* (1859). London, Penguin.

Miller, R. (2002) *Free Schools, Free People: Education and Democracy after the 1960s*. Albany, State University of New York Press.

Mitroff, I. and Kilman, R. (1978) *Methodological Approaches to Social Science*. San Francisco, Jossey-Bass.

Morgan, G. (1997) *Images of Organization* (2nd edn). Thousand Oaks, CA, Sage.

Moustakim, M. (2004) Progress report. London, St Mary's University College.

Muir, C. (2004) *The Establishment and Development of South East Birmingham Community Credit Union Ltd.* Birmingham, West Midlands Social Economy Partnership.

Naidoo, M. (2004) 'I am because we are. How can I improve my practice? The emergence of a living theory of responsive practice'. Paper presented at the British Educational Research Association Symposium 'Have We Created a New Epistemology for the New Scholarship of Educational Enquiry through Practitioner Research? Developing Sustainable Global Educational Networks of Communication', UMIST, Manchester, September. Retrieved 16 January 2005 from http://www.bath.ac.uk/~edsajw//bera04/ mnbera04.htm

Newby, M. (1994) 'Living theory or living contradiction?', *Journal of Philosophy of Education* 28: 119–125.

Noffke, S. (1997) 'Themes and tensions in US action research: towards historical analysis', in S. Hollingsworth (ed.) *International Action Research: a Casebook for Educational Reform*. London, Falmer.

Nugent, M. (2000) *How Can I Raise the Level of Self-Esteem of Second Year Junior Certificate School Programme Students and Create a Better Learning Environment?* MA dissertation, Dublin, University of the West of England, Bristol. Retrieved 30 November 2004 from http://www.jeanmcniff.com

O'Callaghan, I. (1997) *Growing into Principalship*. MEd dissertation, Dublin, University of the West of England, Bristol.

O'Donohue, J. (2003) *Divine Beauty*. London, Bantam.

O'Shea, K. (2000) *Coming to Know my Own Practice*. MA dissertation, Dublin, University of the West of England, Bristol.

Parlett, M. and Hamilton, D. (eds) (1977) *Beyond the Numbers Game*. Basingstoke, Macmillan.

Penny, R., Carr, C., Hafenrichter, J., Johnson, C., McNiff, J., Moreland, J., Moustakim, M., Renowden, J. and Richardson, J. (2004) 'Demonstrating accountability through our self-study practices as teacher educators'. Symposium Proposal at the Conference 'Integrating Multiple Perspectives on Effective Learning Environments', European Association for Research on Learning and Instruction, Nicosia, August.

Polanyi, M. (1958) *Personal Knowledge*. London, Routledge and Kegan Paul.

Popper, K. (1966) *The Open Society and its Enemies. Vol. I: Plato. Vol. II: Hegel and Marx*. London, Routledge.

Pring, R. (2000) *Philosophy of Educational Research*. London, Continuum.

Punia, R. (2004) *My CV is My Curriculum: the Making of an International Educator with Spiritual Values*. EdD thesis, University of Bath. Retrieved 21 January 2005 from http://www.bath.ac.uk/~edsajw/punia.shtml

Rayner, A. (2002) Video clip of Alan Rayner talking about inclusionality and severance. Retrieved 17 January 2005 from http://www.jackwhitehead.com/rayner1sor.mov

Rayner, A. (2003) ' "Nested holeyness": the dynamic inclusional geometry of national space and boundaries'. Retrieved 17 January 2005 from http://www.bath.ac.uk/~bssadmr/inlusionality/nestedholeyness.htm

Reason, P. (ed.) (2002) 'The practice of co-operative inquiry'. Special issue of *Systemic Practice and Action Research* 15 (3).

Reason, P. and Rowan, J. (1981) *Human Inquiry*. London, Wiley.

Rivers, M. (2003) 'How can I create an inclusive atmosphere to support an autistic student in my classroom?', in J. Delong, C. Black and H. Knill-Griesser (eds) *Passion in Professional Practice*, Vol. 3. Ontario, Grand Erie Board of Education. Retrieved 21 January 2005 from http://schools.gedsb.net/ar/passion/pppiii/index.html

Roberts, S. J. (1982) 'Oppressed group behaviour: implications for nursing', *Advances in Nursing Science* July: 21–30.

Roberts, P. (2003) *Emerging Selves in Practice: How Do I and Others Create My Practice and How Does My Practice Shape Me and Influence Others?* PhD thesis, University of Bath. Retrieved 20 January 2005 from http://www.bath.ac.uk/~edsajw/roberts.shtml

Roche, M. (2000) *How Can I Improve My Practice so as to Help My Pupils to Philosophise?* MA dissertation, Cork, University of the West of England, Bristol. Retrieved 26 November 2004 from http://www.jeanmcniff.com

Roche, M. (2003) 'Setting the "what if …?" free. Talking and thinking in an infant classroom: an investigation into one teacher's practice'. Paper presented at the Conference 'Critical Debates in Action Research', University of Limerick, June. Retrieved 30 November 2004 from http://www.jeanmcniff.com

Roche, M. (2004) Working paper. Limerick, University of Limerick.

Said, E. (1994) *Representations of the Intellectual: the 1993 Reith Lectures*. London, Vintage.

Schön, D. (1983) *The Reflective Practitioner: How Professionals Think in Action*. New York, Basic.

Schön, D. (1995) 'Knowing-in-action: the new scholarship requires a new epistemology', *Change* November–December: 27–34.

Sen, A. (1999) *Development as Freedom*. Oxford, Oxford University Press.

Senge, P. (1990) *The Fifth Discipline: the Art and Practice of the Learning Organization*. New York, Doubleday.

Serper, A. (2004) Alon Serper's web pages. Retrieved 16 January 2005 from http://www.bath.ac.uk/~pspas/

Smith, C. (2002) 'Supporting teacher and school development: learning and teaching policies, shared living theories and teacher–research partnerships', *Teacher Development* 6 (2): 157–179.

Snow, C. (2001) 'Knowing what we know: children, teachers, researchers', *Educational Researcher* 30 (7): 3–9. Presidential Address to the American Educational Research Association Annual Meeting, Seattle.

Sowell, T. (1987) *A Conflict of Visions: Ideological Origins of Political Struggles*. New York, Morrow.

Spender, D. (1981) 'The gatekeepers – a feminist critique of academic publishing', in J. Roberts (ed.) *Doing Feminist Research*. London, Routledge.

Steenekamp, K. (2004) *The Improvement of Teaching Practice in Higher Education*. PhD thesis, Rand Afrikaans University.

Steinberg, S. and Kincheloe, J. (1998) *Students as Researchers: Creating Classrooms that Matter*. London, Falmer.

Stenhouse, L. (1975) *An Introduction to Curriculum Research and Development*. London, Heinemann.

Suderman-Gladwell, G. (2001) *The Ethics of Personal, Narrative, Subjective Research*. MA dissertation, Brock University, Ontario. Retrieved 26 November 2004 from http://www.bath.ac.uk/~edsajw/values/gsgma.pdf

Sullivan, B. (2004) 'The transformative potential of an educational practitioner's engagement in emancipatory practices'. Paper presented at the British Educational Research Association Symposium 'Have We Created a New Epistemology for the New Scholarship of Educational Enquiry through Practitioner Research? Developing Sustainable Global Networks of Communication', UMIST, Manchester, September. Retrieved 26 November 2004 from http://www.bath.ac.uk/~edsajw/bera04/bera2.htm

Taylor, K. (2004) *Brainwashing: the Science of Thought Control*. Oxford, Oxford University Press.

Thomas, G. (1998) 'The myth of rational research', *British Educational Research Journal* 24 (2): 141–161.

Thomas, G. and Pring, R. (2004) *Evidence-Based Practice in Education*. Maidenhead, Open University Press.

Todorov, T. (1999) *Facing the Extreme: Moral Life in the Concentration Camps* (trans. A. Denner and A. Pollack). London, Weidenfeld & Nicolson.

Usher, R. (1996) 'A critique of the neglected epistemological assumptions of educational research', in R. Usher and D. Scott (eds) *Understanding Educational Research*. London, Routledge.

VSO (2003) *What's New about the New Curriculum?* Newsletter, Voluntary Services Overseas, Beijing.

Walsh, D. (2004) *How Do I Improve My Leadership as a Team Leader in Vocational Education in Further Education?* MA dissertation, University of Bath. Retrieved 16 January 2005 from http://www.bath.ac.uk/~edsajw/walsh.shtml

Wenger, E. (1998) *Communities of Practice: Learning, Meaning, Identity*. Cambridge, Cambridge University Press.

Whitehead, Jack (1976) *Improving Learning for 11–14 year olds in Mixed Ability Science Groups*. Swindon, Wiltshire Curriculum Development Centre. Retrieved 26 November 2004 from http://www.actionresearch.net/writings/ilmagall.pdf

Whitehead, J. (1985) 'The analysis of an individual's educational development', in M. Shipman (ed.) *Educational Research: Principles, Policies and Practice*. London, Falmer. Retrieved 24 January 2005 from http://www.bath.ac.uk/~edsajw/bk93/5anal.pdf

Whitehead, J. (1989) 'Creating a living educational theory from questions of the kind, "How do I improve my practice?"', *Cambridge Journal of Education* 19 (1): 137–153. Retrieved 26 November 2004 from http://www.bath.ac.uk/~edsajw/writings/livtheory.html

Whitehead, J. (1993) *The Growth of Educational Knowledge: Creating Your Own Living Educational Theories*. Bournemouth, Hyde. Retrieved 21 January 2005 from http://www.bath.ac.uk/~edsajw/bk93/geki.htm

Whitehead, J. (1999) *How Do I Improve My Practice? Creating a New Discipline of Educational Enquiry*. PhD thesis, University of Bath. Retrieved 23 January 2005 from http://www.bath.ac.uk/~edsajw/jack.shtml

Whitehead, J. (2000) 'How do I improve my practice? Creating and legitimating an epistemology of practice', *Reflective Practice* 1 (1): 91–104.

Whitehead, Jack (2003) 'Creating our living educational theories in teaching and learning to care: using multimedia to communicate the meanings and influence of our embodied educational values', *Teaching Today for Tomorrow* 19: 17–20. Retrieved 26 November 2004 from http://www.7oaks.org/ttt/ttt19.htm

Whitehead, Jack (2004a) 'What counts as evidence in the self-studies of teacher education practices?', in J. J. Loughran, M. L. Hamilton, V. K. LaBoskey and T. Russell (eds) *International Handbook of Self-Study of Teaching and Teacher Education Practices*. Dordrecht, Kluwer.

Whitehead, J. (2004b) 'How valid are multi-media communications of my embodied values in living theories and standards of educational judgement and practice?' Retrieved from http://www.bath.ac.uk/~edsajw//multimedia/jimenomov/JIMEW98.html. In Action Research Expeditions, October 2004. Retrieved from http://www.arexpeditions.montana.edu/articleviewer.php?AID=80

Whitehead, Jack (2004c) 'Action research expeditions: do action researchers' expeditions carry hope for the future of humanity? How do we know? An enquiry into reconstructing educational theory and educating social formations'. Retrieved 26 November 2004 from http://www.arexpeditions.montana.edu/articleviewer.php?AID=80

Whitehead, Jack (2005) 'Developing the dynamic boundaries of living standards of judgement in educational enquiries of the kind, "How do I improve what I am doing?" ' Retrieved 17 January 2005 from http://www.jackwhitehead.com/jwartl141015web.htm

Whitehead, J. and McNiff, J. (2003) Proposal to the American Educational Research Association for the symposium 'The Transformative Potential of Individuals' Collaborative Self-Studies for Sustainable Global Educational Networks of Communication', accepted November 2003 for presentation in April 2004. Retrieved 21 January 2005 from http://www.bath.ac.uk/~edsajw/multimedia/aera04sym.htm

Whitehead, Joan (2003) 'The future of teaching and teaching in the future: a vision of the future of the profession of teaching – making the possible probable'. Keynote address to the Standing Committee for the Education and Training of Teachers

Annual Conference, Dunchurch, October. Retrieved 23 January 2005 from http://www.bath.ac.uk/~edsajw/evol/joanw_files/joanw.htm

Whitehead, Joan and Fitzgerald, Bernie (2004) 'New ways of working with mentors and trainees in a training school partnership as practitioner-researchers'. Paper presented at the British Educational Research Association Symposium 'Have We Created a New Epistemology for the New Scholarship of Educational Enquiry through Practitioner Research? Developing Sustainable Global Educational Networks of Communication', UMIST, Manchester, September. Retrieved 23 January 2005 from http://www.bath.ac.uk/~edsajw//bera04/bera3.htm

Williams, M. and Dick, B. (eds) (2004) *Write a Doctoral Thesis About Work: Professional Action Research – A Creative Reader Introducing Rich Modelling.* Cottesloe, WA, Resource.

Winter, R. (1998) 'Managers, spectators and citizens: where does "theory" come from in action research?', *Educational Action Research* 6 (3): 361–376.

Yeaman, K. (1995) 'Creating educative dialogue in an infant classroom – my educational journey'. Action research module, University of Bath. Retrieved 16 January 2005 from http://www.bath.ac.uk/~edsajw/module/kathy.htm

Zimmerman, M. E., Callicott, J. B., Sessions, G., Warren, K. J. and Clark, J. (2001) *Environmental Philosophy: from Animal Rights to Radical Ecology* (3rd edn). Upper Saddle River, NJ, Prentice-Hall.

Index